The Body Owner's Manual

The Body Owner's Manual

An Acupuncturist's
Teachings on Health
and Well-Being

DEBORAH A. DEGRAFF
ILLUSTRATED BY ADELAIDE TYROL

BERKLEY BOOKS, NEW YORK

This book is an original publication of The Berkley Publishing Group.

THE BODY OWNER'S MANUAL

A Berkley Book / published by arrangement with
the author

PRINTING HISTORY
Berkley trade paperback edition / September 1998

The Penguin Putnam Inc. World Wide Web site address is
http://www.penguinputnam.com

ISBN: 0-425-16503-5

BERKLEY®
Berkley Books are published by The Berkley Publishing Group, a member of Penguin
Putnam Inc., 200 Madison Avenue, New York, New York 10016.
BERKLEY and the ''B'' design
are trademarks belonging to Berkley Publishing Corporation.

PRINTED IN THE UNITED STATES OF AMERICA

10 9 8 7 6 5 4 3 2 1

Acknowledgments

The first thing I want to do is thank my legs for patiently sitting for so long while I wrote when often they wanted to be walking, skiing, biking, dancing, just moving in some way. That aside, there are many people I want to acknowledge and thank for their generosity, support and help while I was writing this book. I'll start with Julia, who took me seriously when I said I wanted to write a book. She responded by giving me *Wild Mind: Living the Writer's Life.* Thank you, Susan Meeker-Lowry, for walking into my office at the right time with the right question. Thank you for all you have taught me about the process of writing; your ideas, support and enthusiasm have been invaluable. Thank you to my patients in California and Vermont. Your willingness to share yourselves and your healing processes with me has contributed so much to the genesis of this book. Thank you, Hameed, Michael and Faisal, for what you have taught me about states of Being. It has profoundly affected my life and my work. Thank you, Ivan and the Roy Hart Theater Core Group. Thank you, Janet Adler. Thank you, Miriam Lee and all my teachers of traditional Chinese medicine. I press my hands together at my heart and bow my head to you. I also want to thank the Vermont Studio Center in Johnson, Vermont, for providing me with a quiet place to write, good company and great food. Thank you, Julia Cameron, for writing *The Artist's Way*. And to my friends for their steady love and support, thank you, Madelyn, George, Helen, Joe, Rob, Sue, Merrick, Lee, Denise, Kathy, Karin, Ann, and Tim. Thank you, Hannah, for all you have taught me about blood sugar regulation. Thank you to my guest authors. You can't imagine how wonderful it felt each time one of your stories or pieces arrived. Thank you, Scott Luber, N.D.; Hannah Lewis, nutritionist; Leita Hancock, D.C.; Sue Arbogast, P.T.; Rebecca Deitzel, anatomist; and Ned Farquhar, grammarian, for your suggestions and invaluable expertise. Thank you, Charlie Tritschler, for computer aid in times of panic. Thank you, team Wong, at camp Jindabyne for allowing me the space to complete this. Thank you, Carol Mann and Hillary Cige. And lastly, thank you, Mom and Dad, for all that you have done for me of which I am not aware.

Contents

Part Three: Stories of Healing

Introduction

Western medicine is a science that focuses on disease. Practitioners find what isn't working and do their best to fix it with drugs or surgery. It is the kind of medicine with which most of us grew up. It is familiar, and that, in itself, can make us comfortable.

Traditional Chinese medicine is a healing art. It focuses on the individual and how his or her energy, Spirit and wellness are disturbed or out of balance. The entire theory is based on the existence and behavior of something that is invisible to the human eye. That something is called *Qi* (pronounced chee), or energy. *Qi* does not show up on an X ray, sonogram or CT scan. You can't evaluate it with a blood test and you can't find it when you cut open the body.

It takes a leap of faith to go from the familiar territory of "medicine as science" to the less familiar territory of "medicine as a healing art." Although these approaches offer two different ways of seeing health and disease, they are not mutually exclusive, as long as we are willing to open our minds wide enough to contain them both. In fact, they coexist in the practices of a growing number of Western medical practitioners who are also healers, and in hospitals all over China where

Western medicine and traditional medicine are practiced side-by-side.

To enter the world of medicine as a healing art, it is helpful to be open to the existence of this invisible energy called *Qi*. This may mean saying, "I don't understand this, but that does not mean *Qi* isn't real." I remember being halfway through my first year of studies in traditional Chinese medicine when it occurred to me, if *Qi* really exists, then how had I gotten to be twenty-five and never heard of it? At some point during my studies I made a leap of faith that allowed me, complete with all my Western upbringing, to let in this whole other Eastern world view. To my surprise, and relief, neither one invalidated the other. They were just different, and they could coexist.

The leap of faith that you may find in front of you while reading this book is one that asks you to look at your body in a different way; to listen to the messages your body sends you as helpful signals, as opposed to symptoms to be suppressed or eliminated. It can feel scary to listen to and trust your body, when so many of us have been taught to listen to and trust everyone but ourselves. However, while many things can serve as signposts along the way, each of our paths through life is different, and in the end we must rely on and trust ourselves.

This book is about the foundations of self-care. It is what I teach my patients, and what I see giving the best results. It describes activities that you can do on your own, small adjustments you can make in your day-to-day life that will make a significant difference, specifically in your energy level, your emotional stability, your sense of well-being, and the functioning of your immune system. The book also talks about the kind of help that is available in the field of natural medicine, what different specialties have to offer and when they may be appropriate choices for you to pursue.

I always recommend consultation with your medical doctor when you have a concern or fear about your health condition. One of the strengths of "medicine as science" is the capacity to diagnose physical illness and disease. By all means take advantage of this capacity.

This book will introduce you to the language in which your body speaks as it has been understood in traditional Chinese medicine for thousands of years. In over fifteen years of clinical practice I have developed my own blend of East and West, and that is what you will find in this book. My aim is to empower you with an understanding of your body and a knowledge of self-care skills to help you determine the quality of your life. My wish is that if I help you translate the messages of your body and Heart, and support you in taking steps that will make you stronger, healthier and happier, then you will feel able to meet the challenges of manifesting the particular gifts you bring to life on this planet now.

And who am I who wants to lead you on this exploration of self-care? What path have I walked to arrive here? Well, I grew up in Albany, New York. I studied art in college, and was interested in nutrition, herbs and yoga. I stumbled upon traditional Chinese medicine in Vermont. It was, on the one hand, completely foreign (there wasn't even a Chinese restaurant where I grew up!), and on the other, utterly natural. I took to it like a fish to water. It just made sense.

After studying the basic sciences—biology, psychology, chemistry, anatomy, physiology, medical terminology and some Mandarin—I entered a college of traditional Chinese medicine. Once there, it was *terra incognito*—no Western anything. We went to school six days a week, year round, and had a week off at Chinese New Year. We learned that everything in the universe can be described as being made up of two opposite aspects, called *Yin* and *Yang*. And that while *Yin* and *Yang* are polar opposites, they are also mutually dependent. We learned that the universe can be organized according to five elements. We learned to sing our lists of Chinese herbs to remember their names and what they do. We learned that all stomachaches are not alike and do not receive the same treatment. We treated patients in the school clinic and interned with acupuncturists in the community. We looked at the whole person and his or her life, not just the presenting symptom. We learned that it is not the diagnosis of disease that is important, but understanding how disease is manifesting in a particular person.

During this time I came to believe that when you are in a state of balance, harmonious energy moves outward from you into your life, your work and the lives of those around you. When you are out of balance, everything you do reflects this disharmony. Taking care of the body, mind and emotions becomes not only self-care, but also a political act of bringing harmony into one's life, work and the world.

By way of a send-off, I would like to share with you an experience I had while writing this book. It brought home to me why I was actually writing it. On August 31, 1996, a friend of mine died instantly in a car accident. She had been so full of life: wrinkling her nose, laughing; telling me stories of her cats; talking in her funny voices; talking in her serious, deep voice; red hennaed hair; belly dancer; digeridoo player. Walking into her home was like walking into a sunny harem: beads, silks, curtains, artwork, altars, textures, fabrics, cushions, cats, her garden. She had a strong, wonderful presence in the world and in my Heart. Even though I lived three thousand miles away, after she died, I could feel she was gone. A balance had shifted.

I have always believed that everyone matters, everyone makes a difference. But until Eszike died I didn't realize what a big energetic presence we each have here on Earth. And how when you leave, your energy is gone too and it leaves a big hole. While I can still feel Eszike's presence (it has become big, expansive and less personal), she is no longer a part of the equation here on the physical plane. It is as if she just got off the teeter-totter, and now we have to find our balance without her.

What I am learning from this is how much everyone

counts. We all make a difference. How can I say this so that someone who thinks they don't matter can really get it? Maybe I can't, but I'll try.

You really do make a difference. People in your life may treat you as if you don't. It is only their ignorance, and how someone has treated them that causes them to do this. They simply don't know any better. The reality is that you do make a difference. When you are gone, even people who act like they don't care will feel your absence. They can't help it. You have a presence, your life and your energy are uniquely yours, and you are here for a reason. No one else can do what you are here to do. It may seem little and insignificant to you. It may be private and no one knows about it. But people can still feel it. That you are doing what you came here to do means something.

You may plant a little garden and care for it. You may pray for the world, or for your family. You may go to your job and do the best you can. You may raise your children, write music, or choreograph a dance and never show anyone. You may be kind to people you meet on the street. Who knows what your Spirit has come here to do? But whatever it is, what is important is that you do it. This much I do know.

In a world with problems that can seem overwhelming, it is easy to feel insignificant and powerless. But what I know to be true is this: *that feeling of insignificance is an illusion.* Your intention, integrity, your thoughts and your actions all matter. Evidence of this may not be readily apparent, and you may never know the impact you have on others. This does not mean you are not having an impact. And it is no reason not to do what you are here to do with all your Heart and the fullness of your Being.

You carry within you an energy that is here with a purpose. Loving and protecting that energy is a way to allow that purpose to manifest. Remembering this may remind you to listen to your body and to take care of yourself. The choice is

yours, for you will be the one to take that leap of faith and allow your body to guide you on your own healing journey. And
please remember, it is not just for you, but for the balance of
this teeter-totter, that you do it.

PART ONE

The Basics of Self-Care

If we do not change our direction,
we are likely to end up where we are headed.
—*Ancient Chinese proverb*

CHAPTER 1

Making Peace with Your Body

Think of your body as you would a six-year-old child. It wants basic things in order to be comfortable and content: regular meals, sleep, attention, treats, unstructured time, a sense of safety and security, acceptance, love, respect and someone with whom to play. Six-year-olds like routine, regularity and dependability. Your body will ask for these kinds of things.

You may wonder how you can tell what your body is wanting. It can be hard sometimes, for the body and mind speak in different languages. The key is to recognize that your body is communicating with you all the time through thoughts, feelings, sensations, visions, intuition and dreams. As you begin to pay attention you will start to understand that your body is continually providing you with directions, a map to chart your course through each day and through your life.

Body Language

The body has intelligence and it communicates in both subtle and obvious ways. Subtle communication may take the form of ideas, flashes of insight, coincidences, memories and inexplicable urges. More obvious methods the body uses to get your attention are hunger, fatigue, boredom, dissatisfaction, aches, pains, klutziness, depression and illness. All of these messages tell you how your body is feeling and what it wants. Some of these communications could be labeled negative; they make you feel sick, hurt or afraid. Others could be viewed as positive; they gently nudge you in a particular direction. In reality they are all positive communications with the intention of keeping you on track. It's just that some are easier to hear than others.

There are standard signals the body uses to indicate that its needs are not being met and it wants more attention. We also have our own individual, idiosyncratic distress signals. Some people get sore throats, their gums itch or they become klutzy. Others may have to urinate more frequently, their backs go out or they get rashes. There are messages in these symptoms. They are asking you to slow down and listen.

How you feel about your body, your symptoms, your thoughts and feelings creates an atmosphere that promotes or discourages communication within yourself. Just because you don't hear, understand or acknowledge your body's wants and needs, does not mean they will go away. To the contrary, they will only get stronger and more persistent. If your body must get sick to get what it wants, then often that is what it will do.

You may want to consider what small, nagging symptoms you get when you are tired, hungry or under stress. What bigger problems recur every year or two when your stress level is really high? Notice which parts of your body "speak" to you through pain or dysfunction. Is it your immune system with recurring colds and flus, or your digestive system with stomachaches? If your red flag is a recurring feeling, look for its home in your body. Where do you experience the feeling? Is it rage knotted in your solar plexus, an empty hole of sadness in your chest or fear clamping down on your heart?

You may not feel well, though you don't have a diagnosed illness. Your medical tests may indicate that there is nothing physically wrong with you. However, when you don't feel well, your body is communicating that something is not right. A message of fatigue, pain or dysfunction means something, and it can be frustrating when you don't know what the meaning is. How then can you take steps to take care of yourself? Often a natural health care provider, looking at you and your body from a different perspective than your Western medical doctor, will be able to help you understand and resolve a health problem that "medicine as science" is unable to diagnose and treat.

You may have a diagnosed illness and be under the care of one or several Western medical doctors. Many people in this situation want to make changes in their daily lives to complement and support their Western medical treatment. They want to listen to their bodies, to feel empowered and be active participants in their own healing processes.

Approaching your body, mind and Heart with respect, kindness and understanding constitutes a major step toward health and well-being. Selecting health care providers who treat you with respect, kindness and understanding will support you in this process. Overall, it is easier to listen sooner rather than later. Either way, it is never too late to start a friendship with your body.

When Your Mind and Body Are in Harmony You Feel Better

You may experience a sudden health crisis. Perhaps you have always been healthy and never needed to pay much attention to your body. You may feel confused by messages of pain and dysfunction, and resent the loss of your good health. You may be angry with your body. What it needs may feel completely out of line to you. You may be chronically tired and resent all the care your body requires. "Why doesn't it just act like other people's bodies and let me do what I want?" you may ask yourself. If this sounds familiar, you may be in an adversarial relationship with your body. When you feel like your body is ruining your life, it makes it hard to hear what it is saying to you.

Think of that six-year-old. If her mother is angry and storming around the kitchen slamming cupboards, it will not feel like a safe time to ask for a new pair of shoes or a peanut butter sandwich. If you are angry at your body, step back from your life for a minute and get a new perspective. What are you asking of yourself in your daily life, and what are you doing to nurture yourself? Use your imagination to create a neutral zone where you can listen to the wants and needs of your body *and* the complaints, frustrations and expectations of your mind. Let the neutral part of you be a curious observer and a mediator.

Whether you appreciate your body or resent it, whether you understand your symptoms or are baffled, whether your symptoms are serious or simply nagging complaints, you often have more control over how you feel than you might think. The actions you take on a daily basis to attend to your body's wants and needs, no matter how small, will have a powerful impact on your health. This creates harmony between your body and your mind, and will initiate the process of change.

The Process of Change

From the start, I want to acknowledge that just because you have an understanding of how your body works and what your personal wants and needs are does not mean that you will make any changes in your life, or that the changes you do choose to make will be easy. Many people know they "should" do something to improve their health, yet they don't do it. Human beings are complex; many factors influence the choices we make. A small change made on a daily basis will make a big difference over time. When you understand which changes will be most beneficial for you, it can make the process of change easier.

Generally change happens slowly. You may start eating breakfast, drink herb tea instead of coffee in the morning or take a walk at lunch three times a week. It may not seem like much, but after six months or a year the impact is substantial. Sometimes making a change is straightforward. You decide to make a change and you do it. Other times it is not so easy.

Some changes are difficult and require a lot of preparation. You may know what is good for you, but you just can't seem to do it. This is often when there is work to be done on a subconscious or emotional level. I call this "foundation work," when there are no obvious outer manifestations of change. Such times can be frustrating; all you want is to see results. However, building a solid foundation is essential and it can take time. It is important to have patience with yourself and allow yourself all the time you need for preparation.

The Start of Your Journey

It is natural to be full of enthusiasm at the start of a journey. And this *will be* an exciting, inspiring and fulfilling journey. However, allowing your body to guide you can at times be a slow, frustrating and painful experience. If you feel stuck, discouraged or hopeless, turn to the stories in Part Three for encouragement. As you take responsibility for your health, the slow, steady pace of self-care can try your patience.

Most of us have been raised in a culture where we go to the doctor when we are sick, get a prescription, and expect to feel better in twenty-four hours. And often this is the case; painkillers stop the pain, antibiotics clear up the infection and inhalers allow us to breathe again.

The effects of self-care are rarely so dramatic. More commonly they are gradual; a steady, reliable improvement that you earn each step of the way. Self-care does not mean you will never go to the doctor, need surgery or take drugs again. It simply means that you take care of yourself, day by day, as you would a child that you loved with all your heart. Some days you'll do better than others. The goal is not to be perfect, but rather to learn to listen to yourself and respond with care and attention.

Layers of Healing

The process of healing is a bit like peeling an onion. As you peel away the outer skin, another layer is revealed. If an injury sustained by the body, mind or Heart were superficial, then healing would occur as you peel away the outer layers. If the injury were deeper, you might find it lodged in many layers, exhibited in a variety of symptoms. It can take time and patience to move through these layers to reach the root of an injury and allow complete healing to occur.

As you start healing at deeper layers, all of the experiences and blocks that are stored in that layer will emerge, as well as beliefs about who you are and what is and isn't possible. The more profound a change you make, the deeper the layers it will affect and the greater the influence it will have on your life.

Be gentle with yourself, and patient with your process. Take advantage of books, tapes, classes, workshops, journal writing, friendships, support groups and health care practitioners. If change were going to be effortless, you would have done it a long time ago.

We often think, "Healing is possible, for *other* people, in *other* situations. But not for me. Not in *this* situation." It is natural to discover limiting beliefs in your healing process. Notice them, but don't get attached to them as if they were "The Truth." Recognize that you believe this certain thing in your life will never change, and then acknowledge that you don't know if what you believe is true. Nothing builds faith like the change of something that you considered unchangeable.

Change is a part of life. Seeds grow into plants, winter turns to spring, wounds heal. Life changes, and you are a part of life. With kindness and understanding toward yourself, and with the curiosity and willingness to ask questions and to listen for answers, many things become possible. This opens the door, just a crack. The possibility of change has entered the room.

CHAPTER 2

Where Do We Begin?
The Wish List

I n the language of your body, wanting is a form of communication. Many of us were taught that wanting is wrong or selfish. However, if you don't know what you want, you are like a ship at sea without a navigator.

The more permission you give yourself to notice what you want, the more likely your body will be to "talk" to you. Remember your body is like a six-year-old. Give a six-year-old the space to feel comfortable and accepted, and he or she will tell you all sorts of things.

Knowing what you want may provide information that connects to the root of your complaints. If you look at symptoms alone, sometimes you miss the root of a problem, for emotional wants can express themselves in physical ailments and pain. As your ability to distinguish between your physical and emotional wants increases, you will more easily be able to address each. By considering both emotional and physical concerns, you enhance your well-being as you address your life as a whole.

Making Your Wish List

As an experiment, while you are working with this book, I'd like you not to judge yourself. Instead of finding flaws, be curious. It's the difference between "I did that again!" and "I wonder why I do that." To make changes in your life it is important to see where you are now and where it is you want to go. This can be difficult when you are judging yourself. Suspending judgment and becoming curious enables you to accept things as they are now *and* imagine the possibility of change.

With this attitude in mind, make an inventory of everything in your life that isn't satisfying. It may involve your health, job, relationships or your mental, emotional or spiritual state, your living situation or financial concerns. Particularly look at the messages your body is giving you through discomfort, pain and other symptoms of distress and malfunction. This list may feel overwhelming—but stay curious, and do it anyway. Then set it aside.

The next step is to make your Wish List. Write down anything and everything that you would like to see change in your life. Be unrealistic. Being practical is not the point. As you make your Wish List, allow yourself to write down everything that comes to mind.

If a wish occurs to you, and you think, "Forget it, I'll never get that," write it down anyway. Remember your curiosity. The point is to wake up your inner navigator and get the flow of directions coming. A Wish List gives you access to your directional signals. As you allow wishes to emerge it is helpful to remember that just because you want something does not mean that you will get it. Nor does it mean that someone else should get it for you. Wanting is just that—an urge, a desire, an impulse.

And having a wish does not mean that you have to act on it either. Some directional signals may not require any action—recognition and acknowledgment are enough. Furthermore, just because you want something does not mean that you *really* want to get it, or that if you got it you would be happy. For now, try not to focus on getting. It tends to stir up doubt and fear. Just for now, allow yourself the freedom to want, free of consequences.

As in learning anything new, when you begin working on your Wish List, know that making mistakes is a part of the process. Recall what it was like the first time you went shopping by yourself for clothes. Perhaps you bought something that hung in the closet for years. You never wore it and later could hardly believe your bad taste. But did it harm you to have made a poor choice? And have your shopping skills improved over time? Or have you learned to shop with a friend who has an eye for clothes?

Making a Wish List is no different. Over time, your Wish Lists will become a more accurate reflection of who you are and what you want. You'll learn what sorts of wishes really work for you. So start. Just give it a try. What do you want?

Fear

You can expect fear to arise. It can lead you to deny your wishes for fear of making mistakes, being laughed at, or losing security or approval. Sometimes we fear that we won't get what we want, or we fear the consequences if we do. Please don't let fear stop you. Be curious and ask yourself, "I wonder why this makes me fearful?"

If your wish feels really outrageous, then focus on the motivation underlying it. Look at the inner experience you are after, not the outer image. In this way, even the most unrealistic of wishes can show its achievable aspects. The real issue here is the choice between trusting what you want and following it, or trusting fear and doubt and following them. Guess which of these choices opens opportunities in your life, and which closes your mind and Heart? Even when you take no action, and do nothing more than write your Wish List, just having acknowledged what you want opens your Heart and creates a kinder, more accepting atmosphere in your mind toward your body.

Wants That Just Won't Go Away

Some wants will be a passing fancy, and others will persist throughout your life, patiently reminding you that you want to work with clay, dance, grow a garden, play piano, sing, have a child, build a house, sail around the world, change your diet, make peace with an old friend or start your own business.

Perhaps you want to write a book. So you write on your Wish List: 1. I want to write a book. Your next thought is: "I'm not talented. I can't write, and even if I could, I'd never find a publisher." That voice is not the inner navigator speaking. That is fear, doubt and self-attack. The voice that says, "I want to write a book. I have something to say," that is the inner navigator. This is an important message from your Heart. To listen to the fear and doubt would be to ignore an important communication, a navigational signal.

Your Wish List is a way to invite your body and your Heart to speak to you. Once you have invited these parts of yourself to contribute ideas, it would be disrespectful not to listen to their responses. Just take in the information, in whatever ways it comes. And consider it when you make choices in your life.

Listening to Your Wants When You Are at the End of Your Rope

When you are at the end of your rope, your first wish might sound like this: "I want to leave this house, these kids, my husband and go to Tahiti and live on the beach for the rest of my life." Acknowledging this desire lets the steam out of the pressure cooker. As you settle down, the desire to get away might remain, while the wish changes: "I want a vacation for a week where it's warm. I want to leave the kids with my parents and go away with my husband, just the two of us."

With a sigh of relief, you may pick up the phone and call your mother to see if she can take the kids for the weekend.

Allow yourself to blow off steam without judging yourself. After all, you are at the end of your rope. Give yourself a break. You don't have to do anything about it. Just let the feelings come. Be curious. What do you want right now?

In Summary

Wanting something, whatever it is, opens up a flow of communication within you that increases the connection between your body, your mind and your Heart. When you make your Wish List, first ask yourself what you want. Recognize that your wishes are directional impulses, and judging them is like saying left is better than right. They are simply directional signals. Pay attention, notice them, write them down.

Then, prioritize your Wish List and identify the wishes you want to take action on. What steps can you take toward making that wish come true? These do not have to be big steps. Very small steps will do just fine. What small, nonthreatening thing can you do that heads you in the direction of your wish? Is there someone you could talk with, a book to read or a class to take? Is it one hour a week alone, or more intimacy you seek? List steps you can take to achieve your goals, and one at a time do them. Lastly, leave room for the unknown and unexpected to come into your life.

CHAPTER 3

Choices in Health Care

The most basic level of health care—self-care—is available to everyone. And while a variety of health care systems and practitioners is invaluable, nothing compares with the power of the daily practice of health-building habits. Even health problems resulting from situations beyond your control, such as accidents, environmental pollution or heredity, are affected positively or negatively by the choices you make on a daily basis.

While practicing self-care builds a strong foundation for health, it doesn't guarantee that you will never suffer from physical illness or emotional distress. If your body is communicating through distress, physical symptoms or illness it is important to listen to those messages, and seek medical advice when it is appropriate. To aid you in mapping out your health care program, let's look at four basic categories of health care options.

1. Basic Self-Care:

- **The basics of a healthy lifestyle:** a healthy diet, plenty of clean water, regular exercise, relaxation and ample sleep.

- **Mental and emotional health:** reduce stress, maintain a positive mental outlook, attend to your emotional life and communicate in a straightforward manner.
- **Inner development:** meditation, prayer, journal writing, reading books that inspire as well as address your problems and concerns, listening to music and educational tapes and expressing your creative energy.
- **Expanding personal horizons:** taking classes, attending support groups, participating in the life of your community and travel.

2. **Over-the-Counter Remedies and Supplements:** vitamins and nutritional supplements, herbs, tinctures, homeopathic remedies, flower essences and over-the-counter pharmaceuticals.

3. **Fields of Natural Medicine:** acupuncture, Alexander work, Ayurvedic medicine, biofeedback, body work, craniosacral work, chiropractic, counseling, faith healing, Feldenkrais, herbology, homeopathy, massage, naturopathy, nutrition, prayer, psychic healing, reflexology, rolfing, shamanic healing, Therapeutic Touch and vision therapy.

4. **Practitioners of Western Medicine:** physical therapists, nurse practitioners and physicians' assistants, eye doctors, osteopaths, general medical doctors, psychiatrists and specialists, and Emergency Room medical staff.

Using one level of health care does not preclude the use of another. For example, if you have a sinus infection you can start out by supporting your immune system. Make sure you are getting plenty of sleep, eating a healthy diet, drinking plenty of water, and doing saltwater nasal rinses. A hot shower pounding on your sinuses or hot compresses can increase circulation in your sinuses and relieve pressure. You may want to use a grapefruit-seed-extract nasal spray from the health food store for its antibiotic effect in your nasal passages, and increase your intake of vitamin C. You may want to get acupuncture to drain blocked sinuses, increase circulation and support your immune system. If your symptoms are really strong or not responding to self-care and natural therapies, you may want to consult your nurse practitioner or medical doctor, as a prescription for antibiotics may be appropriate. All of these approaches can work together to support your healing process.

You are a unique individual and your body has its own wisdom. Appreciate your individuality and trust that your body knows best how to heal you. Take the information you gain from observation and introspection, combined with information from natural health practitioners, doctors and medical tests, and select the treatment options and combinations that suit you best. As you learn to recognize, trust and follow your body's advice you will find yourself practicing self-care. This will create your most optimal healing environment.

I encourage you to evaluate your health care needs and goals. This information will affect your priorities and choices. It will also help you choose the type of health care that is appropriate for you. Factors to consider include your age and medical history, your overall health and the severity of any existing conditions. Your choices will also be influenced by your basic values, lifestyle, upbringing and past medical experience.

I want to mention that the principles of self-care and natural medicine apply not just to health maintenance in a healthy person, but also to improving the quality of life in a person with a so-called "terminal illness." In some cases, natural therapies and self-care have even shown themselves capable of extending life and at times reversing what was considered to be an irreversible condition. Oncologist Bernie Siegel cites many examples of this in his inspiring book, *Love, Medicine and Miracles*, where he discusses his study of extraordinary cancer patients.

It is important to recognize that choices in health care are extremely personal. What is appropriate for one person may not be for another. I encourage you to listen to your Heart and its wisdom when making your choices, and to respect and support other people's choices, however different from your own they may be.

CHAPTER 4

An Introduction to Traditional Chinese Medicine

I t is important to respect each person's unique experience in life. While cookbook-style diagnosis and prescribing are tempting, they do a disservice to the individual. They put authority outside of yourself, and take away your opportunity to ask your body for information. Allowing your body to express its innate wisdom in its own language and to take this advice into account is what I find to be the heart of traditional Chinese medicine.

The focus of traditional Chinese medicine is on the individual and not the disease, and the intention of traditional Chinese medicine is to keep the patient well. Traditional doctors were paid only when their patients were healthy and received nothing when a patient became ill. Using skills of observation, the doctor was to perceive imbalance before it manifested in physical, mental or emotional illness. Then the patient was instructed in the use of natural therapies to bring balance back to the body, mind and Heart.

The traditional Chinese doctor knew that health was affected by the patient's thoughts and feelings as well as his or her physical condition. The traditional Chinese system of medicine reflects this understanding. Information is gathered by observing the body and its language. The skills needed are ones most of us are born with: looking, smelling, hearing, touching, feeling and sensing—in short—paying attention.

Today a traditional Chinese practitioner will examine, evaluate, diagnose and treat a patient. Among the treatment methods used are:

- acupuncture,
- breathing and sounding exercises,
- herbal and dietary therapy,
- lifestyle counseling,
- massage,
- moxibustion (burning Chinese herbs over acupuncture points) and
- physical exercises (*Qi Gong*).

Some History

In the 1920s, in an effort to modernize, the Chinese government outlawed traditional Chinese medicine in favor of Western medicine. After the Chinese revolution in 1949 there was a shortage of doctors for the 500 million Chinese people. Mao Tse-tung ordered a reevaluation of the traditional medical system to see if there was anything in it worth salvaging. Studies showed that the traditional system was effective, and in 1958 traditional and Western medicine became equal partners in an integrated medical system in China.

Traditional Chinese Medical Education

For thousands of years the traditional method of education was apprenticeship; thus the training of an acupuncturist began in childhood. The practice of acupuncture could vary greatly from one practitioner to the next, depending on this training. Acupuncture systems developed not only in China, but also in India, Tibet, Korea, Japan, Great Britain and

France. Each country and its practitioners lent their unique perspective to this ancient system of health care.

In the past few decades traditional Chinese medical schools have opened in Asia, Europe, Great Britain, Australia and the United States. There are probably as many ways to practice traditional Chinese medicine as there are practitioners, yet all these approaches are rooted in the same body of knowledge.

The important thing to remember when you consult an acupuncturist is that there are many styles of practice and there is not one right way. A particular style or practitioner may suit you or your health condition better than another. What you want is to find a practitioner who gets results, in whom you have confidence and with whom you feel comfortable and supported.

What Does Traditional Chinese Medicine Treat?

Traditional Chinese medicine was *the* medical system in China for thousands of years. It was used to treat everything. We now have the option of using both Western medicine and natural medicine to complement each other in the diagnosis and treatment of health problems. The following is a list of some ailments that are commonly treated today with acupuncture and traditional Chinese medicine.

Physical Ailments

- headaches,
- migraines,
- ringing in the ears,
- dizziness,
- vertigo,
- sinus infections,
- insomnia,
- depression,

- digestive disturbances,
- ulcers,
- constipation,
- colitis,
- recurring colds and flus,
- bronchitis,
- asthma,
- allergies,
- back pain,
- tennis elbow,
- knee pain,
- repetitive motion syndrome,
- arthritis and
- any stress-related disease or disorder.

Women receive acupuncture for the treatment of

- PMS,
- menstrual cramps,
- ovarian cysts,
- dysplasia,
- fibroids,
- infertility, and
- menopausal symptoms.

Acupuncture helps those who are addressing addictions to

- food and overeating,
- caffeine,
- cigarettes,
- alcohol and
- pharmaceutic and street drugs.

It is important to recognize that receiving acupuncture cannot make you quit something that you do not want to quit. If you do want to quit something, acupuncture can be of great assistance. Let's take smoking, for example. If you do want to quit smoking, acupuncture can make the process much easier. It balances your body energetically, and the result is you will be less attracted to things that knock you off-balance, like cigarettes. This can actually reduce the hold an addiction has on you. Acupuncture also increases your emotional cushion, calms your nerves, counteracts the tendency to overeat and helps clear, strengthen and heal your lungs.

Adjunctive Therapy in Serious Illness

People with illnesses such as cancer, lupus, MS, hepatitis, HIV and AIDS may receive acupuncture along with their Western medical treatments to strengthen their immune systems and their bodies.

Acupuncture and Chinese herbal medicine can counteract the side effects of chemotherapy in cancer patients. They can improve the quality of life experienced during the chemotherapeutic regimen, and can help maintain a patient's strength, so that his or her body can better tolerate the chemotherapy. They can calm nausea, help rebuild appetite and strengthen immunity.

Adjunctive Therapy during Emotional and Spiritual Work

Some people use traditional Chinese medicine and acupuncture to augment their personal growth processes. Emotional processing, while of great benefit in the long run, can also be stressful and demanding for the physical body in the short run. Understanding your body and making small changes in your lifestyle to support it, can help ease difficulties that arise during periods of intense emotional work.

Often when a therapeutic process is challenging there is a tendency to overeat. This is a spontaneous effort to stabilize, ground and calm yourself in the midst of internal change. Over time, this can wear on the body. Acupuncture can help the body rebalance, center and strengthen itself when things are changing and shifting within the psyche.

People doing spiritual work and meditation often find that traditional Chinese medicine and acupuncture benefit their practice. Not only can distracting physical complaints be relieved, but focus, concentration, insight and awareness can increase when your energy is strong and flowing, and your body is energetically supported and balanced.

Some Basic Concepts in Traditional Chinese Medicine

Traditional Chinese Physiology

The traditional Chinese understanding of physiology is different from our current Western view. To discover the inner workings of the human body, more indirect and subtle methods were used than the ones to which we are accustomed today. The focus of traditional Chinese physiology was on clinical observations. Now, with blood tests, X rays, sonograms, surgery, CT scans and MRIs we are able to see many parts of the body that were not accessible to a traditional Chinese doctor. However, the traditional Chinese system contains the wisdom of thousands of years of observation and can often reveal and explain what tests cannot.

An example can be seen in the traditional Chinese view of the Lung. The Lung refers not only to your lungs, but also to your nose and nasal passages, your skin, and the protective energy field that surrounds your body and is an aspect of your immune system. If your Lung energy is weak your protective energy field will also be weak, and you may suffer from frequent colds and flus. When your Lung energy is strengthened, your immune system is strengthened, and your resistance to colds and flus is greatly improved.

Qi

"*Qi*" (pronounced chee) is your life force, your energy. Health, in traditional Chinese medicine, is when *Qi* is strong and flows freely to all parts of your body. Disease is weakness, blockage or disturbance in the flow of *Qi*. The definition of pain is blocked *Qi*. The intention of traditional Chinese medicine is to strengthen *Qi* and encourage it to flow freely throughout the body.

Qi is the energy that makes you alive. It comes from the food you eat, the air you breathe, the water you drink, the exercise you get, and the sleep and rest you allow yourself. The way you live your life directly effects the quality of your *Qi*.

You can observe your *Qi* on a daily basis by noticing how you feel on awakening and where your energy level is throughout the day. When *Qi* is strong and flowing, you feel great. When *Qi* is weak or blocked you feel tired, sick or uncomfortable. *Qi* is invisible, but you can tell when it's there and when it isn't.

Qi internally connects your body, mind and Heart, and externally connects you to all of life. Animals have *Qi*, so do plants, rocks, a forest, a waterfall and a thunderstorm. *Qi* is what makes you feel better after a walk in the woods. The *Qi* in nature strengthens your *Qi*. Understanding and using *Qi* is what allows a martial artist to do seemingly miraculous things.

Emotional upset, stress, tension, repressed emotions, poor diet, overeating, lack of exercise or sleep, physical injury and surgery can all block the flow of *Qi*. *Qi* can also be weakened by insufficient food, sleep, rest and relaxation, poor diet and stress. In Chapters Five through Ten you will learn how to build, maintain and circulate your *Qi*.

Meridians

One way traditional Chinese doctors work with *Qi* is by observing the pathways in which *Qi* flows. These pathways are called meridians. Meridians are invisible. From the Western scientific perspective, meridians are the pathways of least electrical resistance in the body. If we had electricity traveling through us, meridians are where it would travel. Meridians roughly follow the paths of nerves, blood vessels and lymphatic

LUNG MERIDIAN WITH
ACUPUNCTURE POINTS

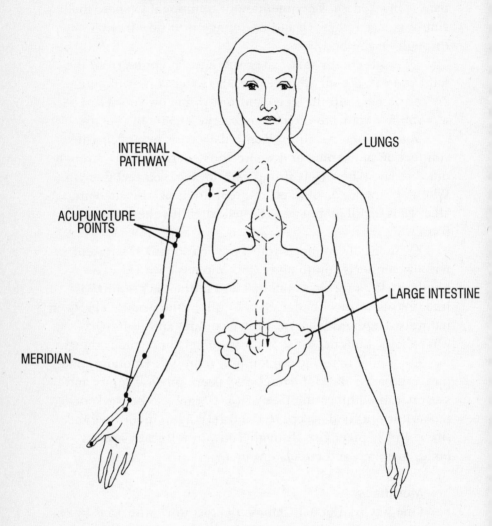

vessels. Treating a meridian will have an impact on these three other systems.

There are fourteen main meridians in the body and they all have acupuncture points located along them. These points are where an acupuncturist inserts needles, or burns Chinese herbs (moxibustion) to affect the flow of *Qi*. These same points are used in acupressure and shiatsu massage. Twelve of the fourteen main meridians connect to organs in the body. For example, your Liver meridian connects to your liver. By needling or massaging points on the Liver meridian the flow of *Qi* is affected along the entire pathway, and in your liver itself.

Wei Qi

Wei Qi (protective energy) describes the field of energy that emanates from your Lungs, permeates your muscles and skin, and forms a protective field around your body. When your *Wei Qi* is strong, your muscles and skin are supple and you are resistant to colds and flus. When your *Wei Qi* is weak, your skin will be dry, you will be sensitive to drafts and cold, and have lowered resistance to colds, coughs and flus. *Wei Qi* also insulates your nervous system and surrounds you with a protective bubble of energy. Sometimes weak *Wei Qi* can make you hypersensitive, as if your nerve endings were exposed and you had no emotional cushion around you.

If your *Wei Qi* is weak, you can strengthen it by dressing warmly and protecting your neck, lower back and ankles. It is best to avoid strong winds, as they can blow this energy field away. Deep breathing and aerobic exercise are good ways to expand *Wei Qi*. Simply taking a walk every day will enhance your protective energy field and strengthen your Lungs.

Wei Qi sometimes collapses following a major loss. The heaviness of grief can weaken the Lungs, so they cannot support the *Wei Qi*. The body then becomes susceptible to respiratory problems like bronchitis and pneumonia. As the weight of grief moves through you and is released, your respiratory condition will improve. Acupuncture can help this process, and will often clear a respiratory infection that does not respond to antibiotics. It strengthens the Lungs and *Wei Qi* and thereby restores immunity. When you are grieving, help your immune system. Dress warmly, keep your house warm and wear extra socks, scarves and sweaters to create *Wei Qi* out of fabric until your body can once again do it on its own. Take walks and breathe deeply to restore your *Wei Qi*.

Another time when *Wei Qi* frequently collapses is following surgery. The most effective remedy I know of for this is an acupuncture treatment.

The Tao (pronounced Dao)

The *Tao* is the traditional Chinese concept that describes the void, non-duality and the ordering principle of the universe.

> *There was something formless and perfect*
> *before the universe was born.*
> *It is serene. Empty.*
> *Solitary. Unchanging.*
> *Infinite. Eternally present.*
> *It is the mother of the universe.*
> *For lack of a better name,*
> *I call it the Tao. . . .*

Lao-tzu (Translated by Stephen Mitchell, *Tao Te Ching*, HarperCollins Publishers, 1988)

All life springs forth from the *Tao* or the void, first appearing as pairs of opposites, the *Yin* and the *Yang*.

Yin and Yang

In the beginning God created the Heavens and the earth.
The earth was without form and void,
and darkness was upon the face of the deep;
and the Spirit of God was moving over the face of the waters.
And God said, "Let there be light"; and there was light.
And God saw that the light was good;
and God separated the light from the darkness.

God called the light Day, and the darkness he called Night.
And there was evening and morning, one day.

   Genesis

   Yin and *Yang* speak of the traditional Chinese concept of dynamic balance. They are opposites and yet they are dependent upon each other, complement each other. *Yin* is dark, cold, damp, descending, inner, slow, passive, substantial and female. *Yang* is light, hot, dry, ascending, outer, fast, active, invisible and male. Night is *Yin*, and day is *Yang*. Winter and rain are *Yin*, summer and drought are *Yang*. The Earth and the moon are *Yin*. The sky and the sun are *Yang*. Your inner life is *Yin*, and your outer life is *Yang*. Rest and fatigue are *Yin*, motion and activity are *Yang*. Your blood is *Yin*. Your *Qi* is *Yang*. Your body is *Yin*, your Spirit is *Yang*.

   Yin and *Yang* are in continuous interaction, always changing. Too much of either *Yin* or *Yang* will cause imbalance. Neither one is right or better. Each requires the other for its very existence. The good health and well-being of not only you and me, but also our planet, are dependent on the dynamic balance of the *Yin* and *Yang*.

The Five Elements
Yin and *Yang* are further divided into the Five Elements: Fire, Earth, Metal, Water and Wood. Fire generates Earth, which generates Metal, which conducts Water, which nourishes Wood, which nourishes Fire. The strength or weakness of any element influences all other elements.

   The Five Element theory provides a poetic and practical way to describe physical and emotional relationships within the body. It is easy to understand. I often use this approach to explain to a patient what is happening in his or her body.

   The Five Elements also apply to life. They encompass a philosophical approach which describes the seasons of nature, human interaction, history, politics and the cosmos. This broad

FIVE ELEMENT GENERATION CYCLE

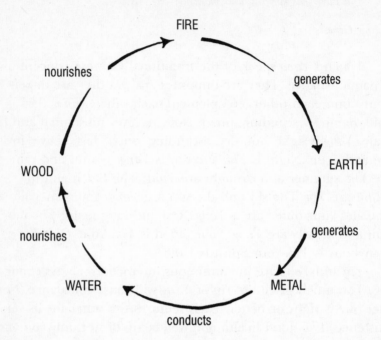

vision allows you to connect what is going on in your body with what is going on in the world around you.

The Five Elements and Their Associations

Each element has an individual personality, and interacts with the other elements creating a functional system. Each element has two organs associated with it, except for the Fire element, which has four. And each organ has a job description which explains its chief functions. When you look at the group of twelve organs with their job descriptions you get a picture of the interdependent functioning system that makes up your body.

When your Heart and Spirit are supported (Fire) you are content by day and sleep well at night. When you are well-rested and content, you will be relaxed and enjoy a healthy ap-

GENERATION CYCLE

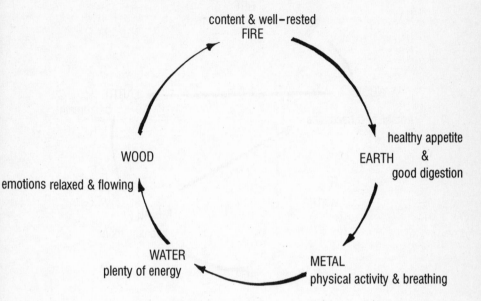

petite and good digestion (Earth). When you are well-fed and relaxed, there is a desire to be physically active. This circulates your energy, increases your breathing capacity and strengthens your Lungs and protective energy field (Metal). In turn, the well-exercised Lungs support abundant physical energy. When your energy is plentiful (Water), it nourishes your emotional state (Wood). And when your emotions are relaxed and flowing, you are content by day and sleep well at night (Fire).

Each part, or organ, is essential to the health and well-being of the whole. For example, constipation (Metal) frequently causes irritability, headaches (Wood) and bad breath (Earth).

Each element is associated with a particular direction, season and type of climate, and governs specific body parts and fluid secretions. Each element has a taste associated with it, as well as a sound, a color and an emotion. For instance, the Earth element governs the digestive organs, the muscles, the mouth

DESTRUCTION CYCLE

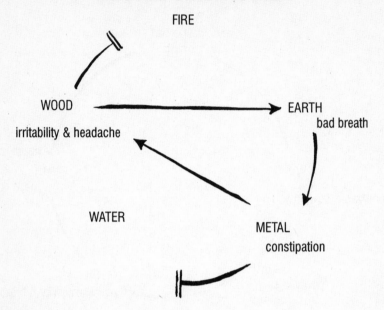

and saliva, and is associated with the center, late summer and humid weather. The taste associated with the Earth element is sweet, the sound singing or singsong, the color yellow or sallow and the emotion compassion.

There are qualities attributed to each element. For example, willpower and ambition are attributed to Water. Specific foods are connected with each element and are said to strengthen it, like millet and beef which help the Earth. In addition, each element governs a particular bodily function like trembling for Water, or belching for Earth.

An excess or deficiency of any emotion can affect you physically by blocking *Qi* in a meridian or damaging and weakening an organ following the destruction cycle. A common example of this is anger and irritability (Wood) causing indigestion and stomach pain (Earth). In Chapter Ten you will find more information on the Five Elements and their emotional associations.

DESTRUCTION CYCLE

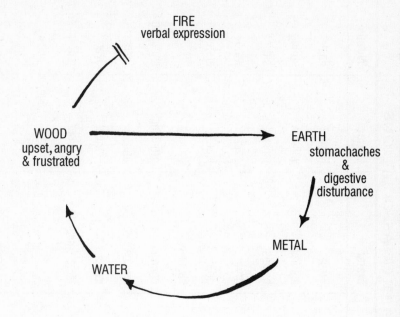

The Body Time Clock

The last traditional Chinese concept I will cover in this chapter is called the Body Time Clock. This maps *Qi* on its continuous travels through your meridians. And like a wave, there is a crest to this flow of *Qi* which moves to a different organ and meridian every two hours. Each organ has a two-hour peak time of day as described by this theory, when the maximum amount of *Qi* is flowing through that organ and meridian system. And conversely, each has a two-hour low, when it has the least energy available to it. For example, *Qi* peaks in the Stomach meridian and organ between 7 A.M. and 9 A.M.— breakfast time. Then the wave moves on to the Spleen between 9 A.M. and 11 A.M. Problems that recur at a given time each day may indicate a problem in the corresponding organ or meridian system.

The Body Time Clock is a system that can give clues to

FIVE ELEMENT CHART OF ASSOCIATIONS

	Fire	Earth	Metal	Water	Wood
Orientation	South	Center	West	North	East
Season	summer	late summer	autumn	winter	spring
Activity	growth	transformation	harvest	storage	birth
Weather	hot	damp	dry	cold	windy
Emotions	joy	meditation, worry	grief, sadness	fear	anger
Sound	laughter	singing	crying	groaning	shouting
Fluid	sweat	saliva	mucus	urine	tears
Organs	heart, small intestine, pericardium, triple warmer*	spleen, stomach	lungs, large intestine	kidneys, bladder	liver, gall bladder

	Fire	Earth	Metal	Water	Wood
Tissues	blood vessels	muscles	skin	bone	tendons
Indicator	complexion	lips	body hair	head hair	nails
Color	red	yellow	white	black	green
Powers	wisdom, concentration, vitality, creativity	obstinance, manifestation, giving	inspiration, justice, vigor	ambition, will, honor	mental clarity, control, patience, spirituality
Sense	tongue	mouth	nose	ear	eye
Taste	bitter	sweet	spicy	salty	sour
Grains	corn, amaranth	millet, barley	rice	beans	wheat, oats
Meat	lamb	beef	fish	pork	chicken

*The triple warmer is an organ system in traditional Chinese medicine that is comprised of three regions of the body: the lower warmer, which includes the organs of reproduction and elimination; the middle warmer, which includes the organs of digestion; and the upper warmer, which includes the heart and lungs. The triple warmer is involved in the circulation of energy and body fluids between these three regions of the body. ◆

THE BODY TIME CLOCK

Large Intestine	5 A.M.– 7 A.M.
Stomach	7 A.M.– 9 A.M.
Spleen	9 A.M.–11 A.M.
Heart	11 A.M.– 1 P.M.
Small Intestine	1 P.M.– 3 P.M.
Bladder	3 P.M.– 5 P.M.
Kidneys	5 P.M.– 7 P.M.
Pericardium	7 P.M.– 9 P.M.
Triple Warmer	9 P.M.–11 P.M.
Gall Bladder	11 P.M.– 1 A.M.
Liver	1 A.M.– 3 A.M.
Lungs	3 A.M.– 5 A.M.

what is going on in your body. Sometimes it provides great insight. Other times it is not applicable. Please don't rigidly adhere to it. It is a tool; one aspect of what traditional Chinese medicine has to offer. It is included in this book because it can be fun to use and it offers one more avenue of exploration in understanding your body.

Attractions and Aversions

You may want to notice which Five Element associations you feel strongly about. In traditional Chinese medicine we seek health through the free flow of *Qi* and the internal balance of the Five Elements. Attractions and aversions are clues to the weaknesses or excesses of the elements within you. Often when you follow a strong clue to a particular element you will discover that your health issues are described by that element.

For example, you may have a hard time each year in the spring. It's not that anything in particular has to happen, you just get depressed, irritable and the joy goes out of your life. When you look up spring in the Five Element chart, you'll see it is associated with the Wood element, the liver and gall bladder, wind, tendons and sinews, the eyes, anger and shouting. It may be that you don't like drafts and wind, you suffer from tight muscles and tendons, and eyestrain. And you may get angry easily, and shout, blaming others when you are irritated. This would indicate that you may benefit from working with your Wood element. Chapter Nine, Cleansing and Detoxification, and Chapter Ten, Emotional Health, both offer suggestions for working with the Wood element.

If you hate cold weather, you may want to look at self-care techniques that support your Water element (kidneys and adrenal glands) such as eating warm foods, regulating your blood sugar with diet and dressing warmly. If you frequently get colds, flus or sinus infections and have repeatedly taken courses of antibiotics, then consider self-care activities that support your Metal element (Lungs, *Wei Qi* and Intestines). Read Chapter Eight, The Immune System.

Attractions and aversions are not to be judged or seen as right or wrong. Rather, they are clues which provide information about who you are. If you fight against your nature and judge that to which you are naturally drawn, you prevent yourself from choosing the environment and the life situations in which you will thrive.

In Summary

This chapter has touched on some aspects of traditional Chinese medical theory. If you want to learn more, I have included a list of books in the appendix which are great resources on traditional Chinese medical theory, and cover it in much greater detail.

Whenever traditional Chinese theory is discussed certain

questions always arise, such as, "How did they figure this out? Why is one thing associated with the Metal element, another with Wood or Fire?" How the system came about and why it works I cannot say. What I can tell you is that it took thousands of years of observation and experience to develop it, and it does work. Try it and see for yourself.

CHAPTER 5

A Basic Healthy Diet

A discussion about food and diet is rarely a simple matter. We all have beliefs, assumptions and expectations about food. Among other things, food is commonly associated with comfort, love, control, power, how we look and feel, how others view us, morality and ethics. Each person's attitude is a unique blend of his or her personal history and experiences.

While reading this chapter, I would like you, as much as you are able, to let go of your assumptions about right and wrong regarding food and diet. For now, let's look at food and diet from the perspective of your body. At the most basic level, you eat to maintain your health and well-being. Food provides you with nutrients to build and repair your body, with sugar to fuel your brain, and with energy, life force, so that you may live.

Different bodies need different things at different times. The only person who knows what you need and want is you. You know this by listening to what your body says. Hard and fast rules simply do not apply. Yet there are some basics about how bodies work that can provide you with some guidelines to start working with food and diet from the perspective of your body.

What Does Your Body Need to Thrive?

The most important thing to understand about diet is that there is no right or wrong to it, yet there are consequences. How you feel is influenced by what you eat. The best foods to build your health depend on many things, including:

- the time of year,
- the climate you live in,
- your body type and constitution,
- your health history,
- your current state of health,
- your lifestyle and
- your digestion.

The most important thing to understand about eating is that the food you eat is transformed into your blood and your energy, also known as *Qi*. Eating good food at regular intervals provides you with a steady supply of *Qi*. Moreover, the quality and life force of the food you eat affects the quality and strength of your *Qi*. Since the *Qi* of fresh foods is stronger than frozen, canned or packaged foods, eating fresh foods is a simple way to increase your energy.

Eating whole foods, as opposed to those that are refined and processed, will also enhance your *Qi*. Food that is grown and raised naturally without pesticides, herbicides or hormones, and is free from additives and coloring will further enhance your health because it won't burden your liver, which has the job of neutralizing the toxins that enter your body.

The closer a food is to its natural state, the more life force it has to give you. Some people take this quite literally and eat only raw foods. From the traditional Chinese perspective a raw food diet is cold and damp, and can cause an accumulation of

Yin in the body. This may manifest as fluid retention, a slow metabolism, a sensitivity to cold and dampness, and poor digestion and assimilation. The excess *Yin* extinguishes what the traditional Chinese called digestive fire. In a hot, dry climate, and with a constitutionally strong body, a raw food diet may be beneficial. However, in a cold or damp climate, or in a body that is weak, sensitive to cold or retains fluid, this can cause imbalance and a deterioration of health.

Spectrum of Foods from Most *Yang* to Most *Yin*

Heating←——————————————————————→Cooling

Yang Foods←——————————————————————→*Yin* Foods

salt red meat grains roots bitter greens vegetables fruit tea alcohol miso poultry beans squashes potatoes lettuce fats + oils coffee drugs eggs fish nuts seaweeds yams sprouts sugar juice

(From Annemarie Colbin's book *Food and Healing*)

How Often Should You Eat?

Physically, the body generally operates best on three regular meals a day. If you have a fast metabolism you may feel better adding snacks at mid-morning and mid-afternoon. If you have a slow metabolism you will still want to eat three meals a day, however you may prefer a light breakfast such as blue-green algae or a protein shake with fruit.

Despite the body's requirement for regular food, many people have irregular eating habits. These habits usually develop over time, for a variety of reasons. The reasons I often hear include:

- I'm not hungry in the morning.
- I don't like breakfast.

• If I eat breakfast I never stop eating all day.
• I prefer coffee.
• There is no food in the house.
• I don't have time for breakfast.
• I don't want to take time during the day to eat.
• I want to lose weight, so I skip meals.

There are people who say they don't need three meals a day. They aren't hungry in the morning and don't need to eat until much later. Or they eat something for breakfast and don't eat again until dinnertime. They seem to do just fine nibbling and eating one or two meals a day.

You can get a lot of things done when you don't take time out to eat; however, the basic needs of your body are not being met. Many people lacking a morning appetite do carry on their life eating a meal or two a day, and often for years. What enables them to do this is that their bodies have backup systems which provide stored energy for stressful situations such as lack of food. But any backup system, if overused, will wear out. Over time, regularly relying on your backup system leaves your body depleted, exhausted and vulnerable to illness.

The pattern of skipping meals sets up an adversarial dynamic between your body and your mind, where your mind gets to do what it wants, while your body's needs are ignored. Your mind can only win for so long before your reserve tank runs dry and your body starts to falter. If you keep ignoring your body's needs, your body will often communicate a protest in the form of exhaustion, discomfort and illness in an attempt to get your attention.

Listening to your body may require a reorientation of your relationship with food, for one of the body's most basic needs is to eat regularly.

Digestion

Another basic need of the body is to digest and assimilate the food you eat. Digestion starts in the mouth with chewing, which prepares food for digestion by breaking it down into small pieces and mixing it with saliva. Saliva contains a digestive enzyme that begins the digestion of starches. Not chewing well interferes with digestion.

From the mouth, food passes down the esophagus and into the stomach where acid secretions start digesting proteins and milk products. The partially digested meal then moves into the small intestine where digestive enzymes from the pancreas and small intestine break down starches, fats, proteins and sugars. The liver and gall bladder add bile salts to aid in the digestion of fats. When your meal is broken down into small enough parts, the nutrients are assimilated into your bloodstream and distributed to your cells. Fiber and undigested food particles then move on to the intestines and are eliminated from the body.

If there are toxins or foreign chemicals in your food, they hopefully are filtered out of your bloodstream by your liver, and excreted from your body by your intestines. If your liver is unable to filter out and detoxify the toxins in your bloodstream, your body will store them, often in fat tissue. Ideally you eliminate *at least* once a day, to prevent the re-absorption of toxic matter into your bloodstream. Less frequent elimination can contribute to sluggishness, low energy, headaches, grouchiness and many more serious health problems. Drinking plenty of clean, non-chlorinated water will help your body eliminate wastes and reduce toxicity.

The Importance of Variety

It is common to eat the same foods over and over again, day after day. When I ask people what they eat for breakfast, most people who eat breakfast respond like this: "Everyday I have . . . " and then they tell me exactly what they eat every morning. Often the only changes are special breakfasts on the weekend, a hot cereal during cold weather and a cold cereal during warmer months.

Eating the same foods every day can contribute to the development of food allergies. If you develop food allergies then the foods you love and rely on can make you feel poorly. Regularly eating foods to which you have an allergic reaction wears on your immune system as it perceives that food as a threat to your system and forms antibodies against it. To avoid this, simply vary your diet. Instead of oatmeal every day, some days have buckwheat cereal, cracked brown rice cereal, or a multi-grain cereal. Check out the cereal section at your local co-op or health food store. You may be surprised at all the options there are. As you vary your cereal, also vary your milk source. Try soy milk, rice milk, oat milk and almond milk. For a real change, try heating up leftovers from dinner for your breakfast. Or have soup, as the Japanese do. Don't drink orange juice every morning, and vary the kind of sandwich you have at lunch. Use a variety of oils for cooking and salad dressing. Even vary your snacks.

Signs and symptoms of food allergy include: asthma, belching, bloating, chronic bladder infections, chronic infections, cramps; dark, puffy circles under your eyes; diarrhea, ear infections, eczema, flatulence, headaches, hives, insomnia, itchy nose and throat, joint pain, low blood sugar problems, rashes and sinus infections.

If you suspect you have food allergies, try eliminating the suspicious food or foods for two or three weeks, and see how you feel. Common allergens include: citrus fruits, corn, dairy, eggs, gluten, nuts, soy and wheat. Or you can eliminate all the common allergens and then slowly add one at a time back into your diet and watch your body's reactions. Particularly watch for bloating, diarrhea, fatigue, food cravings and flatulence after eating. Health food stores and co-ops now carry extensive selections of foods for people with common food allergies. A blood test to determine both immediate and delayed allergic reactions is available through the Great Smokies Diagnostic Laboratory.

Leaky Gut Syndrome

The quality of your digestion is responsive to your actions. While illnesses, medication, genetics and age can all play a part in your digestive capacity, you still can have a good deal of influence over the state of your digestion through the choices you make about how you eat, what you eat and when. Belching, bloating and gas all indicate a digestive disturbance.

If your food is not well-chewed, or if you do not have sufficient digestive enzymes, you may end up with partly undigested food in your digestive tract which can ferment, putrefy and cause gas. While gas is unseemly and inconvenient, more serious problems can develop from incompletely digested food. Some people suffer from what is commonly called "leaky gut syndrome," where the intestinal walls become more permeable than they were intended to be. This allows partly digested protein particles, among other things, to get out of your intestines and into your bloodstream. Here they may be seen as foreign invaders by your immune system, which responds with an allergic reaction. This can give rise to food sensitivities and allergies.

A variety of factors can contribute to leaky gut syndrome, including: poor digestion, nutritional deficiencies, alcohol consumption, non-steroidal anti-inflammatory drugs (such as ibuprofen), an imbalance in the bacteria population of the intestines, and parasites. Health conditions associated with leaky gut syndrome include: eczema, fatigue, food allergies, inflammatory bowel disease, inflammatory joint diseases and autoimmune diseases.

Taking digestive enzymes at the start of any meal containing cooked foods can often improve poor digestion. Plant-derived digestive enzymes such as Similase are comprehensive, acting on proteins, carbohydrates, fats and sugars.

Food Combining

Food combining is not necessary for someone with a healthy digestive system. However, if you suffer from poor digestion, conflicting food combinations can make your condition worse and lead to partially undigested food particles, fermentation and gas. Different foods require different enzymes and different pH ranges to be broken down. The basic rules of food combining are:

- Eat raw fruit alone, at least twenty minutes before a meal, or at least two hours after a meal. Fruit digests more rapidly than other foods and can cause fermentation if it sits around in the stomach waiting for other food to be digested.
- Eat non-vegetarian proteins such as meat, fish, cheese, eggs and milk separately from carbohydrates and starchy vegetables, like potatoes. You may eat them with non-starchy vegetables. So avoid steak and potatoes, or fish and rice. Instead, have your steak with snow peas and salad, or have a green salad with chicken, or a chef's salad.
- Vegetarian proteins such as legumes, beans and tofu can be combined with carbohydrates, starchy vegetables and non-starchy vegetables. Legumes and tofu with grains or potatoes are fine, as is tofu with rice and vegetables, or lentils, couscous and vegetables.

Food combining can interfere a good deal with most social dining situations. However, if you are suffering from digestive problems it can be helpful, as it eliminates digestive stress. If you have a digestive problem, you may want to start out with the first rule. Eat raw fruit separately from other foods and see how that feels. This can be incorporated into most people's lives with little difficulty. If your digestive problems are more severe, you may be motivated to rearrange your diet to accommodate food combining more thoroughly to see if it is a beneficial remedial diet for you.

The Traditional Chinese View on Food

Traditionally the Chinese knew that all food wasn't the same. Some foods built energy, some built blood, some warmed a cold body and some cooled a hot body. Some strengthened the Lungs and some the Kidneys.

They knew that digestive fire is what allows us to transform the food we eat into *Qi* and blood. They knew the way to strengthen digestive fire was by eating cooked foods, warming foods and spices, and by getting physical exercise. They knew cold, raw foods and cold drinks squelched digestive fire.

Think about it. Your body temperature is at about 98.6 degrees Fahrenheit. If you drink a glass of ice water or eat a bowl of ice cream, your body will have to heat that water or ice cream to 98.6 degrees as well. This is a waste of your digestive fire and *Qi*. It can cause stomachaches and diminish your digestive capacity. Experiment by eating only cooked, warm foods and hot beverages. See how you feel. Particularly ask your stomach how it feels.

In cold weather, when the inner fire not only needs to "cook" the food you eat but also heat your body, then warm, cooked foods are most appropriate. In hot weather, raw foods and cool drinks are more appropriate for many people. There are two main exceptions to this rule. If your body is weak and you feel cold or have poor digestion it would be better if you avoided cold, raw food and iced drinks regardless of the weather, until you rebuild your strength and digestive fire. And if your digestion is strong and your body is hot you may benefit from more cooling foods and drinks throughout the year.

What You Can Do to Strengthen Your Digestion

- Relax before you sit down to eat
- Chew your food well
- Drink liquids up to half an hour *before* your meal to allow stomach acid to build up before you eat
- Limit liquids during and right after a meal
- Take digestive enzymes when eating cooked food
- Cook legumes with a stick of kombu seaweed and a pinch of Hing (also called Asfoetida), a mixture of Indian spices that improves the digestibility of legumes
- Experiment with food combining
- Exercise regularly
- Cook with spices that aid digestion
- Avoid cold, raw foods except during hot weather
- Eat salads at room temperature, after the hot part of your meal
- Order hot water or hot lemon water at restaurants instead of iced water

---

Traditional Chinese theory also states that exercise supports digestion. And it is true. Exercise relieves accumulated stress, and when you allow yourself time to relax after the exertion of exercise, your nervous system shifts into relaxation mode. This facilitates digestion as your blood and energy gather in your belly and the secretion of digestive enzymes is stimulated.

Meat

Whether to eat meat or not is a subject about which people have strong opinions. For the purposes of this discussion, "meat" includes fish, poultry, pork, lamb, beef and wild game.

People choose not to eat meat for a variety of reasons including spiritual and political beliefs and health concerns. However, believing in something intellectually or spiritually does not necessarily mean it will be true for the physical body. Some people simply feel better physically when they eat meat, and others feel best on a meat-free diet. This has much more to do with your body type, the climate in which you live, your lifestyle and the state of your health, than it does your beliefs.

Some people who choose not to eat meat argue that our bodies are not designed to eat meat. They compare the teeth and digestive tracts of animals that are meat-eaters with animals that are vegetarians, and assert that our teeth and digestive tracts are similar to those animals that are vegetarians. They conclude that we too should be vegetarians.

This argument is fine on paper. However, in actual practice, many people simply experience better health while eating some meat. For hundreds of years many of our ancestors have been meat-eaters and our bodies are accustomed to this diet. Abruptly attempting to change what has developed over generations can be stressful and not necessarily beneficial.

Addressing the issue of killing animals to survive and thrive is a difficult and personal matter. We are animals, and all animals must eat to live, whether they eat meat, grains, vegetables, nuts or fruit. Where do we draw the line between the life we can take to nourish ourselves and the life we can't? I believe it is a denial of our animal nature, and our connection to all of nature, to say categorically that we *must not* kill animals to eat, even if that is what our bodies need to thrive. I know many people will disagree with me on this point. However, I have seen many unhealthy vegetarians regain health, vitality and balance by adding some meat to their diet.

Traditionally, the Chinese have used meat as a condiment, rather than the focus of a meal. Meat is warming, grounding and strengthening. It fortifies energy and rebuilds tissue. These warming and strengthening qualities give the body a kind of *Qi* that other forms of protein, such as beans, tofu, tempeh, nuts, dairy products and blue-green algae cannot. If you always feel cold and tired, are thin and pale, crave sugar or caffeine, have low blood sugar, live in a cold climate or are experiencing a high-stress lifestyle you may need this kind of energy and will most likely benefit from eating some meat.

The Chinese also taught that eating too much or too little of any one food, or category of foods, creates health problems. Just as those who eat no meat may benefit by adding some to their diet, people who eat a lot of meat may benefit by reducing their meat intake.

Dietary Changes for Vegetarians

If you are a vegetarian and want to experiment with eating meat, start slowly. Eat small quantities and chew thoroughly. If you haven't eaten meat for a while, your ability to digest it may have diminished. Try taking digestive enzymes to help your body digest the meat. Eat small amounts of organic meat several times in one week. How do you feel? If eating meat is beneficial for you, you will feel a difference. You will feel warmer, stronger, crave less sugar and your energy level will stabilize. Let your body be the judge. Do you feel better?

Different kinds of meat have different qualities of *Qi* and support different organs. Red meat has stronger *Yang Qi* than pork, poultry or fish. If you are very weak, there are several approaches to take. You can start out gently with organic chicken broth or chicken soup. Or you can go right to the serious medicine and have some thinly sliced beef in a stir-fry, or cook up a lamb vegetable stew. Experiment with different kinds of meat.

MEAT AS MEDICINE

lamb	beef	fish	pork	chicken
tonifies the heart, small intestine	tonifies the stomach, spleen	tonifies the lungs, large intestine	tonifies the kidneys, bladder	tonifies the liver, gall bladder

You may find that during summer months, or on vacation in a hot climate you desire less meat, or none at all. Listen to your body. Over your lifetime, your meat requirements will most likely change. For example, if you are run-down your body may want more meat to heal and rebuild. As you regain your strength, you may feel better eating less meat.

Dietary Changes for Meat-Eaters

If you are a big meat-eater and you want to make a change in your diet, I recommend eating more poultry and fish, and less red meat to start. Then, find a non-dairy-based vegetarian cookbook that appeals to you. Start experimenting with beans, legumes, tofu, tempeh and nuts. As you find dishes that you like, incorporate them into your diet. Some cookbooks I recommend are:

- Annemarie Colbin's *The Natural Gourmet*
- Amadea Morningstar's Indian cookbook *The Ayurvedic Cookbook*
- Martha Rose Shulman's *Mediterranean Light*

If you are eating meat twice a day, you may want to cut back to once a day. When you have found some vegetarian dishes you like, try having a no-meat day twice a week. See how it feels. Gradually reduce your meat consumption to a level where you feel good, comfortable and are achieving your health goals. If you are a big meat-eater, making these adjustments to your diet can be especially helpful if you have high blood pressure, high cholesterol or a family history of heart disease.

What about Organic Versus NonOrganic Produce, Dairy and Meat?

There are three clear benefits to eating organically produced foods. First, you will receive increased nutritional value from the food you eat if it is raised organically. Second, your body will benefit from a decreased exposure to toxins from the pesticides, herbicides, antibiotics and hormones found in non-organic produce, dairy and meat. Third, you will be supporting organic food producers who farm in a way that does not pollute soil, rivers and ground water with chemical fertilizers, and toxic herbicides and pesticides.

Rutgers University conducted a study comparing the nutritional value of organically grown vegetables to nonorganically grown vegetables. Organically grown tomatoes were over 5x higher in calcium, 13x higher in magnesium, and 1930x higher in iron compared to nonorganically grown tomatoes. Similar results were found when organic and nonorganic snap beans, cabbage, lettuce, and spinach were evaluated. Organic produce can be found at organic farm stands and farmers' markets, co-ops, health food stores and some grocery stores. And you can grow organic vegetables in your yard, on your patio or at your community garden plot if you are the gardening type.

I do not recommend eating meat that is raised on chemically treated feed, antibiotics or growth hormones. Meat is high on the food chain which means that it concentrates pesticide residues, as well as hormones and antibiotics. These foreign chemicals do not belong in your body and are not beneficial to your health. They tax your liver and upset your internal balance. You are not meant to be ingesting pesticide residues, antibiotics and hormones in your food. Organic and range-fed meat is available at health food stores, from local farmers and increasingly at grocery stores. Ask your grocery store or butcher about organic, range-fed meat in your area if you have difficulty finding it.

Dairy

Dairy products are an easy source of protein for vegetarians, but they are mucus-forming, high in fat, and for some people they can be the source of food allergies. Many people feel better reducing their intake of dairy products. Some have an easier time digesting dairy products from sheep and goats.

If you are eating dairy products, choose those that are from organically- or range-fed animals, and free of antibiotics and hormones such as bovine growth hormone, which is used in the United States to increase the milk production in cows. Cows treated with bovine growth hormone are more prone to getting mastitis and are therefore treated with more antibiotics. The repercussions of antibiotic overuse are discussed in Chapter Eight, so suffice it to say here that there are far-reaching health problems associated with the development of antibiotic-resistant strains of bacterium from the overuse of antibiotics.

Our bodies are infinitely delicate and complex and the repercussions of ingesting dairy products from animals treated with bovine growth hormone are not fully understood. Why take the risk, particularly with children, who commonly consume large quantities of dairy products? Request pesticide-free, hormone-free, and antibiotic-free dairy products from your health food store or grocery store whenever possible.

A Word on Sugar and Caffeine

Sugar is not food. It raises your blood sugar level, and so it does give you a quick burst of fuel, but it does not contain nutrients, and actually leeches nutrients from your body. So eating pure sugar is a net loss to your body nutritionally. In the history of human bodies, candy bars are a relatively new phenomenon. There are naturally occurring forms of concentrated sugar, like dates and maple syrup. But in general our bodies are not well-adapted to the frequent ingestion of large quantities of concentrated sugar, like candy bars.

A concentrated dose of sugar puts a big stress on the pancreas. Your pancreas is involved in keeping your blood sugar within a normal range so your brain can function. It does this by secreting insulin into your bloodstream when your blood sugar level is too high. The insulin then makes your cell walls more permeable to sugar, so sugar leaves your bloodstream and goes into your cells much faster than it does when insulin is not present. If your pancreas loses its ability to produce insulin, which can happen by simply overusing it, you may require a restricted diet, and drugs or insulin to keep your blood sugar within normal limits.

Caffeine is also not a food. It is a drug and it has a strong effect on your body. If you are drinking coffee or caffeinated sodas regularly, your liver will become adept at clearing caffeine, which is a toxin, from your body. This means that the better your liver is at clearing the caffeine, the less of a caffeine buzz you will get. You'll need more and more coffee to get you going in the morning. If you stop drinking coffee for a while and then have a cup, you will be amazed at what a strong drug it is. Your body will have lost its capacity to clear the caffeine quickly, and you will probably feel the effects much more strongly than when you were a regular coffee drinker.

I am not saying you should never have sugar or caffeine. But it is helpful to know what they do to you. When and how you use them has a big impact on how they affect you. If you treat them as if they were foods, you will deplete your reserve tank and weaken your digestive capacity. When you eat sugar or drink caffeinated beverages, do so *after* a meal, *not instead of it*. In this way their negative effects will be moderated.

The Basic Health Building Diet

It is generally best that the majority of your diet be comprised of fresh, organic whole grains, vegetables, legumes and fruits, and *at least* two servings of protein per day. Minimize consumption of dairy, with the exception of yogurt containing live acidophilus cultures. Whenever possible, eat meat and dairy products that have been organically raised. Have some of your protein servings come from fish, soy products, nuts and seeds. Use cold-pressed oils, like flaxseed, olive, safflower, sesame and sunflower. Minimize your intake of desserts, candy, chips, sodas, fried foods, fast foods, boxed, canned, frozen and instant foods, alcohol and caffeine. Listen to your body and experiment to find the balance of proteins, whole grains and legumes, vegetables and fruits that feel best to you.

Body Phases

As Marc David discusses in *Nourishing Wisdom: A Mind-Body Approach to Nutrition and Well-Being,* your optimal diet will vary in relation to what he refers to as your body phase. Are you cleansing, building or sustaining?

The cleansing phase is a time of purification, releasing toxins from the body and, in general, letting go. A building phase is a time of strengthening, fortifying and repairing. Sustaining is that phase of balance somewhere between clearing out and building up.

The body has its own wisdom and timing as it moves through these phases, and different styles of eating will contribute toward or distract from the intention of each phase. Raw fruits and vegetables facilitate cleansing, where animal products support a building phase. A diet somewhere in the middle of these two will tend to be sustaining.

Which phase you are in at any given time and what foods support you in that phase are what you will want to discover by listening to your body. Do you crave fruit in the morning, or does it leave you feeling cold and hungry? If fruit feels great in the morning, this may indicate that your body wants to cleanse a bit. If you are craving chicken soup, a hamburger, ribs or a steak, your body is most likely wanting to fortify and strengthen itself. When the simplicity of brown rice, vegetables and tofu appeal to you, or a bowl of miso or black bean soup, you may find you are in more of a sustaining mode. If all you want are stimulants like sugar and caffeine, then your body may well be in a building phase but it is not getting the protein it needs to do its job.

The different foods your body wants can tell you a lot about what phase you are in, and help you make food choices accordingly. When you regularly pay attention to how your body is responding to the food you are eating, it will help you to notice and respond to your body's changing needs. Particularly pay attention during seasonal changes, temperature changes, and changes in the status of your health and stress level.

It is also important to note that the foods that cleanse, build or sustain one person may not work for another. These are individual patterns and no one knows better than you what your experience is in your body.

If you have been steadily eating a building diet for years and you feel an urge to try a lighter, more sustaining diet, you may want to start out by finding a good natural foods restaurant. Discover which whole grains, beans and vegetables you prefer, how you like them prepared and how eating them makes you feel. Alternatively, you can find a new cookbook or take a cooking class. If you have been on a prolonged cleansing or sustaining diet and find yourself cold, weak, fatigued and craving stimulants, you may want to experiment with eating more building foods. Again, eating at a restaurant can be a good way to introduce new foods into your diet. Try ordering meat and see how it feels.

The following is a list of basic food groups to choose from.

Proteins include:

- blue-green algae,
- dairy products
- eggs,
- fish,
- meat,
- nuts,
- protein powders,

- seeds,
- tempeh and
- tofu.

Legumes include:

- aduki beans,
- black beans,
- great Northern beans,
- kidney beans,
- lentils,
- mung beans,
- navy beans,
- pinto beans and
- split peas.

(It is helpful to note that while legumes are often thought of as a good source of protein, many contain much more complex carbohydrate than protein. Therefore, if you are in a building phase and relying on legumes for your protein, you may not experience good results in terms of feeling supported and strengthened.)

Whole grains include:

- amaranth;
- barley;
- brown, basmati or wild rice;
- buckwheat;
- bulgur;
- corn;
- couscous;
- millet;
- oats;
- quinoa;
- rye;

- spelt;
- whole wheat.

Vegetables include:

- starchy vegetables such as potatoes, yams and corn;
- root vegetables such as carrots and onions;
- non-starchy vegetables such as broccoli, green beans, peppers and eggplant;
- leafy greens such as collards, chard and kale;
- salad greens;
- seaweeds

Fresh fruits include:

- apples and bananas,
- berries,
- citrus fruits,
- dried fruits,
- fruit juices,
- melons,
- pitted fruits and
- tropical fruits.

Examples of Meals:

Breakfast Grain with some protein and fat: oatmeal with yogurt and maple syrup, hot brown rice cereal with rice milk and almonds, buckwheat cereal with soy milk and raisins, yogurt with nuts and fruit, or a protein shake.

Snack Grain and/or protein: whole grain crackers or whole grain bread with almond butter, hummus or avocado; or yogurt.

Lunch Grain, protein and vegetable: tuna sandwich on whole grain bread and salad; chicken, vegetables and rice; tofu, rice and vegetables; or soup and salad.

Snack Fruit or vegetable: apple, carrot sticks or fresh fruit or vegetable juice.

Dinner Grain, vegetables and protein: chicken or lentil soup with a baked potato and salad; fish, vegetables and salad; black bean soup and salad; bean and rice burrito with vegetables.

In Summary

Three keys that will help you maintain a healthy diet throughout your life are eating regular meals that include a wide variety of quality foods, eating in moderation and listening to your body.

Regular meals provide a steady source of fuel for your brain which provides you with a stable internal environment and energy level. Variety in your diet will increase your ability to meet your body's nutritional needs and reduce your likelihood of developing food intolerances and allergies. Quality foods provide you with quality *Qi*. Eat a variety of whole, fresh, organic foods, and drink filtered, dechlorinated water whenever possible.

Be moderate in what you eat. Overeating is stressful for the organs of digestion and demands a great deal of your energy. Allow moderation to soften any rigidly held rules and beliefs you may have about food. This better allows you to hear what your body is actually saying.

Listening is perhaps the most important key. Listen to your body. If it is hungry, feed it. If it feels cold, eat something hot. If you feel better eating meat, eat meat. Treat your body as you would a six-year-old who is very precious to you. Be the wise parent who listens to his or her child, but does not indulge every whim. When you eat meat, choose organic meat. If your body wants a treat, eat dinner first, then have a cookie or two. If you are not hungry, then assume your body has a good reason for it, and don't make yourself eat.

In general, give your body a basic routine, so it knows what to expect: breakfast every morning, then lunch in the middle of the day, snacks when you get hungry and dinner every night. This is the kind of dependability that your body wants to relax, to feel safe and comfortable. And when your body is relaxed and comfortable, so are you.

CHAPTER 6

The Importance of Eating Breakfast: Blood Sugar Regulation

One of the most important things that you can do for your health and well-being is to eat breakfast. If you rely on coffee in the morning, sugar to keep you going throughout the day, lack a morning appetite, skip meals, have a history of dieting or an eating disorder, are tired, suffer from headaches or migraines, mood swings, anxiety, allergies, PMS, chronic low back pain or are addressing a drug or alcohol problem, then I recommend you try regulating your blood sugar with diet.

To regulate blood sugar it is best to start by eating a good breakfast. Eating breakfast can be a big hurdle if you don't have a morning appetite. It may take a few weeks of eating in the morning before the body's natural appetite awakens. Persevere for a week or two if this is your case, and see how you feel. Notice if you start to feel hungry in the morning. Are your energy and mood more steady throughout the day? Do you still have energy in the evening? On days when you skip breakfast, do familiar feelings come back, food cravings, energy jags? On days when you regulate your blood sugar with diet, do you feel better?

To regulate your blood sugar with diet, it is best to regularly eat foods that release a slow and steady supply of sugar into your bloodstream throughout the day. This gives your brain the fuel it needs to function, and it puts your body in a healing and repairing mode, instead of a stressed out, degenerating mode.

When your blood sugar levels are too high or too low, your brain can't function properly. This alerts your body to enter an emergency mode of operation to bring your blood sugar levels back within normal limits. The purpose of regulating your blood sugar with diet is to provide your brain with a steady supply of fuel and to take the burden of regulating your blood sugar off your internal organs. This strengthens your immune system, stabilizes your energy level and mood, and improves your overall health.

Running on Empty

Your main source of *Qi* is wholesome food, food with life force in it. In our society many people don't distinguish between sugar, coffee and sodas, and real food containing *Qi*. However, our bodies were designed to be fueled by real food, not caffeine and sugar. Not understanding this causes much unnecessary suffering in terms of fatigue, depression, weight gain and degenerating health.

Real food is digested in your stomach and small intestine and enters your bloodstream in the form of sugar. This sugar fuels your brain. Since your brain must have a steady fuel supply to function properly, your body has a built-in backup system to cover for emergencies when your blood sugar level drops. This allows your brain to keep working even if you haven't eaten anything. When your eating patterns are erratic or when you favor nonfoods, like sugar and caffeine, over real food, your body comes to rely on this backup system as a part of your daily life. This puts enormous stress on your internal organs and body systems.

Regulating your blood sugar by what you eat restores your

body to its natural mode of operation. Your energy comes from the food you eat, and your backup system is there for emergencies. You stop running on empty, and start running on food. It

---

Example of a Stimulant-Based Diet

You ate dinner at 7:00 P.M. and had a little snack about 10:00 P.M., then went to bed at 11:00 P.M. Your alarm went off at 6:30 A.M. At this point, you've eaten nothing for 8½ hours. You get up, shower, dress for work, grab a cup of coffee and run out the door. It is now 7:45 A.M. At 8:30 A.M. you arrive at work and have a meeting in fifteen minutes. So you pour yourself another cup of coffee, grab a muffin and head into the meeting. It is now 8:45 A.M. You are active, needing to think clearly and make decisions, and it has been 10¾ hours since you had any real food. All that muffin did was spike your blood sugar level for a short time. Soon you will be experiencing a blood sugar crash and will need something else to get your sugar level up, a cup of coffee, some more sugar or an adrenaline rush caused by stress.

What has been going on in your body all this time? While you were sleeping your metabolism slowed down. Your body was doing a lot of healing and rebuilding. Your brain was sorting the input of the day, organizing itself, dreaming. Sleep is often the only time during the day when you have your energy and attention to yourself.

When you woke up your body needed fuel to start the day. But you were not in the habit of eating in the morning, so you had a cup of coffee to wake you up and clear your head. While caffeine does clear your head and give you energy, it accomplishes this by stimulating your body to produce adrenaline. This gives you access to stored energy. That cup of coffee allows you to walk right past the digestive center and all its capacities, and go straight into the reserve tank, pouring stored sugar into the bloodstream. The question is, how long can you do this before the reserve tank runs dry?

is a simple process, however it takes some time and planning. A muffin and a cup of coffee won't do it. What you need is serious fuel—protein and vegetables. The good news is that the benefits are immediate, tangible and well worth the effort.

Are You Afraid to Eat Breakfast?

Many people are afraid to eat breakfast because when they do they are hungry all day, can't stop eating, and are afraid that they will gain twenty pounds in two weeks simply by opening the door marked "Breakfast."

If you haven't been eating breakfast, you probably *will* have a big appetite initially and eat more than you usually do. *This is normal and it won't last forever.* As your body gets used to being given what it needs, that body-based panic will subside, and with it the excessive appetite. Remember, you may have been running on empty for a long time. Your body may feel that this is not going to last and it had better take advantage of this fuel stop while it can.

In time, a month or so, your body will trust you more. It will start to rely on the breakfast routine: I'm really going to get breakfast every morning! What a relief!

Things Look Different When You Regulate Your Blood Sugar with Diet

You may discover when you regulate your blood sugar with diet that you are not nearly as weak-willed as you thought you were. Many people feel they simply have no self-control and could never stop eating or drinking their favorite sugar or stimulant. They feel they have no choice in the matter. I'm not saying categorically that this isn't true; however, I often see that in fact it isn't true. The reality is that when your blood sugar is low, your brain is starved for fuel and it *is* a life and death matter. It is not about self-discipline, willpower or inner strength.

It is survival, period. Survival is wired into your system. And one way your body knows how to survive is to raise your blood sugar level.

Think about what you use to raise your blood sugar. It may be sugar from dried fruit, a muffin, a candy bar, cookies, ice cream or a glass of juice or wine. Or it could be caffeine from sodas, coffee or black tea. You may use nicotine from a cigarette or a jolt of adrenaline caused by a stressful event to raise your blood sugar. They all do a similar thing. They are helping you survive by increasing your blood sugar level so your brain can function.

What I'd like you to do before resigning yourself to the "no willpower club" is to regulate your blood sugar by what you eat for a week or two and watch your cravings. I'm not saying they will *all* go away. But I think you will notice they change. And over time, if you stick with it and let your body heal, you will notice there was a strong physiological basis to what you had been chalking up to poor character.

When you start to regulate your blood sugar, your internal world steadies and calms. Sometimes from this new perspective you look out at the world around you and see things differently. You may find yourself more tolerant of the small annoyances of daily life as you stop living at the edge of your emotional cushion. At the same time, as your internal chaos subsides, you often see things that you just didn't notice before. Your sense of personal boundaries and limits may become more clearly defined, more discerning.

The Transition from Sugar and Stimulants to Food

When you start to regulate your blood sugar, a layer of exhaustion may be uncovered. Let's talk about what is happening when this occurs so you won't be caught off-guard. If you have been running on empty for weeks, months or years, then it's going to take some time for your body to adjust to running on food-based fuel instead of caffeine and sugar.

Shifting from reserve to your digestive center is a big change. It is like putting your credit cards in the back of your desk drawer and making a pact with yourself to pull them out only in a *real* emergency. What often happens is you have to scale down your energy expenditures so they are in line with what you actually take in during a day. One reason people often find themselves eating all the time when they first start is that they are frantically trying to make fuel to do all the things they normally do.

For some people, the first month on a blood sugar regulating diet is the most challenging. The exhaustion level or energetic debt that is revealed can be hard to face. However, it's not going to get any easier.

If your reserve tank is empty, you will probably feel tired and out of sorts without your usual stimulant to pump you up. Let yourself sink down into that exhaustion, and you will have the opportunity to heal it. Sleep, stare at the ceiling or out the window. Do nothing, nap, get up, eat and take another nap. Be kind to yourself. You are healing your exhaustion. Stay at home and let yourself rest as much as you can. In the long run you will have much more *real* energy. But you may have to wait a bit. First you have to heal.

At first you will notice that you are getting bursts of energy and you will recognize it as your old self, how you used to feel. It will be different than when you have a cup of coffee in the morning. Your own energy will tend to be steadier, calmer and more focused. You will probably get more done and find yourself being more efficient, concentrating better and having more patience. It will feel good.

You may only get moments of energy at the beginning, interspersed with exhaustion. Gradually the periods of exhaustion will get smaller and the periods of energy will get longer. Soon you will be experiencing a new kind of steady, grounded energy most of the time. When it's used up you'll know it is

BLOOD SUGAR REGULATION

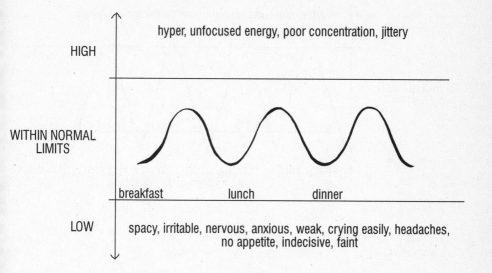

time to eat something, stretch, go for a walk, take a break or nap. It will not be inhuman, limitless energy. It will be exactly how much energy you actually have.

How Long Will It Take?

How long it takes depends on how depleted you are, how much you are willing and able to listen to your body and give it what it asks for, and how quickly or slowly your body heals. You may feel exhausted for a weekend, a week or a month. And it may take six to nine months before your organs recover. There is no right amount of time for healing. Just pay attention to your body and how you feel. In this way you will learn about *your* body, *your* depletion, and *your* healing process.

Follow a blood sugar stabilizing diet until you feel strong, stable and supported by what you eat. Then you may want to shift back to a basic healthy diet. In times of stress, when traveling, and for women during their pre-menstrual phase, revert-

THE BLOOD SUGAR ROLLER COASTER

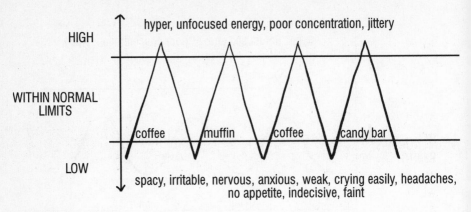

ing to the blood sugar regulating diet can give your body extra support.

The Blood Sugar Regulating Diet— Where to Start?

The idea is to start the day with a strong foundation. It is like putting a big log on the fire instead of a bunch of balled-up newspapers. What we are looking for first thing in the morning is staying power.

Breakfast Eat protein and vegetables for breakfast. This does not have to be a large meal, but eat it as soon as possible after getting up. Leftovers from dinner make it easy.

You eat protein because it digests slowly, which releases sugar into the bloodstream at a slow, steady pace and gives you a steady supply of energy to start the day. The vegetables keep your blood pH in balance, as most proteins acidify the blood and the alkalinity of vegetables balances this.

Some examples of a blood sugar regulating breakfast are: beans, tofu or tempeh with vegetables; bean or chicken soup with vegetables; chicken, beef or fish with vegetables; miso vegetable soup with tofu; yogurt, nuts and seeds or leftovers from dinner.

It can be hard to adjust to eating dinner food first thing in the morning. However, if this diet works for you, you will feel a difference right away, and *that* is a motivator. Your blood sugar level will be stable and so will you.

Mid-Morning Snack After a dinner-style breakfast it's normal to get hungry a few hours later. This is a good time for a whole grain snack. Do not skip this snack if you are hungry. Some examples are: whole grain crackers with avocado or hummus; whole grain bread with almond butter; a nori roll (a Japanese dish: seaweed rolled around rice and vegetables or fish); mochi or oatmeal.

Lunch Have lunch at a reasonable hour. Don't wait until three o'clock. Have protein, vegetable and a whole grain. Try a tuna fish sandwich with salad; tofu, vegetables and rice; bean or meat soup, baked potato and salad; a burrito, tostada or stir-fry vegetables with beef and rice.

Mid-Afternoon Snack If you are hungry in the afternoon, have a healthy snack. Try whole grain crackers with almond butter or tahini and brown rice syrup; yogurt; carrot sticks; almonds or pumpkin seeds or fruit.

Dinner I generally recommend that people eat their usual dinner. However, anyone having trouble sleeping may want to avoid protein at dinner. See if you sleep better with most of your protein in the first half of the day. Try soup and salad, or baked potato, vegetable-flour pasta or whole grains with vegetables and salad.

Once you have started your day with a solid breakfast, mid-morning snack and lunch, there is not much you can do the rest of the day to cause major blood sugar problems. *However, if you miss breakfast and don't get that steady start, there is little you can do the rest of the day to make up for it.* The idea is to give your body enough fuel to carry you through the day without having to fall back on your emergency reserves.

For people with moderate symptoms, I recommend eating a good breakfast, snack and lunch, then eat as you like the rest of the day. The freedom in this approach works well for many people, and the results are good in terms of energy stabilization and strengthening.

If your goal is to give yourself a tune up, then dessert or a glass of wine now and again will most likely be a source of enjoyment and not disrupt your healing process. However, the best way to find out is to try it and observe. How do you sleep after a glass of wine? How do you feel in the morning after eating dessert? Do different kinds of desserts work better for you than others?

For people with strong symptoms of depletion, a stricter approach is appropriate until your symptoms start improving. Avoid all stimulants, sugars, fruits and simple carbohydrates for at least a month. Be sure to eat a good afternoon snack if you are hungry and a healthy dinner at a reasonable hour. If your goal is to address a serious health condition, then a whole grain and vegetable dinner, with or without protein, is appropriate.

If you suspect you have food allergies, avoid corn, dairy, eggs, nuts, soy and wheat for the first few weeks. Then reintroduce them one at a time to watch for reactions.

Whichever approach you choose, gradually you will want to experiment with reintroducing into your diet the things you miss eating. Let your body tell you how it feels. Do fruits work for you now? Do you still need protein for breakfast, or can oatmeal sustain you? As the adrenal glands become rested and restored and your energy reserves increase, your body will become more forgiving and you won't suffer your old symptoms as much when you stray from your diet.

The Three Keys to Regulating Your Blood Sugar with Diet Are:

- eat breakfast shortly after getting up. Have protein and vegetables (dinner food),
- mid-morning have a whole grain snack, and
- eat lunch at a reasonable hour. Have protein, vegetables and a whole grain.

Animal Proteins include:

- beef,
- cheese,
- chicken,
- eggs,
- fish,
- lamb,
- milk,
- pork,
- turkey and
- yogurt.

Vegetarian Proteins include:

- blue-green algae,
- legumes,
- nuts,
- seeds,
- soy-based protein powder,
- tempeh and
- tofu.

Whole Grains include:

- any whole grain (rice, barley, millet, corn, quinoa, oats, bulgur, buckwheat, spelt, couscous),
- whole grain breads,

- whole wheat or corn tortillas or chappatis,
- popped corn,
- rice cakes,
- tortilla chips, and
- whole grain and vegetable-flour pastas.

Supplements That May Be Helpful for You:

- B complex,
- vitamin C,
- multimineral,
- glandular supplements to support the adrenal glands and pancreas, and
- digestive enzymes.

Encouragement

When you start regulating your blood sugar with diet, please don't expect to be perfect. Sometimes you won't have the time, or you won't feel like it. Whatever the reason, please do not beat yourself up. You are not a failure. Don't give up. The whole thing is an experiment. Be curious about what happens when you don't regulate your blood sugar with diet. Pay attention to how you feel. It is the perfect opportunity to see if this diet makes a difference for you.

Do whatever you need to make this feel good. Be moderate. This is not deprivation or punishment. It is not a two-week crash diet. This is your life. The point is to feel better, not worse. Don't set yourself up for a backlash by being *really* good followed by a binge of eating everything of which you felt deprived. You are finding a way to let your organs heal, stabilize your energy and mood, support your immune system and establish a sustainable lifestyle.

What Happens in Your Body When You Use Sugar and Stimulants (More details for those of you who are interested)

Certain organs in your body, the adrenal glands, liver and pancreas, are particularly stressed when you do not regulate your blood sugar with diet. The adrenal glands sit on top of the kidneys and one of their jobs is to raise blood sugar levels. They do this by secreting adrenaline, which signals the liver to release stored sugar (glycogen) into the bloodstream. Your adrenal glands do this throughout the day whenever your blood sugar level starts to drop, or whenever you become stressed or fearful.

The release of adrenaline causes an energy rush. It stimulates your nervous system causing a hyper-alert state, sends additional strength to the muscles of your arms and legs and raises your blood pressure and pulse rate. This is a survival mechanism nature has given you so you can physically respond to emergencies. The energy released by adrenaline is short-lived, as your body burns up sugar rapidly.

When a stress is prolonged, your body needs a more sustained source of energy. The adrenal glands also secrete corticosteroids, other stress hormones, that cause you to break down protein. This gives you the more sustained energy you need to cope with an ongoing stress.

Your body does not distinguish between physical danger and emotional stress. When you get an energy surge during a telephone call, or a business meeting, you do not generally have the opportunity to release it by physically battling your opponent, or lifting your desk and hurling it out the window. You experience an adrenaline rush without physical release, leaving you with an edgy nervous system, exhausted from the energy crash that follows a high.

If this happens regularly, over time your adrenal glands will become depleted, and your ability to respond to stress will diminish. You will feel tired on awakening and need coffee to get going, want sugar in the afternoon, and often desire alcohol in the evening to unwind. You'll be less patient and more irritable, and your body will start exhibiting symptoms of discomfort and distress. Your immune system may become depressed. Women may experience an increase in premenstrual symptoms. In general, your body's ability to spring back to normal after any sort of stress will diminish.

Changing your diet by regularly eating foods that release their sugars into the bloodstream slowly and steadily, and using nutritional supplements that support the adrenal glands, gives them a chance to heal so they can once again function normally.

Your pancreas is also involved in blood sugar regulation. It secretes insulin after you eat. It causes sugar from the food you have digested to move out of the bloodstream and into your cells at a faster than normal rate. The kind of food you eat tells the pancreas how much insulin to secrete. Foods that break down quickly like sugar, and refined foods such as baked goods, white bread and most breakfast cereals cause a rapid rise in blood sugar. If such foods are eaten regularly, particularly instead of a meal, the pancreas will be called upon often to produce insulin to bring your blood sugar levels back to normal. Over time, this exhausts the pancreas and can diminish its ability to produce insulin.

Another problem associated with foods that cause a rapid rise in blood sugar is that the pancreas may overreact by secreting too much insulin to get all that sugar out of the bloodstream fast. This results in lowering the blood sugar too far. Then the adrenal glands must signal the liver to release more stored sugar to get your blood sugar level back up. This is the blood sugar roller coaster. It is stressful and exhausting for your body physically, mentally, emotionally and energetically. It erodes your health and well-being.

As with the adrenal glands, you can support and heal the pancreas by eating foods that release their sugars into the bloodstream slowly and steadily and by taking nutritional supplements to support the pancreas.

In Summary

Of all the self-care activities you can do, regulating your blood sugar is among the most important. If you suffer from fatigue, low immunity, have a history of poor eating habits or an eating disorder, try investing six to nine months in rebuilding your energy reserves by regulating your blood sugar. This will take stress off your internal organs and immune system, allow your body to heal and repair itself, and you will learn about your body and how it communicates. Your energy level, mood, and mental focus will improve, and so will your overall health and resistance to illness.

CHAPTER 7

Restoring *Qi* with Relaxation, Sleep and Exercise

S ome people are born with a strong constitution. It's like getting a big inheritance at birth. Other people are born with a weak constitution, less Kidney *Qi*. Some people can move through life taking abysmal care of themselves and it doesn't seem to have an affect. Other people are like finely tuned instruments and require all sorts of care and attention to feel well. You can resist the way things are, comparing your health and Kidney *Qi* to someone else's, but it won't change the way things are. I recommend you accept your Kidney *Qi* as it is, and do the best you can to nurture and support it through self-care. It is not only what you are born with, but what you do with what you have, that can make a difference in life.

From the traditional Chinese perspective, your Kidney *Qi* is determined by the amount of Kidney *Qi* your mother and father had at your conception. This provides the basis of your Kidney *Qi* for life. It is your reserve tank, your inheritance. Once you have been given it, it is up to you to take care of it.

Throughout childhood and youth most people have abundant energy and take it thoroughly for granted. At some point in their teens or twenties, many people will notice a change in that energy. They just don't have the same resilience they once had. They can't do the crazy things they once could without paying for it. This is the point where your body first starts speaking up, asking for support for its needs to be met—by you.

This is like the first notice you get about an unpaid bill. It is an ideal time to start learning about self-care. However, many of us passed this point long ago without learning how to care for ourselves. Instead, we learned how to tap into our reserve tank and use that backup energy to support us in living our daily lives. To do this we usually found a chemical support like caffeine, nicotine, sugar, diet pills or other stimulants— even stress—to help us.

The problem with this approach is that one day the reserve tank will be empty, our inheritance spent, and then we will really be in trouble. However, there will be warning signs along the way . . . like the red lights on the dashboard of a car warning you to fill the gas tank. Recognizing and heeding these warning signals can alleviate a crisis if you adjust your behavior before the reserve tank is empty.

Each warning signal is like a stronger notice that your bill must be paid. Each time you can again choose to override your body's messages and keep on living as you have been—overextending yourself and your energy. Or you can listen to your body, welcome its messages and accept the fact that you are experiencing some limitations.

See what you can learn from them. This is when your body can start teaching you about yourself and your individual needs. It is also a time when your body will start instructing you on what is true for you as opposed to what society teaches. It can be a time of differentiation and individuation from group norms. The current norm is toward doing and accomplishing. Your body, however, may have a more relaxed agenda in mind. If you listen to your body and give yourself enough sleep, regular meals, rest, relaxation, vacations and the slower pace your body may prefer, you will be choosing to cultivate a harmonious relationship with your body.

This is not to say that there won't be conflicts, particularly with other people. As your priorities shift you may find yourself in conflict at times with other people's expectations. "What do you mean you are doing nothing?" a friend may demand, as if it were a criminal act. Let people have their reactions. Some people may be jealous when they see you taking care of yourself and being kind to yourself in a way that they aren't to themselves. They may wonder, why does *she* get to rest and I don't?

It is a good question. The answer lies in your choices and priorities. People will often say, "Oh, *I* couldn't do that!" But look at their priorities. Look at the choices they make instead. If you have made the choice to begin respecting your body's messages, you may find yourself the object of curiosity and criticism. Simply living your life in alignment with your body will give permission to those around you to do the same.

If you notice you do not want to do something and you force yourself to do it anyway, you might want to notice how long it takes you to complete the task. How many mistakes do you make? Then another time when you do feel like doing the same task, notice how that feels. What is it like to work *with* your energy as opposed to working *against* it? Is there a difference? This is something you can experiment with to start developing a more trusting relationship with your body. If your body says, "I want to nap," and you say, "No, we are going to do this chore," just notice. If your body says, "I want to nap," and you say, "Okay, we'll nap," notice that. Then pay attention to your daydreams during that nap. How do you feel when you get up?

See what happens when you trust your body's messages. Start small. Pick a little message that won't make a big problem in your life if it doesn't work out. Do as your body asks, and then see how you feel. What happens? Are you surprised? Allow yourself to start experimenting with trusting your body as a friend, an ally, someone who is in this life *with* you, supporting you, providing you with help and guidance.

For Those Who Long Ago Stopped Noticing the Warning Signs

As you read this you may look back and recognize that, yes, you had plenty of energy in your youth and you may also see the point at which that changed. You may recognize that your body asked you to slow down long ago and you didn't. You may go through the list of chemical supports you have been using ever since. You may realize that there was a critical juncture that you passed years ago. You may see that you have been overextending yourself and draining your reserve tank for many, many years. So what now? What happens if you've already missed many warning lights?

The important thing is to recognize that you have been pushing yourself beyond your true capacity. Once you see that, if you choose to make some changes, then this book is full of suggestions about what you can do to bring yourself back into balance. First you will want to go on a blood sugar regulating diet and back off your chemical supports. Then you will see how far you have pushed yourself. The most common repercussion of depleting your reserve tank is exhaustion. You will want to rest and get enough sleep. Resting is when you allow yourself to simply be, as you are, in that moment. Enough sleep is when you wake up on your own, without your alarm clock, and you feel rested and are ready to get up.

It can be a huge challenge to let yourself sink into your exhaustion and rest. It can feel like it will never end, like it is totally interfering with your life. "Why me? Why now? No one else feels like this!" It is easy to start whining about exhaustion. "I work so hard. I'm barely getting by now, and you want me to sleep more! Where am I going to get the time for that?" Listen to the way you talk to yourself inside your head. Imagine yourself as a small child, a six-year-old, listening to someone talk to you that way. We can be so hard on ourselves.

If you notice yourself whining about how exhausted you are, then step back a minute and take some time to get an overview of your life. Where are your time, energy and attention going? Who or what are you nurturing and supporting? What is supporting and sustaining you? Are you eating regularly and sleeping enough? Do you drink enough water during the day? Are you taking time for yourself? When was your last vacation?

Often when you are in a "poor me" mind-set, you are living your life in an unsustainable manner. You are expecting more of yourself than is reasonable. This is an important thing to recognize and address. There is an excellent book I recommend to anyone who is overwhelmed and living at an unsustainable pace. It is called *How to Organize Your Life When You Don't Have the Time*, by Stephanie Culp.

When you are living in an unsustainable fashion it can be hard to take an overview of your life. Reality may not be easy to face, but it is often not as impossible as your "poor me" mind-set would have you believe. Read *How to Organize Your Life*, and follow Stephanie's suggestions.

Warmth and the Restoration of Kidney Qi

If your Kidney *Qi* is deficient, it is important to eat warm foods and keep your body warm. Eating warm foods means eating and drinking nothing colder than room temperature, preferably eating all cooked, hot foods and drinking only hot beverages, including hot water. Putting a slice of fresh lemon in hot water improves the taste. To avoid iced water in restaurants try ordering hot lemon water. Have lightly steamed vegetable salads instead of cold, raw salads. And avoid ice, ice cream, cold sodas and cold sandwiches. In the world of Chinese medicine, eating meat, walnuts and black beans are three traditional methods of strengthening Kidney *Qi* with food.

Keeping your body warm means wearing enough clothes. Are you going sockless a bit late in the season? Are you ignoring the message that your ankles are feeling cold? Notice if there is a draft between the bottom of your pants and your socks. How do your neck and chest feel? Is there a draft or sensitivity to cold there that you have been overlooking? If so, wear turtlenecks, scarves and jackets with collars and hoods. Wear a hat. Do you feel chilled and sensitive to cold around your lower back? Is there a draft that comes in there? If so, wrap a warm scarf around your lower back and abdomen underneath your clothes or wear a jacket that covers your buttocks.

Avoid walking barefooted in cold weather or on cold floors. The first point on your Kidney meridian is located on the ball of your foot. Walking barefooted on cold floors allows your Kidney *Qi* to be drained out through this point and into the cold floor. Protect your Kidney *Qi* by wearing warm socks, leg warmers bunched around your ankles and slippers or shoes in cold weather. When you are dressing to go out, ask yourself if you would let your six-year-old go out dressed the way you are.

Sleep, Dreams and the Restoration of Qi

It is important to recognize and give the body what it requires to enjoy good health. One request your body will often make is for adequate sleep. It is essential to your health, well-being and the restoration of *Qi*. Not getting enough sleep is one way to use up your reserve energy. Without ample, deep, restful sleep, your body will not thrive and your immune system will not function at its best.

Regularly getting less sleep than you need is like regularly using a credit card to buy things you can't afford. In time you'll have to pay off your debt, and the longer you wait the harder it will be. Taking a daily nap can be a good way to make up for a backlog of sleep deficiency.

Not only is sleep important to your health, but so are your dreams. Dreams can bring you in contact with your body and its language. You might want to keep a dream journal by your bed and write down your dreams first thing in the morning or when they wake you in the night. Then in the light of day you can read them over and start to learn the language in which your dreams speak. Paying attention to your dreams is a good way to connect with and listen to your inner voice, your inner navigator. When you are sailing off course, your dreams will often warn you. Keeping a dream journal is one more way to understand what your body is saying to you.

Sometimes When You Stop and Rest You Feel Worse

Sometimes when you stop to rest, relax and take some time off you will feel worse, especially if your life is normally busy and stressful. A deep layer of exhaustion may be revealed. You may get headaches, stomachaches, "catch" a cold or feel depressed. This is normal. You are decompressing, and it can be uncomfortable. However, if you allow yourself to go through the discomfort, you will get to a place of true relaxation and your body will be able to recharge on a deep level.

You may notice whenever you have some down time that there is a recurring theme to your discomfort. You may always get a cold, a headache or a familiar depression may settle in. As your body relaxes, specific areas of deeply held tension may be uncovered. Particularly if the same pattern repeats itself, you can bet that you are carrying this tension around every day, but that your normal hectic pace keeps you from noticing it. Take advantage of these times when deeper tensions are revealed. What is the message? What are these stomachaches about? What is the theme of this recurring depression? This is a great time to explore the messages in your tension and holding patterns. Get a massage, have a counseling session, spend some quality time with yourself, really pay attention to your feelings and what your body is saying.

If you get sick when you take a week-long vacation, then arrange a longer vacation next time so that you have a chance to enjoy the relaxation that follows the release of tension. If a longer vacation does not seem possible, then consider doing a weekly or monthly vacation day. Unplug your phone, stay in bed, read a good book, rent a bunch of movies, stare out the windows, or go out into nature and allow your body to soak up the *Qi* in your surroundings. Spend a day in silence. Get away from the concerns of your daily life. When you allow your body to decompress on a regular basis it's like letting steam out of a pressure cooker. The intensity of your next big decompression will be lessened and you'll be able to enjoy your next vacation more.

Restoring Your Qi *with Exercise*

Exercise helps your body cope with stress. It strengthens your muscles, improves your sleep and digestion, and strengthens your digestive fire by raising your body temperature and increasing your metabolism. It decreases fat and builds muscle, which improves your body's ability to burn and use the food you eat. While moderate exercise can cause a short-term increase in stress on your body, the longer-term results are a release and reduction of stress.

Exercise is the motor that helps your body clean house. The contraction and relaxation of muscles that occurs when you exercise is what causes your lymphatic fluid to circulate. The circulation of this fluid is important for healthy immune function. The garbage that has been gathered from all parts of your body must be pumped through the lymphatic system into your bloodstream so that your liver can filter the garbage out and send it down through your intestines to be eliminated from your body.

Not only does exercise support your immune system, it also alleviates depression and increases self-confidence. Most people look and feel better when they are getting regular exercise.

A word about strenuous exercise. People who are doing intensive physical training, racing and marathon work sometimes get into a pattern where the short-term stress of their workout is greater than the long-term benefit. They find themselves in an ongoing deficiency pattern where their body will regularly break down with a physical injury or illness after a certain amount of training. Recurring colds and flus are an example. If you are doing serious training and are having repeated physical injuries or health problems it is important to listen to your body. You are getting a strong message that something is out of balance. This does not mean you should stop, but rather that it would be beneficial for you to incorporate your body's signals into your workout. Learn to exercise *with* your body as an active partner as opposed to someone who limits you.

A book that may help you to find this balance *and* improve your competitive edge is John Douillard's excellent book on exercise called *Body, Mind and Sport.* In it he explains how to improve your health and athletic performance, decrease stress, recharge your body, and prevent injury based on the Ayurvedic approach to exercise. Whether you are a tri-athlete, a regular at the gym, a weekend tennis player, or a full-blown couch potato, the information in this book can help you develop an exercise program that is right for you and your body.

There are also people who don't really like to exercise. They know they *should* exercise but they just can't get motivated or find the time. If this sounds like you and you are planning to start an exercise program, beware of inflated expectations. They can lead to frustration, disappointment and injury. They also provide a great excuse to stop your fledgling exercise regime, reminding you why you don't like to exercise. Why suffer through a high-impact aerobics class or start out trying to run three miles? Instead, start slowly. Do something that appeals to you. Walking is perfectly good exercise; so is putting on music and dancing around your house or taking a ballroom dance class. Try to find a class that is specifically intended for people who are just starting out with exercise. Meet some kindred spirits as opposed to being terrorized or turned off by the athletic scene at the gym. Try taking a fifteen-minute walk every other day. Notice if there is a difference between your walking days and your non-walking days. Be a scientist; see for yourself if there is anything to all this exercise talk.

If you tend to be overzealous with exercise, then read *Body, Mind and Sport* and learn to recognize your limits. Do not exceed them. Allow your exercise routine to develop over time as your body becomes accustomed to more activity.

Some people want to exercise, but when they do they end up more tired than when they started. Some people even get sick whenever they start exercising. Then, in discouragement, they give up. If you want to exercise, yet feel too exhausted, then I recommend you hold off on exercise for now. It is as if your car were running on fumes, and you decided to go for a long drive. You won't get far.

Instead focus on your diet. Regulate your blood sugar through diet until you feel strong and supported. Then, when you have more energy, your body will naturally be interested in more physical activity. At this point, choose an activity that appeals to you. Start slowly and only do as much as you can without getting tired. You want to feel energized and relaxed after exercising. If you are exhausted, then you have done too much. The next time you exercise cut your routine in half. Keep reducing your activity level until you can exercise without depleting your energy. Once you have established a routine that works for you, you can gradually increase it if you want.

Stress Reduction to Restore Qi

Stress contributes to many health problems by disrupting the flow of energy in your body. You may experience this dis-

ruption as weakness, tension, pain, stiffness or other body sensations. Wherever energy flow is disturbed, you will be
vulnerable to illness and injury. Repressed, blocked or excessive
emotions can cause internal stress and, according to traditional
Chinese medicine, make specific organs prone to malfunction
and illness.

Change and stress are a natural part of life. Any major
change, regardless of whether you view it as positive or negative, adds stress to your life. Health problems and emotional
distress sometimes occur around major transition points such
as birth, death, graduation, marriage, divorce, moves and job
changes. Paying attention to your body's messages during such
transitions can help you cope with the stress of change. Even
adopting one small self-care activity during a period of transition can help you stabilize, and ease the impact of stress on
your body. In times of change and uncertainty, health-building
habits can give you a sense that you have some power in deter-
mining the quality of your life and your future.

When you are under stress, the last thing you want to hear
is one more suggestion about what you *should* be doing. Stress
can be all-encompassing. It is easy to become completely identified with it and sometimes even defensive about it. To simply
recognize and acknowledge to yourself that you are under
stress is important. It begins the process of disidentification
with the stress. "I am me and I am experiencing a stressful
event or circumstance." This is different from "I am stressed!"
When you are "me" experiencing a stressful event, you can
also be a person who eats and sleeps and can solve problems.
When you *"are stressed,"* you have no other identity than the
stress, it defines you and controls you. As you disidentify with
the stress you become bigger than it. You can see ways to manage the situation, resolve the stress, get help, and do whatever
you need to adapt.

THE NERVOUS SYSTEM

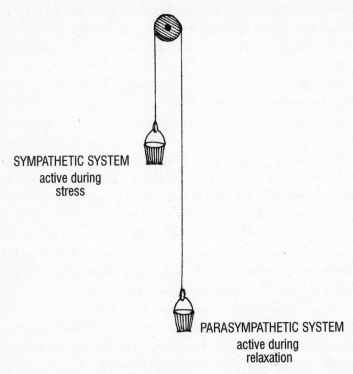

SYMPATHETIC SYSTEM
active during
stress

PARASYMPATHETIC SYSTEM
active during
relaxation

Your nervous system is like a pulley with a bucket on each end of a rope. In one bucket you have the sympathetic nervous system. This is your on-the-go, active, "I have errands to do, places to go, people to see" mode. Stress stimulates the adrenal glands to secrete hormones that activate this aspect of the nervous system. In the other bucket you have the parasympathetic system. This is the laid-back, relaxed, eat a good meal, have a good talk, all your blood is in your stomach digesting your food, "Now I feel sleepy" kind of mode. The parasympathetic nervous system is active during times of rest, relaxation, digestion, meditation and sleep. Your immune system functions best when the parasympathetic system is activated. During deep sleep your immune system is especially active.

Stress activates your sympathetic nervous system. With prolonged stress your sympathetic nervous system is repeatedly stimulated and you can become stuck in stress mode. This can make it hard to remember how to soften, rest and relax. Moderate exercise, yoga, meditation, massage, body work, acupuncture and biofeedback can all help remind your nervous system how to flow between active and passive modes.

Activities that bring you into the present moment, causing a shift in consciousness, will also help you reduce stress. This involves slowing down enough to break out of your habitual, task-oriented routines. Be open to your environment, pay attention to details, and allow new ways of thinking, seeing and behaving to surface. Allow room for your curiosity to emerge. Experience the world with new eyes. This increases pleasure and enjoyment of the simple things in daily life. It can revive and recharge you, and give you a new outlook. Sometimes in that open-minded state you discover creative solutions to problems that, when faced head-on, seemed unsolvable.

You can practice shifting your consciousness anytime and anywhere: On a simple walk, notice the colors of the clouds at sunset. Observe the buds on the bushes in your neighbor's yard. Become absorbed in the dancing shadows of leaves blowing in the wind. Appreciate the patterns the frost forms on your windowpane. Listen to the crunch of your boots in the snow. Watch the wind silently howl through the trees as you look out a window. Feel the air against your cheeks as you walk to your car.

When Stress Hits Hard

Even people who habitually take good care of themselves find their good habits go out the window when they experience a big stress. During a stressful time you may find yourself doing all sorts of things you know are not going to help you in the long run, but for the moment feel good. If the stress is short-lived, you will probably get through it just fine with whatever coping skills your body suggests. To ease your distress, your

body may crave what is familiar and comforting. You may gravi-
tate toward certain foods, more sleep, hot baths, old movies or
watching TV.

Be kind to yourself, and ask for support. It can be helpful
to talk with a kind listener, a trusted friend, family member or
counselor. Be thoughtful of your body. Speak kindly to yourself
and about yourself, and don't expect to perform at top level
during a period of stress. Get a massage, rent an old movie
and order take-out. Go for a long hike, go out to eat, curl up
with a book all weekend, take a day off work. These are the
kinds of things that can make a difference, so your body won't
need to get sick.

Prolonged stress can lead to overuse of food, alcohol and
drugs. If you are or have been under prolonged stress, the cumulative affect of activities that temporarily make you feel better can over time start to cause more stress and health
problems. To minimize the damage caused by coping mechanisms that become bad habits, find out how the stress is impacting your body. What part of your body is being hit the
hardest? How the stress is expressing itself in your body will
give you an indication of what you can do to manage it, and
what self-care techniques you might want to try.

Are you waking up with stomachaches? Have you lost your
appetite, or are you eating every piece of chocolate you can get
your hands on? Are you sleeping? Do you feel wired and
jumpy, or depressed and apathetic?

If you are having stomachaches, try aerobic exercise, yoga
or meditation. Or lie on your back on a comfortable surface
and put your hands on your belly. Start breathing into your
belly, really puff out your belly. Then let your breath travel up
into your chest puffing out your rib cage. If one spot is particularly tense, breathe into that area. Let sounds come out as you
exhale. Let the stress out of your belly with sound. If your
stomach hurts at night and warmth feels good, try sleeping
with a hot water bottle. If the stress is ongoing, set up a regular
exercise plan and make it a high priority in your life.

If you have lost your appetite, again I recommend exercise. A daily walk will help ease your body out of an overstimulated state so your nervous system can settle down. Listen to some quiet music, stretch or do yoga and breathe deeply before you sit down to eat. This will help your nervous system shift from active to relaxed mode. This will improve both your appetite and your digestion.

If you aren't sleeping, try the homeopathic remedy Calms Forte. It is a nonaddictive homeopathic remedy you can take half an hour before bed for sleeplessness. Or try herbal sleep remedies like hops, passion flower, skullcap and valarian. Some people respond well to melatonin. This is a hormone that helps regulate cycles of sleepiness and wakefulness. Melatonin is produced by the pineal gland and its release is suppressed when light enters the retina of the eye. You may want to ask your health care practitioner if melatonin might be appropriate for you. I recommend taking 0.5 to three mg one hour before bed for insomnia, frequent waking in the night and jet lag. If you feel groggy in the morning, reduce your dosage of melatonin the next night. None of these remedies should make you groggy in the morning or interfere with your dream sleep or dream recall. There are also supplements that combine herbs, minerals and melatonin. One I like is called SleepBlend.

You might also want to find a yoga class. Doing yoga will help you let go and relax in the midst of stress. If you are still sleeping poorly, take one yoga posture that you like and do it every night before going to bed. Do some gentle yoga breathing, like alternate-nostril breathing, to calm your nervous system and mind before sleep.

If you find you are wired during the day with adrenaline running through your system, consider joining a gym, an aerobics class, or start running, swimming or biking. Find an aerobic form of exercise that will allow you to discharge the adrenaline that has built up in your system. Breathe deeply during your workout.

If you feel depressed and apathetic, it can be helpful to

find some regular support, a place to talk about how you feel. Is there a support group in your area that you could join, or a counselor with whom you could talk? Gentle exercise may help. Is there someone with whom you could make a walking date every other day?

When you are under stress, find one thing to do that makes you feel better and do it as regularly as you can manage. The point is to minimize the damage caused by the stress.

For some people the problem is not that they get sick during a highly stressful period. To the contrary, they report how well their bodies perform during periods of prolonged stress. For some people, health problems frequently arise *after* a stressful period.

Health Problems That Arise After Prolonged Stress

People often exclaim when they are falling apart that they can't believe this is happening, they just went through the most horrific year last year and had no health problems whatsoever! Now all the stress is resolved and with indignation they list the complaints that now plague them. It makes no sense, they assure me.

To me it makes total sense. When your body has held up admirably during a stressful time, it has been a good friend to you. When the stress dissipates, your body wants to get the attention it has been missing. If you bounce back to a demanding life without acknowledging your body and what it went through, it may do something to get your attention. This may involve exhaustion, illness or falling apart. Do not berate your body for this. Thank your body for holding up so well until now and find out what it wants and needs to regain health and vitality.

What *did* you go through last year? Appreciate how your body supported you when you pushed yourself to your limits and had no time or energy to take care of yourself. Notice how patiently your body waited to ask for what it needed. You are not a robot. You are a living, breathing human being with needs, wants and desires. Now it is time to slow down and listen to your body. Does it want exercise, a better diet, more fun, more sleep, a good book, a vacation? Take care of yourself. You have made it through a big stress.

How Long Does It Take?

Depending on how prolonged and serious the stress was and how deeply depleted your body is, your decompression time will vary. Some people find their bodies respond quickly and enthusiastically to any positive changes they make. Other people feel exhausted and nothing seems to make much difference for a while. This can be discouraging and require patience, patience and more patience. Please remember how long it took you to get this depleted.

It is like building a house. First you lay the foundation. If you are hoping to see walls, windows and doors when the foundation has not been laid, then you will be disappointed. Laying your foundation means restoring your Kidney *Qi*. When your foundation is solid, then your health will improve quite quickly, and you will see and feel clear and obvious signs that you are healing and returning to your normal self.

In Summary

Sleep is essential to restore your Kidney *Qi*. Rest and relaxation are also important. Dreams are important. Down time is important. Not doing anything but *being* is important.

Just as goals, accomplishments and achievements are productive and of value, so too are periods of doing nothing, loafing and staring out the window. Our society tends to overvalue structured time and accomplishments. It tends to view idleness with suspicion. You must be *doing* something. Even young children are often overscheduled and pushed to accomplish and achieve, as if outer success and achievement were the sole ingredients of a healthy and fulfilling life.

What constitutes a healthy and fulfilling life is unique to each person. There is no set way. Each of us is different and have different needs, dreams and desires. We all come to life with a unique path, different abilities, struggles, tasks and gifts. Our souls are drawn to different places, people, activities, foods, lifestyles and work. Recognizing and respecting what resonates for you, what supports you, what your needs and desires are is important to finding satisfaction in your life.

Unstructured, quiet time can allow you the opportunity to evaluate your life and get the "Big Picture." Give yourself time away from your daily life to build a connection between your internal guidance and your mind, to hear your inner navigator's instructions. I recommend you write down any feelings, ideas and guidance that emerge. These are seeds asking for nourishment, guiding and directing you.

It can be easy to overlook, dismiss and forget these seeds when you return to the busy routine of your life. Please don't. This tendency is why I want you to write them down. When you receive guidance and instructions, sometimes they are so clear that you think you'll *never* forget them. But don't trust this to memory. Write it down so you can remind yourself, read it regularly. Pick one of your inner navigator's suggestions and pursue it. Let the wisdom that emerges filter into your daily life. This is a powerful way to recognize and respect your *Qi* and reorient your life to support yourself. It initiates a process of deep change and strengthens the connection between your inner navigator and your conscious mind.

CHAPTER 8

The Immune System

Your immune system is like your internal army. It is dedicated to maintaining your health and physical integrity. It fights off foreign invaders like bacteria, viruses and toxins, and eliminates domestic problems like cancer and internally generated toxins.

Your immune system is made up of many parts. First you have *Wei Qi*, a protective energy field that surrounds your body. Then you have skin. Skin acts as a physical barrier protecting your internal body from the external environment. Inside your body is a lymphatic system in which circulates a fluid called lymph. The lymphatic system includes a network of lymphatic vessels, numerous lymph nodes found in the neck, armpits and groin, and the adenoids, appendix, spleen, thymus and tonsils. Lymph nodes act not only as a filtering system for cellular trash removal, but also as sentinels for your body. They alert your system to the presence of specific problems such as an injury, burn or pathogen so that your body can respond appropriately to the specific situation. For example, you may notice that when you have a cut on your thigh, the lymph nodes in your groin swell while your body attends to and heals the cut.

THE MANY ASPECTS OF THE
IMMUNE SYSTEM

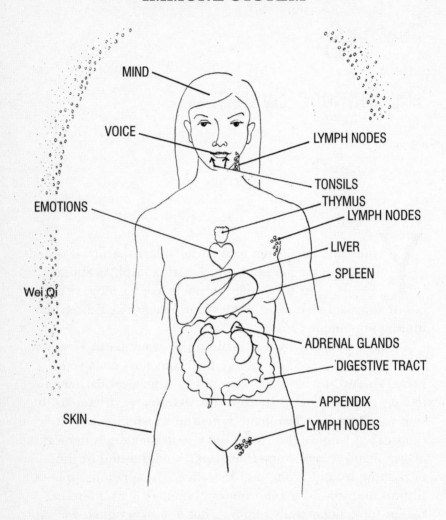

You have roving white blood cells that eat bacteria and tumor cells. Others clean up the mess after an infection by en-
gulfing the dead tissue. You have natural killer cells that attack
and destroy cancer cells, and cells that have been invaded by
viruses. Other white blood cells are involved in allergic reactions.

Your adrenal glands are involved in immune function. They secrete hormones in response to stress. These hormones signal your body to produce more energy so you can cope with an ongoing stress such as fighting an infection. Your liver is also involved in immune function. It filters toxins out of your blood and changes them to less toxic substances that your body can eliminate.

Your digestive tract is also involved in your immunity. The acids produced in your stomach kill nonbeneficial bacteria that might be in your food. And healthy bacteria in your intestines fight off nonbeneficial bacteria and yeast. They also produce B vitamins, which are necessary nutrients for the functioning of many other aspects of your immune system. Your digestive tract is permeated with lymph tissue that is extremely important to your immunity. This tissue produces antibodies that destroy or weaken bacteria and neutralize organic poisons.

Not only does your immune system have physical components, but it also has mental and emotional components. When you are relaxed and calm, your nervous system is relaxed and calm, and this supports your immunity. Your state of mind, attitudes, beliefs, stress level and emotional experience all affect the strength of your immune system.

Stress and Immunity

When you are under stress your nervous system can get stuck in the on-the-go mode and forget how to shift back to relaxation. Without that natural dynamic flow between action and relaxation, your body starts suffering from symptoms of stress, like feeling wired and tense, and being unable to eat or sleep. This creates more stress and depresses your immune system.

In response to stress, your adrenal glands produce hormones that stimulate a quick release of stored sugar into your bloodstream to raise your blood sugar level. In this way your body responds to small daily stresses, a difficult phone call, a near miss on the freeway, or not eating lunch until 3 P.M.

If stress is prolonged then your body will need more than a sugar burst from adrenaline to cope. So the adrenal glands secrete other stress hormones that give you access to more energy by breaking down protein. If the body operates for too long under stressful conditions, the adrenal glands become depleted and shrivel, and you lose your ability to respond to stress. This leaves you exhausted and vulnerable to illness and disease.

During stressful periods it is important to support your immune system with vitamins, minerals and antioxidants. Drinking fresh, organic vegetable juice is an excellent way to support your immune system. Sugar consumption will suppress your immune system by reducing the ability of some of your white blood cells to kill bacteria. If you are under stress or experiencing a bacterial infection, it will help your immune system if you avoid eating sugar.

Digestion and Immunity

What you eat and how you eat affects your immunity. When you are relaxed, your parasympathetic nervous system is activated and your body is ready to digest and assimilate food. When you are experiencing stress your body is under sympathetic nervous stimulation and is not ready to digest or assimilate food. The result of eating while under stress can be incompletely digested food that is prone to fermenting and putrefying. This can cause bloating and gas, and can be the source of internally produced toxins which increase the workload for your liver and immune system. Digestive problems such as bloating, gas, constipation, diarrhea, indigestion, stomachaches, overeating, candida, leaky gut syndrome, food allergies and parasites all indicate a digestive imbalance that may be putting an additional burden on your immune system.

Daily bowel movements support your immunity. Your liver

detoxifies toxins and prepares them for elimination by wrapping them in bile and sending them into the intestines. Daily bowel movements and eating plenty of fiber will aid your body in eliminating these toxins in a timely manner so they do not get reabsorbed into your body. A diet high in whole grains, fresh vegetables and fruit, and plenty of clean water, combined with daily exercise, promotes regular elimination. Psyllium seed husks, oat bran, flaxseeds, guar gum and bentonite all support your immune system by adding bulk to your stool, absorbing toxins and bile from the digestive tract and improving elimination.

Emotions and Immunity

Your immune system is affected by your emotional and mental state, the way you feel about yourself, the way you talk to yourself and the way you are in the world. Depression suppresses the immune system. Moderate exercise alleviates depression, releases stress and promotes sound sleep, all of which support your immune system. Recent studies show that laughter increases the immune system's ability to kill viruses and cancer cells. Norman Cousins wrote a wonderful book called *Anatomy of an Illness* about healing himself from a serious illness by taking intravenous vitamin C and doing laughter therapy. To keep himself laughing he watched Marx Brothers movies and reruns of *Candid Camera*.

In his book, *The Immune Power Personality: 7 Traits You Can Develop to Stay Healthy*, Henry Dreher addresses seven traits that contribute to strong immunity. He defines the Immune Power Personality as ". . . an individual who is able to find joy and meaning, even health, when life offers up its most difficult challenges. The Immune Power Personality handles stressful events not with denial but with acceptance, flexibility, and a willingness to learn and grow."

Some of the traits he discusses are:

- paying attention to what your body and mind are saying;
- taking control of your life and meeting challenges;
- being able to confide in others and share your inner feelings and secrets;
- being assertive about your needs and feelings.
- developing the trait of altruism, healthy helping;
- being able to connect to others and form relationships based on love and trust and
- developing many aspects of yourself so that when there is a stressful event you have multiple strengths to fall back on when one part of yourself is lost or wounded.

To Support Your Immune System

- keep your blood sugar balanced, eat three regular meals a day;
- eat fresh, organic foods as much as possible;
- eat fiber-rich foods like fresh fruits, vegetables and whole grains;
- avoid foods treated with pesticides, chemical sprays, preservatives, dyes and radiation;
- minimize the use of caffeine, sugar, alcohol and drugs;
- relax before, during and after mealtime to aid your digestion;
- address digestive disturbances;
- drink plenty of clean, filtered water. This means at least six to eight cups of water each day;
- get enough sleep;
- get regular exercise;
- get a massage;
- relax;
- laugh;
- speak up, say how you feel and what you want and need;
- address the stresses in your life;
- do a cleanse when your body asks for it;

- supplement your diet with vitamins, minerals and antioxidants;
- take fiber, oat bran, flaxseeds, guar gum and bentonite and
- use herbs to support your immune system when necessary.

Antibiotics and Immunity

Antibiotics kill bacteria. If you have a bacterial infection and your immune system is unable to fight it off, then antibiotics are quite literally a lifesaver. When prescribed by your doctor and used as prescribed they are an important form of medical treatment. However, antibiotics should not be used without good cause, or when a gentler form of medicine can be effective. If you are prescribed antibiotics, it is important to finish the full course as your doctor prescribes. Some people stop taking their antibiotic as soon as they feel better. This doesn't allow the drug to complete its job, and you run the risk of developing antibiotic-resistant bacteria in your body. Then you may need another course of a stronger antibiotic to clear up your bacterial infection. Follow each course of antibiotics with a course of friendly bacteria to replenish the beneficial bacteria colony in your intestinal tract.

Sometimes people take repeated courses of antibiotics without eliminating their infections. In such cases, I recommend consulting a natural health care provider, and making lifestyle changes that support your immune system. Dietary changes, herbs, nutritional supplements and therapies that support your immunity, like acupuncture, biofeedback, visualization and other stress reduction techniques, can all help to resolve an otherwise persistent and unresponsive infection.

Antibiotics do not kill viruses. If you have a viral-caused illness than it is important to support your immune system to fight it off, for an antibiotic cannot do it for you. There are herbs and nutritional supplements that can help your immune system fight a virus. Consult a natural health care provider about what will be most effective in your particular situation.

Antibiotics Have Side-Effects

Antibiotics do not distinguish between the harmful bacteria they are intended to kill, and the friendly bacteria that are an important part of your digestive tract. Your friendly bacteria produce B vitamins and act as "good guys" policing your digestive tract to prevent the "bad guys"—unhealthy bacteria and yeast—from setting up shop. They act as the first line of defense for your immune system in your intestines. When you take an antibiotic these friendly bacteria are killed.

Yeast—*candida albicans*—occurs naturally in the human digestive tract. It is not beneficial. However, when kept in check by friendly bacteria, it does not cause problems. Problems arise with yeast overgrowth. A common cause of yeast overgrowth is the ingestion of antibiotics. When antibiotics kill both the friendly and unfriendly bacteria, they eliminate the yeast's natural competitors and this enables a yeast colony to flourish. For many people, an imbalance in the digestive tract begins with a course of antibiotics. As time goes by, if this imbalance is not corrected, the yeast colony takes a firm hold in your body and undermines your immune system in a condition commonly referred to as "candida."

Your body is not meant to host a flourishing yeast colony. If you have yeast overgrowth, your immune system will be subject to continuous stress. This can manifest in a wide variety of physical, emotional and mental symptoms. People often become sensitive to airborne irritants, pollutants and toxins like cigarette smoke, artificial scents and perfumes, and vapors from construction materials, paints and finishes. Many people become reactive to yeast, molds and fungi (which are all in the same biological family). Exposure to moldy environments, wine, aged cheeses and mushrooms may cause physical symptoms. The ability to deal with toxins decreases as the immune system becomes overloaded with candida and its internally produced wastes. An immune system so internally preoccupied has less energy and ability to defend against external pathogens. This can result in chronic poor health. Look under Yeast Overgrowth in the Self-Care Dictionary for more information on symptoms and treatment of candida.

What About Eating Yogurt After Taking Antibiotics?

Yogurt and kiefer with live acidophilus culture and fermented foods like sauerkraut and miso contain some of the friendly bacteria your body needs. However, antibiotics are medicine and these are foods. Using food as medicine is effective for health maintenance, but expecting food to rebalance your intestines after a course of antibiotics is underestimating the strength of antibiotics. For bacteria to arrive alive in your large intestine, they must survive the acidic environment of the stomach (which is meant to kill bacteria in food as well as enhance protein digestion) and the alkalinity of the small intestine. This means tolerating a large fluctuation in pH, and ordinary friendly bacteria from your food may not survive these conditions.

Antibiotics powerfully change your body chemistry. It is important to take a course of strong, beneficial bacteria to repopulate your intestines after a course of antibiotics. If you have taken repeated courses of antibiotics, or were on antibiotics continuously for months or years, as in the treatment of acne, you can be sure that the balance of your intestines has been altered. Even if it has been years since you took antibiotics, if you did not rebalance your intestines then, your health will have been heading off course ever since. The main body system that is undermined by this ongoing imbalance is your immune system.

If you have never taken antibiotics, but you eat non-

THE IMPACT OF ANTIBIOTICS ON HEALTH OVER TIME

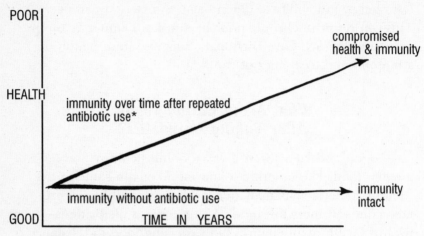

*This assumes the intestinal bacteria were not replenished after taking antibiotics.

organic meat, dairy products and eggs, then you may be ingesting antibiotics. Nonorganically raised meat, including chickens, are fed antibiotics to prevent them from getting sick while being raised in crowded, stressful conditions and to promote growth. These antibiotics pass from their meat into your body when you eat them. So you may be getting a dose of unwanted medicine along with your meal. As much as possible eat range-fed, organic meats and dairy products.

What to Do if You Are Currently Taking Antibiotics

If your stomach is upset or you are having diarrhea from taking your antibiotic, I recommend taking a strong bacterial supplement during your course of antibiotics, but at a separate time of day. This will not help to reestablish your bacterial colony, but it does seem to help the stomach upset and diarrhea some people experience while taking antibiotics. After you finish the full course of antibiotics, it is important to take a full course of beneficial intestinal bacteria to reestablish a healthy environment in your intestines.

You will find strong beneficial bacteria in the refrigerator section of most health food stores, or ask your health food store owner which is the strongest bacterial supplement they carry. You can also get beneficial bacteria from your natural health care provider. Take them for a month. By supplementing daily you are reestablishing your friendly bacteria colony and restoring balance in your intestines.

I also recommend that you minimize your sugar intake while you are on antibiotics. As the yeast proliferate they will want sugar, as it is their food source. You may find yourself craving sugar to feed them. To counteract this, increase your protein intake and keep your blood sugar stable. This is a good time to go on the blood sugar regulating diet for a month. It will help you avoid an overgrowth of intestinal yeast and avert many health problems down the road.

Most people like taking bacteria, or "bugs" as they are fondly called. Your bowel movements may change in regularity, timing, color and consistency. Over time as the bugs settle in, your new rhythm will establish itself. Most people notice better, easier and more regular bowel movements. Initially some people get gas and bloating from the introduction of friendly bacteria to their colon. If this happens to you, reduce the dose of bacteria to a level where you are comfortable, even if this means breaking open a capsule and taking a few sprinkles every other day. *The most effective dose is the one you can take comfortably and with regularity.* The idea is to slowly rebuild the bacteria colony, not to do it all in one swallow and suffer the consequences. Go at your own pace; your body will let you know what you can comfortably handle.

If you took antibiotics in the past and are experiencing health problems now, I recommend reading Yeast Overgrowth in the Self-Care Dictionary.

Birth Control Pills, Yeast and Immunity

Birth control pills raise your blood sugar levels and thereby give a yeast colony more food upon which to thrive. If you have taken antibiotics without a follow-up course of friendly bacteria, you probably have some level of yeast imbalance. If you go on birth control pills you will probably exacerbate that imbalance.

Regardless of whether you find it advisable to stay on birth control pills or to go off of them, there are two things I recommend doing. First, reintroduce friendly bacteria into your intestines. Second, regulate your blood sugar with diet to prevent blood sugar surges which provide lots of nourishment for yeast. These two steps will help counteract the negative effects of birth control pills on yeast overgrowth.

Stress, Yeast and Immunity

When you are under stress your adrenal glands secrete hormones which cause your blood sugar to rise. This gives a thriving yeast colony more food to live on. When you are under stress it is also common to crave sugar, refined flour products, coffee and alcohol—all things that cause a rapid rise in blood sugar and exacerbate yeast overgrowth. To counteract this tendency, increase your protein intake, especially at breakfast and lunch. This will support you in avoiding sugar and refined flour products like cookies, snacks and junk food. Think of a protein source you really love, one that makes you feel comforted. It could be chicken soup, meat loaf, chicken pot pie, poached eggs, smoked salmon, baked tofu, lamb stew. Whatever it is, get some, make some and eat it. Increase your protein intake in such a way that you feel taken care of. Remember, you are under stress. Be good to yourself.

Antibiotics, Infants and Children

I recommend supplementing friendly bacteria for infants and children after they have been given a course of antibiotics. If they repeatedly take antibiotics, they should repeatedly take friendly bacteria. In this way you can help keep their health in balance and their immunity strong, preventing many health problems as they get older.

You may want to find a homeopath and a naturopath in your area who have experience working with infants and children. Establish relationships with them so that you have a variety of sources to turn to for medical advice when your children are sick.

Some Broad-Reaching Concerns about Antibiotics

Stuart B. Levy, M.D., writes in *The Antibiotic Paradox: How Miracle Drugs Are Destroying the Miracle,* "As I stated in a recent editorial, 'Antibiotics are unique among pharmaceuticals in that they treat populations as well as individuals. One's bacteria are not solely one's own. Rather, they are shed, excreted, and otherwise spread into the environment, where they become part of a common pool.' In fact, the individual's flora probably reflect the environmental flora in which that person lives—the kinds of bacteria and the frequency of antibiotic resistance there." (page 228)

Levy's comments bring to light the fact that what we do as individuals has an impact on the health of our communities as a whole. We are not isolated. He cites a study that measured the antibiotic resistance of common intestinal bacteria in infants and small children in three different cities on three different continents. The intestinal bacteria of the children who had never taken an antibiotic were tested for antibiotic resistance to eight different drugs. The results varied greatly be-

tween the cities. While what caused the difference is not
completely understood, it was known from the start of the
study that the use of antibiotics in these three cities varied considerably. It was in those cities where antibiotics were both easily attained and widely used that the children who had never
taken an antibiotic carried many more intestinal bacteria with
resistance to the antibiotics tested.

Antibiotic resistance in bacteria is a phenomenon that was
evident in the early years of antibiotic use in the 1940s when a
British bacteriologist was able to grow mutant strains of antibiotic-resistant bacteria in the laboratory. Antibiotic resistant bacteria are bacteria that have adapted so that an antibiotic that
normally would kill it, no longer has that impact. Over time it
has become apparent that not only can bacteria become resistant to an antibiotic to which they are exposed, but also they
can pass resistance information among themselves. Bacteria can
carry resistance to multiple antibiotics, including antibiotics to
which they have never been exposed, as evidenced in the study
Levy describes. This can seriously limit the ability of antibiotics
to successfully treat bacterial infections, and it creates a situation where a common infection may require repeated courses
of a variety of antibiotics which may or may not get the infection under control.

By this discussion I in no way intend to discourage appropriate use of antibiotics. Antibiotics are clearly indicated for
many bacterial infections and can be miraculous drugs when
used appropriately. They should be used when prescribed by
your physician, physician's assistant or nurse practitioner, and
they should be used correctly, which means completing the full
course of treatment. What is and is not appropriate use is best
determined in conjunction with your health care providers.
However, the use of self-care techniques for health maintenance and prevention, as well as the natural alternatives that
are often appropriate for minor bacterial infections or unresponsive infections can do much to reduce the use of unnecessary antibiotics in your family and community.

The big picture with regard to antibiotics can be frightening. As a society, it is important to be conscious of the corner into which we are painting ourselves. With so many antibiotics in circulation not only in our human communities but also in the food chain, bacteria have ample opportunity to develop resistance to whatever antibiotics are in current use. This means that when you are suffering from a truly life-threatening bacterial infection, there may be no antibiotic to help you. In just fifty-eight years we have so misused and overused the great power of antibiotics that we now run the risk of losing that power.

Alternatives to Antibiotics

In the case of mild bacterial infections that do not require immediate treatment with antibiotics, try taking grapefruit seed extract (not to be confused with the antioxidant and less powerful antibacterial grape seed extract). Grapefruit seed extract is a natural supplement available at most health food stores and from natural health care providers. It is the oil pressed from grapefruit seeds and is very potent. It comes in liquid, tablets and capsules. The liquid should never be taken without first diluting it in water or juice.

Grapefruit seed extract is effective against many bacteria, yeast and some parasites. It works more slowly than antibiotics, so give it four or five days to start getting an infection under control. You will probably need to stay on it longer than you would antibiotics. However, the grapefruit seed extract does not kill friendly bacteria the way antibiotics do. And rather than causing digestive problems, it seems to clear them up. It supports your immune system in doing its job, in contrast to antibiotics which override your immune system and then leave your body out of balance.

For a viral infection echinacea, when taken in adequate doses, can be effective. I recommend its use for colds, flus, sore throats and bronchial conditions. Start taking it at the first sign of a cold or flu at the highest dose recommended on your bottle. Garlic is also a great bacteria, virus and yeast killer. The best results come from raw garlic. However, to take a high dose and to avoid garlic breath, there are garlic tablets and capsules available at health food stores and from natural health care providers. Some of these products are deodorized and some not. Berberine, found in goldenseal, is also excellent for treatment of numerous bacteria, yeast and parasites.

If you have a viral condition such as herpes, shingles, chronic fatigue syndrome or Epstein-Barr you may want to look into garlic and lauric acid to support your immune system. Garlic is a natural virus killer, and lauric acid is a natural antiviral nutrient found in mother's milk. It interferes with the replication of viruses, thus decreases the number of viruses your immune system has to contend with. This is also known as decreasing your viral load. It gives your immune system a leg up in its battle to overcome the virus. Discuss these treatment options with your natural health care provider.

For both bacterial and viral infections, taking vitamin C is helpful to your immune system. When taking vitamin C it is important to take it regularly. When you take vitamin C your immune system comes to rely on it and to suddenly stop taking it will cause a temporary dip in your immunity. Taking a regular daily dose is best. If you start feeling sick, increase your dose. As you recover, decrease your dose slowly back to what you normally take on a daily preventive basis.

Xenobiotics

Xenobiotics are chemicals that do not belong in your body. Examples of xenobiotics include pesticides and herbicides. Water, air, soils and food are frequently polluted with these chemicals, some of which can mimic estrogen when they get into your body. They latch onto estrogen receptor sites and trigger estrogen-related activities, such as cell growth. Some researchers feel that women, men and children are all showing signs of artificially elevated estrogen levels. Health problems that are being attributed to these chemicals include: young girls beginning to menstruate at an earlier age, PMS, infertility, breast cancer, difficulty with menopause in women and reduced sperm count and prostate cancer in men.

Common sources of xenobiotics include indoor air pollution and chemical residues in food. To decrease your exposure to xenobiotics, decrease your exposure to indoor air pollutants such as carpet fumes, glues, solvents and the like, and eat an organic diet as much as is possible.

Paint, Building Supplies, Carpeting, and Household Chemicals Can Affect Your Immune System

Reactions to what used to be considered common household chemicals and building supplies are becoming increasingly common; and our immune systems are compromised daily by the pollutants in food, water and our environment. If you have a tendency toward any kind of allergy or asthma, and are planning construction in your home or workplace, consider using less toxic or nontoxic building supplies, paints, finishes and carpets. Consider choosing nontoxic household cleaning products. It may cost more in the short run, but long-term medical bills aren't cheap! Consider plain wood floors and throw rugs as opposed to the off-gassing of synthetic wall-to-wall carpeting. Try water-soluble paints instead of oil based, and buy nontoxic varnishes and finish. Spend as little time at the construction site as possible. Wear a mask to protect yourself from inhaling toxic vapors and construction dust.

Children can be especially sensitive to toxins. If you have small children and are remodeling or adding an addition to your home, move out during the project. Do not spend nights inhaling the vapors from toxic paints, finishes and glues. This may seem like an inconvenient and expensive suggestion, however prevention is worth a lot when it comes to the breakdown of an immune system. Most of our bodies are already coping with enough stress. Do not push the edge to see what will be the straw that breaks your immune system. Once it has been pushed too far, the repair is not easy. Before moving back in, fully air out your home. The toxic chemicals in building supplies, glues, paints, finishes and carpets can be the final insult to an immune system already taxed by stress and the toxic load from pollutants in our water, air and food. One more insult can be what pushes your immune system into overreactivity. Make a wise choice and walk around trouble, not right into it.

Support Your Immune System When You Travel

When you travel to a foreign country where the food and water may cause stomach problems, there are several supplements I recommend taking along with you. They may make your travels more comfortable. They include:

- **Grapefruit Seed Extract** A natural antibiotic that can be used for bacterial infections. Take three tablets daily, one with each meal, to help prevent diarrhea from bacteria in food and water. If you will be cooking your own food, you can get liquid grapefruit seed extract and put several drops in water to soak and wash fruits and vegetables.
- **Friendly Bacteria** Acidophilus, bifidus, streptococcus faecium and fructooligosaccharides (FOS) all support the healthy bacteria in your digestive tract. You can get them at your health food store or from your natural health care provider.
- **Curing Pill** This Chinese patent medicine is great for upset stomach and diarrhea. You can get it from your acupuncturist or at an herbal pharmacy.
- **Charcoal** These tablets or capsules absorb toxins in your digestive tract. They are great for indigestion, diarrhea and stomach upset. You can find them at health food stores and drugstores.

- **Rescue Remedy Cream** Bring a tube of this homeopathic cream for abrasions, burns, cuts and sores.

It is best not to expose beneficial bacteria to temperatures above seventy degrees. They are alive and at warm temperatures they begin to die. If you will have no refrigeration while traveling, still bring your bacteria along. Just don't bring the whole bottle. Take only as much as you will need for your trip. This way the rest of the bacteria can stay at home in your refrigerator and not be subjected to erratic temperatures. If you develop a digestive upset, continue taking your bacteria when you return home until your body readjusts.

If you have trouble sleeping in a new environment or will be traveling to a different time zone, I recommend taking along:

- **Calms Forte:** a safe and effective homeopathic remedy that can help you relax and get to sleep when you are in a strange bed. It is also effective for settling down over-excited children.
- **Melatonin:** melatonin, or a melatonin and herbal combination supplement like SleepBlend or MetaRest, can help your body adjust to changing time zones so you get a good night's sleep.

If you are traveling during cold and flu season, particularly if it is during the holidays when stress levels tend to be higher, and if you will be traveling on crowded public transport like airplanes, I recommend taking three more things with you.

- **Oscillococcinium:** homeopathic cold and flu remedy that comes in small vials filled with lactose pellets. This vibrational remedy boosts your vital force to prevent colds and flus. Take a vial at the first sign of a cold or flu, or take prophylactically when your immunity is low and you are in contact with people who are coughing and sneezing. Oscillacoccinium is available at health food stores and from natural health care providers.

- **Raw Apple Cider Vinegar:** put several drops of vinegar in your water (use a dropper bottle). This supports your immune system by raising your potassium level and alkalinizing your bloodstream, making it inhospitable to bacteria. Raw apple cider vinegar is available at health food stores and should be refrigerated.
- **Zinc Lozenges:** suck on zinc lozenges at the first sign of a sore throat or cold to support your immune system.

In Summary

Your best defense against illness is to keep your immunity strong. The best way to keep your immunity strong is to take good care of yourself. This includes eating a healthy diet that supplies adequate protein and is rich in whole grains, fresh fruit and vegetables, and is low in sugar, caffeine, refined flour products and alcohol. Drink plenty of clean water. Get enough sleep, rest, relaxation and play. Regular exercise reduces stress and keeps your lymphatic fluid circulating. And use whatever stress-reduction techniques work for you.

CHAPTER 9

Cleansing and Detoxification

Your body is like a house. Your Heart and Spirit live there. Most of us keep the outside of the body pretty clean—we bathe, brush our teeth and wash our hair. But in general, the inside of the body does not get much attention. What house would you live in for forty years and never clean?

Think for a moment of all the junk food you have eaten, containing dyes and preservatives. Think of the chemical fertilizers in the soil and the pesticides sprayed on your fruits and vegetables. Consider the preservatives in lunch meats, bacon and sausage, and the hormones and antibiotics in meat, dairy products and eggs. Think of the drugs you have taken—over-the-counter, prescription and recreational (including alcohol and caffeine). Then consider the environmental contaminants to which you have been exposed in the water, air, soil, and home and work environments. Toxins can be emitted from household cleaners, building materials, paints and carpets. There may be lead and chlorine in your tap water, not to mention protozoans, like giardia or cryptosporidium. The air contains fumes from car exhaust, aerial spraying, particulates from industry, woodstoves and fireplaces.

Now, think of your bloodstream as a swimming pool, and your liver as the water filter. When the filter becomes clogged with dead bugs and leaves it doesn't work well. Then the swimming pool starts looking pretty dirty—that's your bloodstream when your liver is overloaded with toxins and things that don't belong there. When your liver can't clean your blood, then your body stores the toxins away in various corners of your body, especially in fat tissue. When your bloodstream is not properly cleaned, health problems can occur throughout your body.

One way to keep your bloodstream clean is to eat a clean diet, maintain good digestion and avoid exposure to toxins and pollutants. Another way is to cleanse the organs of your body that are involved in detoxification and elimination, particularly your liver and large intestine.

Even if you have a clean diet, it is difficult to avoid exposure to contaminants in the air and water, particularly if you drink unfiltered tap water. However, since the most common source of exposure to foreign chemicals comes through food, if you have eaten a clean diet, the cleansing process will probably be easier for you. If you have eaten foods containing pesticides, dyes, preservatives and other toxic chemicals, the cleansing process may be more of a major overhaul, a slow process to be taken one step at a time.

The Organs and Systems of Detoxification and Elimination

There are several parts of your body that are involved in processing and eliminating toxins: the liver, the large intestine, the kidneys, the lungs, the skin and the lymphatic system.

As I have said, the liver filters your blood. The large intestine eliminates waste through bowel movements. The kidneys also filter your blood. They filter the toxic by-products from protein digestion out of your bloodstream so they can be eliminated through urine. The lungs eliminate waste products through exhalation and the skin through sweat. The lymphatic system transports wastes from all parts of your body to the bloodstream so your liver can pull out all the toxic chemicals, hormones and other substances that do not belong in your body, break them down and prepare them for excretion.

For optimum health all of these systems should be working well. This means a healthy liver with adequate nutrients to carry out its detoxifying functions, daily bowel movements to prevent waste from building up and being reabsorbed, ample clean water intake to flush the kidneys and regular exercise to stimulate breathing, sweating and the circulation of blood and lymph.

Things to Consider Before Starting a Cleanse

There are many choices to make when you are planning to do a cleanse. What is your intention in cleansing? Are you planning a daily period of cleansing, or a weekly, monthly, seasonal or yearly cleanse? And for how long do you intend to do this cleanse?

Since fruit is a naturally cleansing food, a daily cleanse may involve eating only fresh fruit in the morning, or only fruit at dinnertime. This allows the digestive system a period of time to rest and cleanse. A weekly or monthly cleanse may be one day long and again focus on mild cleansing, giving the digestive system a rest. If you do a seasonal or yearly cleanse over a long weekend or for a week, not only does your digestive system get a rest, but you can also cleanse on a deeper level.

In choosing your frequency, time frame and focus I recommend you listen to your body. Do what *feels* right, *when* it feels right, not necessarily what your mind thinks you *should* do. Consider your overall health, the amount of time and energy you have, competitive demands in your life and your support system.

Also consider the weather. When the weather is cold, your

body needs more fuel to maintain itself—this is traditionally not a good time to cleanse. If you feel a strong urge to cleanse during winter months in a cold climate, you can choose to eat a simple cooked-food diet, like brown rice and cooked mung beans, which will allow your body to cleanse and provide you with warmth and nourishment as well.

This leads to the question of what you will eat and drink on your cleanse. When you are cleansing it is best to avoid meat, dairy, eggs, butter, caffeine, sugar, sodas, chocolate, alcohol, fried foods, salt, and refined and processed foods. Do you want to drink only liquids, or will you have both food and liquids? Again, listen to your body, assess your life situation at the moment and choose the approach that feels right to you now.

Keep in mind what foods are accessible. When doing a cleanse you will want to have access to as much fresh organic produce as possible. You do not want to find a fresh pineapple juice cleanse that sounds perfect, only to discover that fresh, organic pineapple is not available where you live at this time of year. And you do not want to be juicing a fresh pineapple sprayed with pesticides when you are cleansing your body.

Try different styles of cleansing and see what works best for you. In the spring you may want to do a week-long cleanse that focuses on your liver. In the fall you may want to try a week-long cleanse that focuses on your intestines. After a holiday celebration you may want to eat only brown rice and cooked mung beans for several days. In the summer you may want to try a fresh fruit and vegetable juice cleanse. Experiment. Listen to your body. Follow your instincts. There are many methods of cleansing, and there is no one right way. The best way for you is the one that works for you.

Cleansing As a Part of Your Daily Life

One approach to cleansing is to eat cleansing foods on a daily basis. This can be as simple as increasing your daily intake of fresh vegetables and fruit, and whole grains (all preferably organic). Fruits and vegetables stimulate your cells to release stored toxins and whole grains ensure daily bowel movements to remove these toxins from your body.

Another way to incorporate cleansing into your daily life is to eat only fruit until noon, as is recommended in the *Fit for Life* diet. This allows your body to do a small cleanse each morning. If you follow the *Fit for Life* program you will follow a food-combining diet for the rest of the day as recommended in that book. Or you can simply eat a basic healthy diet for the rest of the day. Some people when eating only fruit in the morning feel great. However, if you live in a cold climate, have blood sugar problems or feel cold, weak or hungry when following this approach, then it is probably not a positive lifestyle choice for you, at least not now. You may benefit from using it in the hotter months, while on vacation in a hot climate, or in small doses as a cleanse for a few days.

Some people will do well on a simple fresh juice fast or raw vegetable diet, while others doing the same thing would feel cold, weak and hungry. Some people do well eating plain cooked foods, like brown rice and mung beans for several days. Others prefer to go on a longer cleansing program designed to clean out a specific organ like the large intestine or liver. They will take herbs and supplements to stimulate particular cleansing processes.

If you have been eating a standard diet containing chemicals and preservatives, and you are interested in cleansing, I recommend you first follow the approach of cleansing as a part of your daily life. In this way your diet will naturally improve and your body will start to cleanse gradually. After adjusting to these dietary changes for a period of months, you will be ready for a more intensive cleanse, and will experience less discomfort when you do it.

Cleansing As a Break
from Daily Life

You can also take from one to ten days to take a break from the routine of your daily life and do a cleanse. If you have never done any sort of cleansing, you will want to start slowly. You may want to look through books on cleansing at your health food store or bookstore, or find a natural health care provider with whom you can work. You not only will be learning about cleansing in general, but also about how *your* body responds to cleansing.

A one-day juice fast is not a major disruption to your life, does not require a big commitment of time and energy, and it gives your digestive system a rest. A longer cleanse requires more planning and commitment, and usually does not easily fit into your daily routine. It works more deeply and is best done gradually; take time to move into the cleanse, then take time for the cleanse, and again take time to ease your body back out to a normal diet.

You can mix and match. Do a longer cleanse in the spring and follow it by eating a basic cleansing diet throughout the summer when fresh fruits and vegetables are abundant. Choose a longer cleanse when you feel strong, have the time, space and energy, and are ready for a change. Do a shorter cleanse when you have a busy schedule or aren't feeling as strong. The important thing is to listen to your body.

Psychological Aspects of Cleansing

While cleansing is a physical process it also strongly influences many other aspects of your life. For example, you will probably notice changes emotionally, spiritually and in the way you relate to food, your environment and people in your life.

Initially the idea of doing a cleanse can be exciting. A word of caution . . . have you ever gotten *really* excited about cleaning your entire house only to get halfway through one closet to find yourself overwhelmed with stuff? You find letters from an old lover, journals, emotional attachments to clothes you don't wear but can't throw out, things you just don't know what to do with. Well, physically cleaning the inside of your body can be similar.

Be moderate in your expectations; don't attempt to clean out a whole lifetime of junk food in one cleanse. Just as there is value in reading old letters and journals, the feelings that come up during a cleanse are important as well. Cleanse a little and see how it feels. If you feel better, do a little more in a couple of months. Give yourself time to integrate your experience.

The Cleansing Process

One thing you'll learn while cleansing is that digestion takes an enormous amount of energy, and eating lightly actually frees up a lot of energy. Your body will be using this energy to clean house.

There are two phases to the cleansing process. The first is when your cells release stored toxins into your bloodstream. This is the easy part. When given the chance, your body generally knows how to do this. It is like when everyone in your neighborhood puts their garbage cans by the side of the road on Thursday night for the garbage truck that comes on Friday morning. What facilitates this phase of cleansing is to eat lightly, eat simply and eat foods that stimulate cleansing. These include:

- fresh fruits and vegetables,
- fresh fruit and vegetable juices,
- vegetable broths,
- blue-green algae,
- seaweed,
- brown rice,
- mung beans,

- plenty of clean water and
- certain herbs and nutritional supplements.

The second and more difficult stage of cleansing is detoxifying and disposing of the garbage. This part is trickier. It takes place in the liver where toxins and chemicals are broken down and prepared for elimination. The reason toxins are broken down before excretion is that many toxins are fat-soluble and hard for the body to eliminate. The liver breaks them down so they are water-soluble, generally less toxic substances that your body can more readily eliminate.

To accomplish this detoxification, the liver requires an ample supply of specific nutrients and energy. There are two phases to this process. The important thing to understand about this two-phase process is that some of the toxins that are broken down in phase one become more toxic than they were originally. They require further action during phase two to transform them into a state where your body can eliminate them. Phase one reactions also generate free radicals which can be injurious to your cells. Therefore, after a phase one reaction, adequate antioxidants are necessary to prevent tissue damage. And the nutrients and energy required by phase two reactions must be available to render these more toxic compounds less toxic, to prevent tissue injury, immune system damage and mutation.

In short, the liver has a lot of work to do during a cleanse, and it requires the presence of certain nutrients to accomplish this work. So while the rest of your digestive system gets a rest, your liver may be overwhelmed with toxic matter to detoxify and prepare for excretion.

When you are cleansing, you will want to evaluate each system in your body. Choose which ones require the most attention, and what activities, supplements and foods you want to use as supports for these systems. If you have been exposed to a lot of chemicals or drugs, experience emotional congestion in the form of anger, frustration and depression, suffer from headaches, menstrual problems or have sleeping difficulty, there's a good chance your liver needs cleansing.

If you have a history of flatulence, constipation, diarrhea, hemorrhoids, general digestive disturbance, suffer from allergies or have used antibiotics repeatedly at any time in your life, your large intestine probably needs cleansing.

Recurring colds, flus, allergies, sinus infections, bronchitis, pneumonia or a history of smoking or exposure to airborne contaminants all indicate that your lungs may benefit from attention.

A dull, lifeless complexion, acne, cysts, eczema, psoriasis and other skin eruptions indicate that your liver and colon are not working efficiently and your skin, as an avenue of elimination, is clogged.

If you have a sedentary lifestyle your lymphatic system will become sluggish and not work properly. Your lymphatic system is an important part of your immune system. It is comprised of a bodywide network of vessels and lymph glands which, among other things, collect garbage from your cells, transport it into the bloodstream and on to the liver so it can be detoxified and filtered out.

Unlike the circulatory system, which has an internal pump (the heart) to keep the blood moving, the lymphatic system lacks a pump. Lymph (the fluid circulating in the lymphatic system), therefore, does not circulate on its own, but relies on the contraction and relaxation of your muscles to keep it moving. This is one reason why daily exercise is so important. Without it, the garbage just sits there in your lymphatic system, stagnating.

No matter what the focus of your cleanse, it is important to drink plenty of filtered water to flush out your kidneys. And what exactly do I mean when I say "plenty of water"? Plenty of water is six to eight cups of water each day. Drink it slowly to allow the water to be well absorbed and circulated before being excreted. During cold weather or if you have a cold body, make sure the water you drink is warm or hot. If you are taking an intestinal bulking agent it is important to drink even more water to allow the bulking agent to work properly.

What About Fasting?

To me, fasting is having nothing but water. While a water fast is an effective way to get your cells to dump stored toxins into your bloodstream, it is not supportive of detoxification, which is necessary to rid your body of these toxins. A water fast does not provide your body with nutrients to fuel the detoxification processes in your liver. This can result in partial detoxification, the production of more toxic by-products which your body is unable to eliminate, and which therefore go back into storage in your cells. *A water fast, particularly a prolonged one, can actually cause more damage than good.*

During weight loss, toxins that were stored in your fat cells will be released back into your system to either be filtered out and eliminated or returned to storage in other fat tissue. It is interesting to note that fat tissue not only includes what we normally think of as fat around our stomach and thighs, but also the brain and nervous system.

Instead of fasting, I recommend cleansing. By cleansing I mean abstaining from foods that contain toxins or produce toxic by-products, and focusing on foods that stimulate cellular cleansing. When you cleanse you allow your body to choose how much and what you will eat and drink. I also recommend nutritionally supporting your liver during any cleanse or fast, to ensure it has adequate nutrients to fuel its detoxification pathways. There are several products listed in the appendix that work well for this.

How to Fine-Tune Your Cleanse According to Your Body's Needs

If you know of a particular weakness in your body system, or if you have been having trouble in a specific area, the following recommendations can help you fine-tune your cleanse.

Liver Cleansing

In traditional Chinese medicine, the Liver is associated with emotions, especially anger, depression and irritability. It is also associated with physical problems such as headaches, skin rashes and allergies. It is intimately connected to a woman's reproductive system, her menstrual flow and any menstrual disturbances, including PMS.

From Western physiology we know that the liver has many biochemical responsibilities and can be likened to a chemical manufacturing plant. It is responsible for the production and breakdown of thousands of different chemicals and hormones in the body. When your liver is clogged and overworked, this compromises its ability to do its job. Then you can end up with substances in your bloodstream that should have been filtered out, broken down, recycled or excreted, but weren't. Hormones are one example. If your liver is overloaded and/or is lacking the nutrients and energy it needs to fuel its estrogen detoxification pathways, there may be excess estrogen circulating in your blood. This can cause numerous disturbances in the reproductive system.

Another source of stress for the liver is the onslaught of the enormous numbers and quantities of foreign chemicals that we are producing and dumping into our soil, water and air, and spraying on our food. Exposure to and ingestion of these foreign chemicals may be having a devastating effect on our health and our environment. Many petrochemical residues can latch on to estrogen receptor sites in our bodies in both males and females. This artificially elevates estrogen levels and overloads the estrogen detoxification pathways in the liver.

Your liver plays an important part in detoxifying both foreign chemicals and internally produced toxins that don't belong in your body. Before you ask your liver to become involved in a major cleanse you will want to be sure that your other organs of elimination are up and running, to ensure that the toxic matter actually gets out of your body. This means having daily bowel movements, drinking plenty of clean water and getting regular exercise.

Certain foods can be incorporated into your daily life that will have a gentle cleansing effect on your liver. These include:

- apples and apple juice,
- artichokes,
- asparagus,
- beets and beet juice,
- blue-green algae,
- broccoli,
- brown rice,
- brussels sprouts,
- burdock root,
- cabbage,
- carrots and carrot juice,
- collards,
- daikon,
- fresh fruits and fresh fruit juices,
- kale,
- kohlrabi,
- lemons and limes,
- millet,
- salad greens,
- seaweed,
- wheat grass juice and
- yams.

When you are cleansing your liver, you'll want to eliminate chemicals, preservatives and food additives from your diet. Eating organically grown foods at this time is especially important.

Liver cleansing herbs include:

- roasted dandelion root,
- barberry,

- oregon grape root,
- yellow dock,
- goldenseal,
- cayenne,
- echinacea,
- milk thistle and
- gentian.

Nutrients that support liver detoxication and protect your cells from damage associated with these processes include:

- B vitamins,
- vitamin A,
- vitamin C,
- vitamin E,
- beta carotene,
- minerals,
- antioxidants and
- numerous amino acids including glutathione, choline, methionine and inositol.

There are excellent products which combine many or all of these nutrients and antioxidants to help your liver do its job. Much research is being done now in this area and available products will change following developments in the research. Currently, there are supplements in capsules and tablets, as well as powders that you stir into water or juice to support liver function. UltraClear, and supplemental powders like it, are designed to support the liver detoxification pathways and can be used along with a fruit and vegetable cleanse. They will provide protein and nutrients for your liver and help stabilize your blood sugar. I highly recommend the use of such products when you are cleansing, particularly when you will otherwise be consuming little or no protein. The only drawback I have found with these products is they are a bit expensive. However, I feel the benefits are well worth the price. Your natural health

care provider will be able to recommend nutritional supports
to ensure you a safer and more comfortable cleanse.

Large Intestine Cleansing

Bowel bulkers that add bulk to your stools and keep your
bowel movements regular will help clean your large intestine.
Bentonite, or clay, absorbs many times its weight in toxic debris
which helps get toxins out of your system. Abdominal massage
can help loosen whatever is clogged in your intestines. If your
cleansing focuses on your intestines, try:

- abdominal massage,
- bentonite,
- brown rice,
- enemas (in moderation),
- flaxseed, either whole or ground,
- guar gum,
- herbal formulas that are designed to clean the large intestine (you can find these at your health food store or
  from your natural health care provider),
- oat bran,
- pectin,
- plenty of clean water,
- psyllium husks,
- triphala, a traditional Ayurvedic herbal formula that normalizes elimination, enhances digestion and cleanses the
  large intestine.

Bulking agents such as psyllium husks, flaxseed and oat
bran do not work well unless you take them with plenty of water. With flaxseed, if you take the seeds whole in water, they
are effective in keeping your bowels moving; if you take the
seeds ground in water they not only keep your bowels moving,
but also have an antiinflammation effect on the intestinal walls.
Water enemas can be helpful during a cleanse as they

eliminate bile and food residues from the intestines. You can take an enema while lying in a bathtub or sitting on the toilet. Retain the water and massage your abdomen for as long as is comfortable, then release.

Kidney Cleansing
Your kidneys also filter your blood. You can help them by:

- Drinking lots of clean water,
- eating barley, which is a natural diuretic,
- getting plenty of sleep and
- keeping warm (especially the lower back; wrap your lower back with a soft cloth or scarf if it feels cold while you are cleansing).

Lung Cleansing
- aerobic exercise,
- deep breathing,
- fresh air,
- walking and
- yoga, *Tai Chi* and *Qi Gong.*

Skin Cleansing
- aerobic exercise,
- clay facial masks,
- drinking plenty of clean water,
- dry skin brushing,
- hot baths in apple cider vinegar, epsom salts or baking soda,
- saunas and steam baths and
- sweating.

Lymphatic System Cleansing
- bouncing on a trampoline-type bouncer (the movement of your feet and ankles while bouncing is particularly effective at increasing circulation in the lymphatic system),

- deep breathing,
- drinking plenty of clean water,
- exercise,
- lymphatic drainage massage,
- skin brushing and
- yoga, *Tai Chi* and *Qi Gong.*

How Do You Feel During a Cleanse?

How a cleanse sounds when you read about it and what it feels like to actually do it are two separate things. Please do not get caught up in an idea about cleansing and try to stick to it despite communications from your body. With cleansing, it is important to take your time, go slowly and check in with your body regularly. Even if you don't complete a cleanse according to your expectations, it does not diminish the work you have done. It may take you a series of cleanses over a period of months to do what you initially set out to do in a week. Please acknowledge that whatever cleansing you do is an accomplishment.

Some people feel great when they are cleansing. They have lots of energy, are mentally clear and feel light and alive. Some people don't feel so great, however. They feel tired and irritable, have headaches, feel klutzy, spacy, angry, frustrated, nauseous and, if they are cleansing too quickly, really toxic.

You may taste nicotine on your breath, though you haven't smoked for years. You may crave foods you haven't eaten since childhood. You may feel old drugs that were stored away in your body tissue as they come into circulation to be released. Sometimes a childhood illness may reappear. If this happens, it can be a good idea to see a natural health care provider to help you resolve and release the old imbalance.

Physical cleansing is frequently accompanied by emotional cleansing. Old feelings, sensations and memories may arise. Your dreams may be emotionally charged, reflecting the cleansing you are doing. Give yourself time to pay attention to your dreams, feelings and whatever arises to be released.

It is best when you are cleansing to have plenty of time for yourself. However, this is not always possible. Children, family, friends, social and work obligations and demands all make cleansing more difficult. It can be helpful, if you decide to do a cleanse in the midst of family and work life, to let people know what you are doing and ask for their support. Some people will be able to support you and others may not. Changing your habits can disturb others and make them uncomfortable. Some people may even try to dissuade you or lead you astray. Choose your social contacts with care during a cleanse. Give those who cannot support you the space to have their reactions, and draw your attention inward to your own process. You do not need anyone's approval but your own to do this. It is also helpful to minimize social events that revolve around food.

Take as much time as you can to rest, nap, walk, write, paint, clean house, exercise, take hot baths or saunas—in short, to do whatever it is that nurtures you. Taking time to be with yourself is part of the process. Your body will probably have a lot to say to you. Give yourself time to listen.

If You Feel Badly While Doing a Cleanse

The best approach to cleansing is to go slowly. If you do start feeling badly, then slow the cleansing process down. You may feel nauseous, have diarrhea, a terrible headache, fuzzy thinking, be exhausted, unable to function and experience irritability and anger. You may wonder if you should keep on going and tough it out. My answer is no. If you start feeling badly, then by all means *slow down*. If you are working with a natural health care provider, you can call your health care provider for advice. If you are cleansing on your own and feel uncomfortable, I recommend you slow the process down. Either way, the first thing to do is *drink more water*.

Uncomfortable symptoms generally mean that you have succeeded in the first phase of cleansing—the release of toxins from your cells into your lymphatic system and bloodstream. They also indicate that the second stage of cleansing, detoxification and elimination, is overloaded. It will not serve you to push your body to release more toxins until you have eliminated the ones already in circulation. Generally it takes a few days to clear whatever you have already released. So if you have been cleansing for three days, and feel badly now, you may be feeling the effects of what you released a few days ago. This means you may still have yesterday and today's garbage to clear. So slow down. Be kind to your liver and let it catch up.

Slow the process down by not eating so many cleansing foods like fruits, vegetables and cleansing herbs that stimulate toxin release. Instead, eat brown rice and take psyllium husks and bentonite to absorb and escort the toxins out of your body. *Drink lots of water,* exercise, take baths and saunas to induce sweating and get a lymphatic drainage massage.

Coffee enemas can facilitate the rapid clearing of toxins from the liver. This can quickly relieve uncomfortable symptoms caused by a backup of toxins in your bloodstream. The faster you get them out of your body the better you will feel.

To do a coffee enema, use ground, organic caffeinated coffee. Boil three tablespoons of coffee in two to four cups of water for a few minutes, then simmer for fifteen minutes. Strain and cool to body temperature. Follow the directions included with your enema kit which you can purchase at a drugstore. Retain the coffee enema for as long as is comfortable, up to fifteen minutes.

When you feel better, you can start eating more fruits and vegetables. Go slowly, pay attention to your body signals and make sure you keep drinking plenty of water.

When to Cleanse

In traditional Chinese medicine, spring is the natural time to cleanse. The fall is also a good time to cleanse, but then a gentler cleanse is more appropriate. Your health, the climate you live in and your lifestyle are important factors to consider when cleansing. You should not expect to just fit a cleanse into your busy schedule. Make special time for it.

Doing a cleanse may be just the thing for you if you:

- feel the urge to do a cleanse,
- feel toxic,
- feel stuck,
- suffer from skin eruptions,
- are ready for a change in your life or
- are doing meditation or other spiritual work.

After you have done your first cleanse, you may feel really good in your body and about yourself. You may like some of the changes that have occurred in your diet and lifestyle. You may feel inspired to do regular seasonal cleanses. Then that phase may pass and you may only have the urge to do a cleanse every year or two, perhaps in the spring, or when you feel out of touch with your body, or when you've slipped into some poor eating habits.

A cleanse will often clear the slate and give you the opportunity to start over again in whatever it is in your life that feels stuck, stale or blocked. As with everything, you and your body will change, and what will work for you now may not work for you next year. Pay attention and see what it is your body is asking for *now*.

The Temptation to Overdo with Cleansing

There is something about the cleansing process that is deeply satisfying. As with anything that feels satisfying, one can become greedy for more. But more does not necessarily mean more satisfaction. The satisfaction comes from giving your digestive system a rest and allowing your body to self-clean—both things your body naturally wants to do at certain times. Greed comes into the picture when your body has cleaned enough and wants to shift gears back to eating more food to build and strengthen, and you override that message in an attempt to clean out just a little more. Your body knows how to maintain its balance. There are times when it wants to strengthen and build itself up and times when it wants to cleanse and let go. Both are essential to good health and balance. It is important to listen when your body says, "Enough."

When Not to Cleanse

I do not recommend cleansing if you:

- suffer from low blood sugar,
- are recovering from a debilitating illness,
- are under severe stress or
- are emotionally exhausted.

I do recommend that you follow the blood sugar regulating diet discussed in Chapter Six to allow your organs to heal and rebuild themselves. Later, when you are stronger, a cleanse will be more appropriate and the process much easier on your body.

If you are recovering from a stimulant-based lifestyle, have been drinking excessively or using drugs, again I recommend you first balance your blood sugar, rebuild the strength of your organs and replenish your energy reserve tank. With this accomplished, you will be able to benefit from a cleanse.

Cleansing tends to bring about change. If you are already in the midst of upheaval, then cleansing may not be right for you at this time.

The Benefits of Cleansing

Cleansing can give you a new outlook on life and the world. It is effective in breaking old patterns, often ones you were not even aware of having. New options simply appear as your habitual ways of thinking and feeling change. What you like to eat and how much you eat may also change.

Cleansing will change the quality of your *Qi*. It eliminates toxins from your system and allows your body to function more easily and effectively. Old health problems may start to clear up. Your skin may look better. You may lose weight.

After cleansing, your appetite for and tolerance of sugar, caffeine, chocolate, fatty foods and alcohol may change. If you go back to your old habits, your body will once again adjust to a less than optimal condition. However, if you allow your habits to be influenced by your cleanse, then gradually, over time, you may find your diet improving quite naturally.

Once you start cleaning your inner body, the urge to clean often extends to your environment. You may discover the urge to clean up stuff that has been accumulating for years. You may start cleaning your house, your closets, the garage or the garden—throwing out things that you don't use, that don't fit or you simply don't want anymore.

How you feel about your home, your work or your life may change. Your artwork may change or your exercise routine. You may *start* exercising, meditating or writing.

You may not change, but be prepared, you just might . . .

CHAPTER 10

Opening Your Heart and Emotional Health

O ur aches, pains and illnesses often have an emotional message, a story to tell. The traditional Chinese understood this. They did not separate the mind and the body. Rather, they looked at emotional symptoms to gain insight into what was going on physically, just as they looked at physical symptoms to gain clues to what was going on emotionally. You can use this same approach in learning to better understand your body.

The Five Emotions According to Five Element Theory

According to Five Element Theory, each element has an emotion associated with it. You will notice as you look at the elements and their corresponding emotions that the Fire and Earth elements have what we would normally consider positive emotional associations, and that Metal, Water and Wood are not nearly as appealing. However, each element has both "positive" and "negative" attributes, and they are all found in each of us. It is natural for a certain element to predominate. How-

THE FIVE ELEMENTS AND EMOTIONS

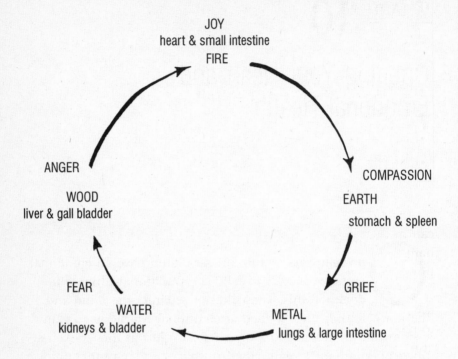

ever, when this is taken to an extreme it can contribute to imbalance and ill health.

I have found it useful to expand the traditional chart to include a wider range of emotions. You will also find in the descriptions of each element a discussion of the strengths that are attributed to it. This will help balance the tendency to think of some elements as better than others. Each of the elements is important, and all are a necessary part of the whole.

Love and the Heart

When Heart *Qi* is strong and flows freely, you have understanding for yourself and the world around you. Laughter comes easily. You experience love, joy, happiness and pleasure. A lack of these feelings can weaken Heart *Qi*. Envy and hatred

THE FIRE ELEMENT

Emotions	Sound	Facial Coloring	Organs
• Love • Joy • Happiness • Pleasure • Envy • Hatred	• Laughter	• Ruddy, flushed or red	• Heart • Small Intestine

can restrict the flow of *Qi* to the Heart. Laughter, on the other hand, can open the Heart, fill it with joy and reestablish the flow of *Qi*.

In traditional Chinese medicine the Heart is the Home of the Spirit. When the Heart is disturbed the Spirit has no place to rest. This causes malaise during the day and disturbed sleep at night. In traditional Chinese medicine the Heart is also considered to be the ruler of the body. When you listen to the wisdom of your Heart, you are guided by your Spirit, your inner navigator.

Your voice is a channel from your Heart to the outside world. In many people this channel is blocked. This is particularly noticeable around the expression of individuality and feelings. Feelings are the domain of the Liver and the Liver and the Heart are closely connected. If your Heart is closed your feelings will be expressed without understanding, and the Liver will tend to speak in anger, attacking and blaming others. This is when shouting, meanness, cruelty, shaming and belittling occur.

On the other hand, speaking from the Heart means saying how you feel and expressing your inner experience to the outside world. One way to practice this is by speaking in "I" statements. This allows your Liver energy to flow through your Heart.

For example, notice the difference between these two statements: "If you slam that door one more time you'll go to bed without dinner!" and "I feel angry when you slam the door. I want you to shut it quietly." In the first statement the Liver is speaking. The second uses an "I" statement, channeling the anger in the Liver through the Heart. At first the idea of using "I" statements to express anger may seem artificial. However, if you give it a try, you'll find that it is an effective way to communicate and you'll be much more likely to get what you want. It also becomes more natural over time.

If you have an emotional communication to make, an "I" statement will offer your listener the opportunity to understand how you feel, and what you would like to be different. And most importantly, it will keep your *Qi* flowing freely, maintain congruence between your inner experience and the outside world, and let your Heart know that you love, honor and respect yourself. In this process you may also find that you are honoring and respecting your listener as well. Not only will *your* energy flow, but the energy *between* you and your listener can also start to flow, making your relationship more healthy, fluid and alive.

Emotions and the Immune System

The voice of your Spirit that resides in your Heart is also the voice of your immune system. It is telling you how to keep your *Qi* strong and healthy. How to respect your *Qi* and yourself.

When I think of the immune system I think of the body's inherent sense of limits. Your body knows what is and is not okay for you. It knows when to say no, when to say I want that, or I need that, and when to say yes, that feels good. You may not have been encouraged to listen to and respect your own needs, wants and dreams, or to trust yourself. Instead, you may have been taught that if you speak up you will be punished, abandoned or unlovable. But regardless of what you were taught, no one else can be your voice for you. In repressing your inner voice you are denying the wisdom of your body and your immune system. Assertiveness is one of the seven traits that Henry Dreher attributes to the "Immune Power Personality." Being able to express your feelings and needs supports your immune system, and makes it stronger.

It is best when you can recognize your own needs, wants and desires, and dare to ask and reach for what you want. Articulate it. I need ... I want ... I dream ... This requires taking risks, changing old patterns, speaking up, exposing yourself. When it feels too scary, imagine sticking to your old routine, remaining silent, carrying on, burying your dreams and desires. How does that feel in your body? Can you live with it?

THE EARTH ELEMENT

Emotions	Sound	Facial Coloring	Organs
• Compassion • Centeredness • Groundedness • Confidence • Worry • Spaciness • Lack of confidence • Stress	• Singing or sing-song	• Sallow or yellow	• Stomach • Spleen

Compassion and the Stomach

When Stomach *Qi* flows freely you feel compassionate, centered and grounded. A natural sense of self-worth, value and belonging arise. You are at ease in your body and on the planet.

Worry, stress and lack of confidence can weaken and block the flow of Stomach *Qi*. This disturbs your grounding and center, and interferes with feelings of calmness and inner peace. When Stomach *Qi* is weak, the Stomach becomes vulnerable to being bullied by the Liver which may harbor anger and frustration. The traditional Chinese called this "Liver attacking Stomach," describing the emotional energy of the Liver bypassing the understanding of the Heart and moving directly to the Stomach, attacking it. "Liver attacking Stomach" can cause indigestion, stomachaches and diseases of the digestive tract.

Meditation is a good antidote to worry, stress and lack of confidence. It can build your center, ground you in your body, remind you of the "Big Picture" and give you respite from the worries of your day. It relaxes the nervous system, supports the immune system and can restore inner peace. Meditation helps cultivate compassion, both for yourself and others. It can also bring clarity to your feelings and situation so you can communicate effectively by speaking from your Heart.

The Earth element also governs your muscles. Strengthening your muscles through exercise can strengthen your Earth element. Exercise can also ground you in your body, build your sense of center, increase your self-confidence and decrease the effects of worry and stress both physically and emotionally.

It is important to find a form of exercise you like. If you like to walk, then walk; don't force yourself to go to the gym. If you need the support of other people, find a class or an exercise buddy. Create the situation that will support you in getting regular exercise. This is not meant to be punishment. The point is to make you feel better. What activity would you enjoy?

LIVER ATTACKING STOMACH

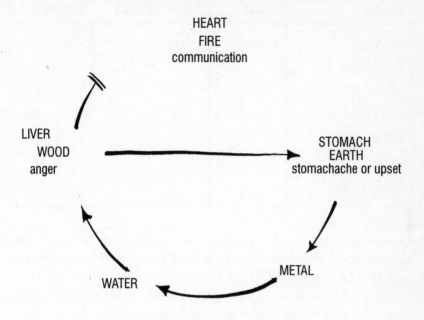

HEART
FIRE
communication

LIVER
WOOD
anger

STOMACH
EARTH
stomachache or upset

METAL

WATER

Grief and the Lungs

When your Lung *Qi* is flowing freely you experience your-self as a full, expanded presence in the world. You are an inte-gral part of the universe and experience ample space to be. There is a fullness to your energy field that allows the irrita-tions of the day to roll off your back. This expanded energy field also acts as part of your immune system and protects you from colds and flus.

Sadness, melancholy, resignation and apathy, along with grief and the depression that can accompany it, all cause a dis-turbed and weakened flow of Lung *Qi*. As Lung *Qi* weakens and breathing becomes shallow, your protective energy field collapses and your body is left vulnerable to respiratory illness. It is not uncommon to develop a respiratory illness, like bron-chitis, when one has sustained a loss and is grieving. If you are suffering from recurring lung problems, and you are not re-

THE METAL ELEMENT

Emotions	Sound	Facial Coloring	Organs
• Sadness • Melancholy • Grief • Loss • Resignation • Apathy • Depression	• Crying	• Pale or white	• Lung • Large Intestine

sponding to antibiotics, you may want to consider having some acupuncture, breathwork or bodywork to see if there are feelings that have lodged in your Lungs that want expression. In the case of an ungrieved loss, getting help moving through your grief will often resolve an otherwise persistent lung problem.

Just as grief makes the lungs vulnerable to infection, full breathing can encourage the release of grief and help the lungs heal. Full breathing can also loosen a depression and lift the cloud of melancholy.

Aerobic exercise will naturally expand your breath and alter your emotional state. You do not have to wear leotards and do high intensity aerobics at the gym. Just take a walk for half an hour. Break a little sweat. Feel the air on your cheeks and notice your surroundings. Daily exercise will restore the flow of *Qi* to your Lungs and strengthen your entire energy field.

Letting Go

Associated with grief and loss is the experience of acceptance and letting go. Letting go has to do with both the lungs and the large intestine. Exhaling fully before inhalation is a way to practice letting go. Constipation is a way the large intes-

THE WATER ELEMENT

Emotions	Sound	Facial Coloring	Organs
• Fear • Fright • Terror • Insecurity • Stress • Anxiety	• Groaning	• Dark, blue-black or gray	• Kidneys • Bladder

tine doesn't let go. An emotional catharsis can sometimes be accompanied by a release of abdominal tension and improved bowel movements.

Loss, death, grief and letting go are a natural part of life. Some losses are clear. When a loved one dies it is clearly a great loss, and often one that will change your life forever. There are also losses that are less clear. Loss can be associated with a job, a relationship, your passing youth, a pet, a missed opportunity, a dream that doesn't come to pass, a home, your health. It does not matter if others perceive your situation as worthy of grief. It is *your* experience and feelings that matter. If you have experienced a loss, give yourself the time and space to feel it. When you reach a place of acceptance, and you are ready, you will let go.

Fear and the Kidneys

When your Kidney *Qi* is flowing fully and freely you have endurance and stamina. Your willpower and ambition naturally support you in achieving your goals. You feel internally supported.

Lack of sleep, irregular eating habits and reliance on sugar and stimulants, like caffeine, diminish Kidney *Qi*, as do stress and fear. In Chinese medicine we call this Kidney deficiency. In Western medicine, it's called adrenal exhaustion. Both describe what occurs when the adrenal glands become so depleted they can no longer respond to stress and support your body. This leaves you exhausted and prone to insecurity, anxiety and fear. In Chapters Five and Six you will find dietary suggestions for healing adrenal exhaustion, as well as dietary measures which can protect your body when you are going through periods of stress or fear.

Activities that support the kidneys and adrenal glands include: getting plenty of sleep; eating regular, well-balanced, warm meals; drinking plenty of clean water and getting moderate exercise. Rest, play and relaxation are also important for healing your kidneys and adrenal glands. Dress warmly, and protect your neck, lower back and ankles from the cold and drafts. When your kidneys and adrenal glands feel weak and the weather is cold, wrap a soft wool scarf underneath your clothes, around your belly and lower back for support.

Fear

Fear tends to justify itself. When you are afraid, your fear convinces you to believe in it. Now there are plenty of times when fear is appropriate. But many of us also walk around with a low level of fear that permeates the way we see the world and experience life. It can be a specific, deep-seated fear, or a general feeling that life is dangerous. There is certainly enough around us to support a fearful worldview.

However, fear disturbs your Heart and makes it difficult to hear the voice of your Spirit. When fear speaks louder than the Heart, the Water element is ruling your body. This will cause imbalance for your Heart, not your Kidneys, is the natural ruler of your body. The job of the Kidneys is to provide stamina and support throughout your day and to help you respond to potentially dangerous situations, not to rule you.

There is an important connection between love and fear. When we experience fear, it closes the Heart. When the Heart is closed, we shut off our understanding. Without understanding it is easy to view the world as a dangerous place. This further encourages us to close our Hearts. Then we carry this closed Heart into our lives, our work and our relationships. Worst of all, we close our Hearts to ourselves. With a Heart closed in fear, it seems there are no choices. But really, we have a choice at any moment to open our Hearts, to listen to our inner guidance, and speak from a place of love, understanding and compassion.

It takes courage to speak from the Heart, from your own experience and vulnerability. Yet it also allows the opportunity for change, growth and transformation to occur. And when you think about it, what is the real risk? In speaking from fear you are usually not expressing what you want; instead you are most often attacking or defending. This puts your listener on the defensive as well, making him or her less liable to speak from the Heart. A vicious circle is established. Yet there is a door that offers the possibility of change, real contact, communication, and the connection of one human being to another.

Speaking from the Heart enables us to be more humane in a world that can seem hostile and inhumane. When we speak from our Hearts it gives others permission to do the same. Speaking from your Heart is the antidote to fear. Our world will not become a saner, safer more humane place until individuals take the risk of becoming more loving, compassionate and understanding with themselves and the world around them. Opening your Heart makes a strong statement. It affirms your belief in the possibility of a humane world and acknowledges your own humanity and the humanity of others.

Feelings and the Liver

When Liver *Qi* is flowing freely you have an innate sense of your own needs and wants as well as your boundaries and limits. Anger naturally arises from your Liver when someone or

THE WOOD ELEMENT

Emotions	Sound	Facial Coloring	Organs
• Frustration • Irritability • Anger • Blaming • Attacking • Rage • Aggression • Violence • Depression	• Shouting	• Greenish	• Liver • Gall Bladder

something approaches or oversteps these boundaries. With freely flowing Liver *Qi* you naturally know how to communicate this and establish a more appropriate relationship. You know when to say "no" and when to say "yes." Further, you know you have every right to determine what does and does not work for you and your body.

Watch a two-year-old. If they don't want you to touch them they will let you know loud and clear. If they don't want to eat carrots they will push them away, turn their head, and assert "No!" Their Liver *Qi* is flowing and they communicate without editing. Like a two-year-old, the Liver is not capable of judiciously guiding you through your life. Like a two-year-old, the Liver requires firm and loving support, guidance and direction. The two-year-old gets such support from parents, family, and other caregivers. The Liver gets it from the Heart, the ruler of the body. Although two-year-olds are generally not good models for appropriate behavior, their clarity on their right to control their bodies and their lives is admirable. They do not get wrapped up in guilt or second-guess themselves after saying "no." They simply move on to the next thing in life. These traits are well worth cultivating and keeping. Often when two-year-olds become socialized, they forget these strengths, and learn to tell people what they think they want to hear.

When your innate sense of autonomy has been interfered with, when you feel powerless, repress your anger and learn to compromise your natural boundaries and limits, your Liver *Qi* becomes congested and blocked. When *Qi* is blocked or congested in the Liver there is a tendency to feel moody, irritable, frustrated, depressed, angry, aggressive, enraged or violent. Doing therapy or talking with a friend can help move blocked energy. Physical exercise can also move blocked energy. It can give you a break from your anger or depression, and clear your mind and thoughts so you gain a new perspective on life.

Whether your Liver *Qi* is congested from emotional toxins (like unprocessed or unexpressed feelings) or physical toxins (like alcohol, drugs, chemicals, pesticides and junk food), it will affect both your emotional and your physical state. It will also create a distortion through which you experience life.

At the risk of sounding like a broken record, using your voice is once again a powerful way to move blocked Liver *Qi* and release anger or depression. You are the only one who can use your voice and express yourself. No one else knows how you feel. It is one way as an adult you can be a good parent to yourself. In using your voice, you can stand up for yourself, ask for what you want and make yourself comfortable.

Coping Mechanisms

When an experience occurs that is more than you can handle, and if you do not have someone to help you learn how to handle it, your body has a natural coping mechanism. It stores the experience or feelings in your body to be dealt with at a later time.

This storage process involves blocking the natural flow of *Qi*. Your *Qi* is literally tied up in knots holding that experience in place. This can manifest as body aches, pains and tension, and if the blockage accumulates long enough, physical illness.

If you are not allowed or encouraged to feel and express your feelings as a child, storing them becomes second nature. If you have adopted this coping mechanism, it is often easier to say "I have a headache" or "My stomach hurts," than to say "My feelings are hurt. I am in pain." But if in fact your pain is emotional in nature, then treating your headache or stomach-ache with drugs will only cover the real issue. If you sense that some of your physical symptoms may be emotional in nature, you might benefit from exploring the messages contained in your symptoms. Take time to be with the part of your body that hurts, ask how it feels, find out what it wants, listen to it.

Listening to your body can take many different forms. Some-people like to draw or paint how they feel inside. You do not have to be an artist to do this. The point is to let your body express itself, not to produce a masterpiece. You may want to buy some big paper and crayons, watercolors or markers. If you like to write, let the part of you that hurts write you a letter. "Dear Susan, I feel like this. Love from, your Stomach." You can express yourself in clay, you can dance your experience, you can close your eyes and do a visualization, you can sing, sound and tone. You can play music, write a poem or pound pillows.

Some body messages may seem profound and some may seem silly. Please do not judge them one way or another. Just hear them and see if the request is something that you might be able to honor. The important thing is to make time to lis-ten to your feelings.

There are numerous body-based therapies that can help you access and release energy and feelings that are stored in your body. It is important to have support in processing the emotions that may be released by bodywork. Depending on the nature of the release, support may range from a hot bath, an extra-long night's sleep and some journal writing or a talk with a friend, to seeking counseling with a trained therapist. When you release blocked energy, traumas and injuries, the overall result is an ability to process and let go of the past and bring more of yourself and your energy into the present.

Counseling and Body-Based Therapies

Therapy can involve the slow and arduous process of rebuilding trust, self-confidence, will, compassion and understanding. It may involve recovering parts of yourself that have long been forgotten and buried. You may have to dig down to uncover and heal old wounds, to remember you have a right to exist and to have your feelings. Yet allowing your inner world and experience to be seen, witnessed and heard by someone who accepts you as you are creates a strong healing environment. Talking with a compassionate and understanding therapist is a powerful way to connecting the feelings of the Liver with the understanding of the Heart.

Many times when you are undergoing a course of therapy your body will crave comfort foods and activities to ease your discomfort and pain. I recommend listening to your body. However, during a long course of therapy, repeatedly listening to and following the voice desiring comfort can lead to imbalances, like overeating. At times it can be helpful to physically balance your body while doing emotional work.

You can help yourself by regularly taking a walk, run or bike ride, working out at a gym or doing yoga. You can also maintain your balance by paying attention to your diet, keeping your blood sugar regulated, getting plenty of sleep, taking hot baths and enjoying a favorite creative pursuit.

Sometimes you may want outside help. This is when the numerous body-based therapies like acupuncture, breathwork, massage, network chiropractic, osteopathic treatment, rolfing and shiatsu can support you in moving blocked energy and restoring your inner balance. Homeopathy and nutritional work can also be of great support in increasing your stability, strength and vitality. Respecting and attending to both the physical and emotional wants of your body will deliver you at the end of your emotional work in a more balanced and whole state.

Going Through the Darkness

Sometimes you may find yourself in a very dark hole. Something happens and it comes upon you. It is often triggered by a disappointment, a major loss, the breakup of a relationship or the death of a loved one.

If you are in a dark hole, please know that benefits can come from dark places. Deep healing can occur. Fairy tales and myths from all cultures tell of this. The most precious aspects of yourself can be hidden in the deepest darkness.

The important thing to remember when you are in a dark place is that there *is* a way out and you *will* find it. This is a good time to seek support. Find a counselor who is comfortable accompanying you in your dark places, who will accept your pain, be your anchor and not judge or condemn you. Find someone who will make a safe space for you to explore your dark hole. Trust that inside the hole, underneath the pain, is a part of yourself that you will treasure more than anything in the world.

You may find comfort and support in some of the stories that are included in the Stories of Healing section of this book. As you go through pain you will often come across old feelings. As you release these feelings you make space for more of yourself to emerge; for the very nature of who you are, your Beingness to surface. This can feel like a birth process—like you are being reborn.

Singing, Sounding and Toning to Reestablish the Flow of Qi

One way to get your *Qi* circulating freely is to open your voice and your Heart. Singing is a powerful way to do this. It is also a good antidote to any emotional blockage. Singing increases breathing which helps the Lungs, it encourages self-expression which connects the Liver and the Heart, and it allows your energy to flow. Vibrations from toning, singing and chanting can break up congested energy and make you feel better both physically and emotionally.

If you are shy about singing, sing in the shower or the car. If you are feeling a bit brave, take a class, join a choir or get together with friends who also want to play with their voices.

This is a story a friend told me. After I heard it, I asked him to write it down, and he did. This happened years ago in our voice group in San Francisco. The assignment had been to pick a song that expressed a hidden side of ourselves and to sing it to the group. Here is Bob's story:

> "If I loved you, time and again I would try to say
> all I'd want you to know . . ."

> I was in love with Elizabeth. I knew that. Yet, I was afraid to go forward. I felt stuck. Afraid of what? I didn't know.

> We (Elizabeth and I) had known each other for years. We were friends—but this was different. She was asking me to open up in a whole other way. It was tempting, but I had been hurt before. I'd been married for six and a half years, and also had been in some long relationships. The most recent was nine and a half years. Those HURT when they ended. I certainly didn't want to go through that again.

> There were other fears that I was less conscious of, but I felt them, even though I couldn't (can't) articulate them. Something about opening up, the way one does with a TRUE LOVE. Dare I show the real me? Dare I risk rejection from this very important person? What if she saw

the real me and said, "No. Now that I see who you really are, I'm no longer interested."

My conflict was that I didn't want to be so hard, so rigid. What good is it to protect myself so much that I'm not open to joy? Also, what if she realized that her desire for me would never be met, because of my fears? Mightn't she leave? It was a painful conflict.

We, the Roy Hart Theater Core Group, had decided to take some risks with each other. We would each pick a song, something personally important, and sing it. We would go further, show more of ourselves to each other. We'd been working in that way for years. We all felt safe. I trusted you. I was willing to take chances in that context. I didn't have to defend any position and you weren't urging me to do anything in particular, as Elizabeth was.

I was afraid, I felt hard. I began to sing.

"If I loved you . . ."

You and Karin were so caring, so loving, so soft. I could feel my shell begin to crack. I felt total acceptance from you. Amazing! Maybe it was okay to show myself, to be ME.

It was becoming easier. I was softening. You and Karin were encouraging me, stroking me. I felt filled with your love. I was crying, joyful, singing out, speaking from my heart, my soul. It was okay, I was okay. I felt good. I dared to open.

It was a profound experience. Elizabeth and I got married. I am very happy and very grateful.

On Developing the Underdeveloped Parts of Yourself

It is important to realize that when you start to develop parts of yourself that have been in hibernation, it is natural to feel uncomfortable, ashamed and like you are missing an important piece. It is also natural to grieve that somehow this part of you has not been welcomed or nurtured in your life. Allow your feelings to surface, and know that feeling stuck, cut-off and wounded is often an integral part of your healing process.

Be open to the possibility that you can grow like a seed that has waited for the right conditions to germinate. Tolerate feeling awkward and being a beginner. Give yourself permission to not know, to make mistakes and be a bit clumsy. Trust that in time these unacknowledged and undeveloped parts of yourself will make you more balanced and complete. They are there for a reason, even if you don't yet know what that reason is. If you don't nurture these parts of yourself, you will be missing important tools to do your work in the world. If you don't nurture your buried dreams, who else will?

CHAPTER 11

The Ten-Question Checkup

A simple way to do a self-checkup is to regularly ask yourself these ten questions, eleven for women. Your answers will give you a good deal of information about how your body, mind and Spirit are doing. A picture will often emerge from your answers to these questions. Your answers may direct you to certain chapters in this book.

For example, you may complain of having no energy. When you go through the ten-question checkup, you may find you are skipping breakfast, drinking coffee, sleeping poorly, and eating lots of sugar in the afternoons. Your fatigue is suddenly transformed from a mysterious malfunction of your body, to an understandable result of your daily actions. Then you may see in the question on emotions that your stress level is high. You may realize that this is probably the root of your poor sleep, poor diet, and resulting poor energy. Your thoughts may shift from an angry "I *never* have enough energy!" to a guilty "I've been *so awful* to my poor body," to a compassionate and understanding "Oh my gosh—this stress is really affecting me. This *is* a lot to handle. How can I take better care of myself?"

The ten questions address the following aspects of your health:

1. *Qi*
2. appetite and diet
3. digestion
4. bowel movements
5. urination
6. sleep
7. exercise
8. headaches
9. body aches
10. emotions
    and for women:
11. menstrual periods

1. Qi

How is your energy? Is it steady, erratic or hyper? Does it crash in the mid to late afternoon? Do you need coffee or sugar to feel awake? Are you always exhausted? If so, how long has it been since you had any energy?

If your energy is good, move on to the next question. If your energy is erratic or hyper, refer to Chapter Six, blood sugar regulation. If you have absolutely no energy, also refer to Chapter Six. You may want to consult a natural health care provider as well, to help you gather enough energy so that you can take care of yourself. As you answer the following questions, you will probably determine the aspects of your lifestyle that are causing the biggest drain on your energy. Making changes in these areas will give you the best results.

2. Appetite and Diet

Do you have a good appetite? Are you hungry in the morning? How many times a day are you eating? Do you eat when you are hungry? What are you eating, and when do you eat? Are you eating a lot before you go to bed? How long has it been since you had a good appetite? Are you suppressing your appetite? Do you drink coffee, diet sodas or smoke cigarettes when you are hungry?

A good appetite is considered basic to good health in traditional Chinese medicine. It is one sign of a strong Spirit, and it is the first step in building strong *Qi*. Your appetite is your body's way of telling you what it needs to make energy for you. Your hunger is a healthy message from your stomach saying your body needs food to raise your blood sugar level, nourish your cells and create energy. Please do not bemoan a healthy appetite. You may want to rein it in a bit, but please don't wish it away. And do not try to silence it with coffee, sodas, cigarettes or whatever else seems to work for you. Rather, review Chapter Five on the basics of a healthy diet and Chapter Six on regulating blood sugar. Give your body the nourishment it is requesting, allow your internal world to calm down, become steady and stable. If you are eating a lot before bed, look and see what you are eating earlier in the day. Make sure you are eating a good breakfast. Try keeping a food diary for a week. Write down everything that you eat and drink. The more thorough you are, the clearer your dietary picture will be.

3. Digestion

How is your digestion? Does food sit in your stomach like a brick after you eat? Do you belch a lot? Do certain foods upset your digestion more than others? Do you feel bloated, or pass gas a lot? If so, when? Do you have stomachaches? Probably more than any other question I regularly ask my patients, this one elicits the question, "What do you mean? How would I know how my digestion is?" To answer this question, start paying attention to your stomach after you eat. How does it feel? Is your food sitting in there like a lump? Do you dash to the bathroom with diarrhea? Do you

burp, have a burning reflux, or start passing gas? If you are experiencing such symptoms, refer to the section on digestion in
Chapter Five.

Do you get stomachaches? If you have stomachaches, when
do they come? Are they daily? How severe are they? Are they
associated with emotional upsets or worries? Does food help or
do you lose your appetite?

If you have chronic stomachaches consult with your physician or nurse practitioner for a diagnosis. You may want to
consult a natural health care provider for dietary recommendations or relaxation therapy. If you suspect that emotional stress
is the cause of your digestive problem, you may want to consult
with a counselor to explore your emotional distress.

4. Bowel Movements

Do you have daily bowel movements? How many times a
day? Are they loose, or are you constipated? Do you have only
one bowel movement a week? Do you have to drink coffee to
have a bowel movement? Is there blood in your bowel movements? Is it fresh red or old and tarry looking? Do you have
hemorrhoids?

Daily bowel movements are important. It is the primary
way your body disposes of wastes and toxic matter. If waste accumulates in your large intestine for a week before being eliminated, it provides ample opportunity for toxins to be
reabsorbed into your bloodstream. This does not contribute to
good health. If you are not having daily bowel movements,
look under Headaches in the Self-Care Dictionary where constipation is addressed. Are you drinking enough water? Getting
daily exercise? Breathing into your belly?

If you have diarrhea, does it occur after eating certain
foods? Have you tried avoiding those foods for a week or two
to see how you feel? Does it seem related to stress? Have you
discussed it with your medical practitioner or naturopath? If
you find blood in your bowel movements, be sure to tell your medi-

cal practitioner about this. If you have hemorrhoids, acupuncture can be an effective treatment for them.

5. Urination

Do you wake up in the night to urinate? If so, how many times? When you feel the urge to urinate, is there a lot there, or just a few dribbles? Do you have to urinate more frequently when you are under stress or are nervous about something? Has there been a recent change in what you consider normal with regards to your urinating habits? If you are a man over forty, when was the last time you had your prostate checked?

This question about waking at night to urinate seems to intrigue people. "Why do you ask if I wake to pee?" my patients ask. "Is it good if I do?" In traditional Chinese medicine, the Kidney energy governs the sphincter of the bladder. When Kidney energy is weak or depleted, it will take a smaller amount of urine accumulation in the bladder to exert enough pressure on the sphincter to give you the urge to urinate. Waking to urinate in the night usually means that either you had a lot to drink before bed, or your Kidney energy is weak. Some people wake to urinate every night, and have for as long as they can remember. This could indicate that they always drink a lot before bed, or more likely that they constitutionally have weak Kidney energy. Following the dietary suggestions in Chapter Six for a few months may replenish your Kidney energy enough to decrease the frequency of your nighttime urination.

If you suddenly start urinating at night, or start urinating more frequently during the day, it may indicate that stress is accumulating and taking a toll on your Kidney energy. This can be a red flag to slow down and look at what is going on in your life. What is stressful for you now? What are you doing to make your situation better or worse? For example, if stress is causing you to sleep poorly, are you drinking coffee during the day to stay alert which contributes to another night of poor sleep? Are you getting some exercise, a walk after dinner? Have you tried a calming tea before bed, or a homeopathic remedy like Calms Forte to help you sleep while avoiding caffeine during the day? How can you support your body?

6. Sleep

Do you sleep well? Do you get enough sleep? Do you feel rested when you wake? Do you need an alarm clock to wake up? Do you need coffee to get going? Do you stay up too late? Do you routinely feel sleep-deprived? Do you have young children? Do you think getting only six hours of sleep makes you a better person, even when your body needs eight? Do you wake up worrying in the middle of the night? What in your life is disturbing your sleep? Is it a child? Your job? A relationship? Money worries? Health worries?

Getting enough sleep is important for the maintenance of good health. Your answers to this question may reveal why your *Qi* is low, where your priorities lie, and unconsciously held negative beliefs about giving yourself what you need. They may point to problem areas in your life that truly need your attention.

7. Exercise

Do you exercise regularly? Too much? Too little? Never? What kind of exercise are you getting? What kind of exercise do you enjoy? Do you feel better when you are more active? How does exercise affect your appetite, mood and sleep? Why are you not exercising more? Why are you exercising too much? How can you change that?

Your answers to these questions often reveals priorities in your life. Try not to judge yourself if you aren't exercising and you want to be or think you should be. Acknowledge what you are doing, how you are spending your time. What is getting a higher priority than exercise in your life right now? Is this a temporary situation or long-term? If it is temporary, make an agreement with yourself about when you will get more exercise. And by all means keep your agreement with yourself. If it is a long-term situation, then you may want to rethink your priorities, particularly if you really want to fit exercise into your life. Continue to check in with yourself. Hmm . . . how do I feel about taking a walk today? No. Okay, maybe tomorrow. Make enough space so that you have a choice.

8. Headaches

Do you get headaches? If so, how often? Do you take anything for them? Do they relate to fatigue, low blood sugar, allergies, stress, hormones, eyestrain, or spending too much time in your head and not enough in the rest of your body?

Getting enough sleep and eating regular meals can clear up many headaches. Start out with the diet recommended in Chapter Six. Clearing up any allergies with natural medicine can also resolve some headaches. Stress reduction and exercise can address stress-related headaches. If eyestrain is causing your headaches, have your vision checked with your eye doctor and follow eye exercise suggestions recommended in the Self-Care Dictionary under Vision Problems and Eyestrain, or consider consulting a vision therapist. Hormonally related headaches may sometimes respond to liver cleansing, herbal treatment or natural progesterone cream. Ask your natural health care provider about these possibilities.

9. Body Aches

Do you have body aches? Are they acute or chronic? Do they roam around your body, or are they always located in the same spot? Are they worse in cold, heat, damp, with activity, after sleep or sitting?

If you have neck and shoulder aches, do you get regular relaxing exercise that gently brings your energy into the lower part of your body? If you have lower back pain or stiffness, knee pain or weakness, or ankle or heel pain and weakness—think about your reserve tank energy. How is your Kidney *Qi*? Do you eat regularly? Get enough sleep, rest and relaxation? How is your stress level? Are you relying on stimulants throughout the day?

There are many suggestions in the Self-Care Dictionary for addressing body aches of all kinds. Refer to the section on the part of the body that is causing you discomfort.

10. *Emotions*

How are you doing emotionally? How is your stress level? What is giving you pleasure in your life these days? How are you nourishing your Spirit?

Answers to these questions can help you identify what is worrying you. What needs your attention? Are you spending all your time and attention on pressing but unimportant tasks, and overlooking less urgent but absolutely essential pleasures, things that feed your Spirit and Soul and contribute to your long-term values and goals.

Chapter Ten may be a helpful resource if this area of your life is calling for your attention. Meditation, exercise, a blood sugar regulating diet or a cleansing diet may also contribute toward improvement in your emotional health.

For women:

11. *Menstrual Periods*

How are you periods? Are they regular? How is your flow? Are there any changes in your periods? When was your last gynecological checkup and PAP smear? Are you experiencing PMS? If so, for how long? What are the themes of your emotional upsets when your have PMS? How are you addressing these issues in your life? Are you getting headaches before, during or at the end of your period? If you are having problems with your period, you may want to read the Women's Health section in the Self-Care Dictionary. Regularly consult with your nurse practitioner or gynecologist about any changes or problems with your periods. Reproductive health is an important aspect of self-care for women.

Summary

After you get an overview of the current state of your life and lifestyle, it can be helpful to ask yourself, "When was the last time I took a real vacation?" By real vacation I mean one that involves doing exactly what you want to do, what restores you, what makes you happy, and reminds you of what is important to you in life. The value of really getting away from your daily life to recharge and renew your body, mind and Spirit, as well as to gain perspective on your life, is not to be underestimated. Sometimes it is when you can least afford it, either in money or time, that you need a vacation the most. Sometimes you just have to go away anyway, for a real vacation can replenish your energy, rest your mind, relax your body, feed your Spirit and bring joy to your Heart. It can restore your emotional cushion and remind you of what you value. It allows perspective, so you can rethink your priorities.

If it has been too long since you took your last real vacation, it just may be time to pull out your calendar and set aside some time for yourself.

PART TWO

The Self-Care
Dictionary

Introduction to Self-Care

I see our bodies on a spectrum that ranges from the gross physical level of an arm or a stomach, to the more subtle energy level of a thought, intuition or feeling. If you think a thought often enough you can make it a physical reality. This brings something from the intangible plane of pure energy into the physical plane of matter. When an illness or dysfunction is developing, it often manifests energetically before it appears physically.

While Western medicine excels in detecting and attacking full-blown physical disease, in traditional Chinese medicine we are trained to detect imbalances before they develop into physical illnesses. Our methods of treatment—diet, exercise, herbs, acupuncture and moxibustion—are meant to address these imbalances and prevent the development of more serious illness. This is the heart of preventive medicine: to detect an energetic imbalance before it has the opportunity to manifest physically, and to correct that imbalance. This allows treatment to be more subtle than the invasive and heroic measures that are often required to address physical disease. This explains the reasoning behind the old tradition of paying traditional Chinese doctors only when they keep their patients healthy. If a patient became physically ill, the doctor was not doing his or her job.

Today there are many approaches to healing that attempt to detect disharmony before it causes physical damage. Some better-known approaches include Ayurvedic medicine, chiropractic, counseling, herbology, medical intuition, naturopathy, nutritional medicine, psychic healing and traditional Chinese medicine.

An important aspect of self-care involves consulting with your medical doctor for an evaluation of any medical condition that concerns you. This includes acute problems, ongoing problems and nagging concerns or fears. When you are pursuing self-care, it is especially important to rule out a serious medical condition or organic illness that may be underlying your complaints. For example, what you may think is a muscle spasm may in fact be a problem in an underlying organ, for the tissue over an organ will respond to distress in that organ. A red flag that your condition may be more than a muscle spasm is when it does not respond to treatment. If a muscle spasm feels hot to the touch, it can also be an indication of an organic problem beneath that muscle. The deeper a problem is in the body, the less of a sense we often have of *where* the problem is actually located. Even if you choose not to pursue the treatment your medical doctor recommends, his or her diagnosis can be valuable, and ruling out organic illness can alleviate many fears. When in doubt, consult your doctor.

This section does not intend to give you medical advice, and it cannot provide you with the individual attention that you will want from your medical and natural health care providers. However, I can share with you some of the self-care tools I recommend to my patients. As you read this section you will see the same basic self-care practices recommended over and over again. I cannot stress enough how important these basic self-care practices are for strong immunity and good health. Eat well. Regulate your blood sugar. Slow down and listen to your body. Get plenty of sleep. Exercise regularly. Drink plenty of clean water. These are the cornerstones to a strong immune system and a healthy body.

If natural medicine is new for you, be aware that it may require more patience than you are accustomed to with Western drugs. More will be expected of you than swallowing a pill. However, the more you do to take care of yourself, the more empowered you will feel in your life.

If you are using Western pharmaceuticals you may notice that your symptoms clear up while you are on the medication, but they return when you stop. Sometimes repeated courses of medication yield less and less effective results. If you are getting less satisfying results from stronger medications, you may want to consider consulting a natural health care provider to learn about strengthening your immunity and rebalancing your body.

For some people Western medicine's drugs and surgery are the most appropriate forms of treatment for distress, dysfunction and disease. For others, they are the choices of last resort after self-care and natural medical alternatives have failed to bring about the desired results. For some, the two systems are interdependent and complementary aspects of health care and treatment, each providing a point of view, information, support and care that the other lacks. I recommend you consult a medical doctor whenever you are worried about an organic illness or disease.

Aches, Pains and Injuries

Accidents and Injuries Can Have an Emotional Impact

A person often experiences stress around a physical injury, especially when it interferes with his or her life. When you are on crutches or in a cast, it is hard to get around, and you are limited and more dependent on other people. This can be a difficult adjustment both physically and emotionally. In addition to physical pain and inconvenience, being involved in an accident or injury can cause shock and emotional trauma. When you don't release these feelings, they are often stored in your body tissue. Releasing this emotional charge is an important part of healing.

Gentle massage, laying on of hands and subtle energy work are especially effective in allowing shock, trauma and upset to surface and be released. This usually doesn't involve a lot of treatment. One or two sessions with a friend or compassionate healer can release a lot. Let the warmth of the hands on the area where you were injured help bring your attention to that spot. Breathe, relax and feel. Perhaps you will want to cry, or tell this person what happened. Often what is needed is to have someone be there to support you in a way that no one was when the accident or injury occurred. Simply having a compassionate person be with you, listening to and acknowledging your experience and feelings can release the blocked energy. Gentle presence and touch can be powerful healers.

Acute Pain As a Warning

Acute pain often follows an accident or fall. It can be a wake-up call, a message to slow down, pay attention, and watch where you are going. Sometimes we go through clumsy phases, like an adolescent who grows four inches over the summer. We walk into chairs, drop things and are not well-oriented in space.

A friend of mine says we go through psychic growth spurts throughout our lives and that these are just as disorienting as physical growth spurts. One way to know your psyche is expanding is when you are suddenly clumsy and accident-prone. Rather than beating yourself up for being such a klutz, slow down and look around you. You may be at a crossroads; pay attention to what is going on inside of you and around you.

Such times can be especially fruitful, and operating in a habitual business-as-usual mode may result in your missing important signals and opportunities as they present themselves. This is a time to listen deeply to your inner navigator.

All My Aches, Pains and Injuries Are on the Same Side!

Often a person will remark that all of his or her injuries and physical problems are on the same side of the body, and it does not always correspond to their dominant side. I don't know why this is such a common occurrence, however, I do have a recommendation for it. Yoga.

Yoga postures work with balance between the sides of your body, front to back, and side to side. They work to strengthen muscles equally on all sides of your body, and to increase the range of motion in your joints. Each side is challenged in strength and balance during balancing postures; to bend, stretch and open in side bending postures; to stretch and open the front and back of the body in forward and backward bending postures; and to integrate in twisting postures. An additional benefit to all this bending and stretching is a deep internal massage of your inner organs.

There are many different styles of yoga. Some are more meditative and focused on relaxation, while others are more strenuous and aerobic. Find a style that suits your needs. If you have a lot of energy to burn an Ashtanga- or Iyengar-style class may be for you. If your aim is stress reduction and relaxation, a Hatha- or Kripalu-style class might be more appropriate.

You will experience the best results from doing yoga regularly during the week. If you take a class, ask your teacher to recommend two or three postures for you to do each day to bring your left and right sides into balance. If you do these postures daily you will start to feel a difference in a week or two.

Broken Bones

Acupuncture can be helpful in healing breaks as it activates the flow of energy, increases circulation and facilitates healing. If you are in the cast, you can have acupuncture on parts of your body that aren't in the cast, or be needled above and below the cast. Once your cast is off, do physical therapy or neuromuscular training to strengthen the injured limb and reverse any atrophy that has occurred. This prevents the development of compensatory patterns that can lead to further physical problems.

Some broken bones don't heal well, and some people continue to have pain around an old break, particularly when the weather is bad. Acupuncture, moxibustion and energy work are all helpful in such instances.

Self-Care Toolbox for Broken Bones

- Acupuncture.
- Moxibustion. For pain around an old break, particularly when weather is cold and damp, see an acupuncturist for moxa treatment.
- Energy work. Have a friend or a massage practitioner place his or her hands on the broken area. Relax and feel the warmth of the hands on your injury. The flow of this energy can help restore the flow of your energy.
- Physical therapy or neuromuscular training. To restore mobility and strength.

Chronic Pain As a Doorway

Chronic pain can be a doorway into an expanded experience of yourself. When you are in pain this is probably not what you want to hear. You want the pain to go away, and you are not alone in this desire. Look at the aisles of pain-killing and symptom-suppressing drugs at pharmacies and grocery stores. Many people are buying them or they wouldn't be there. But when pills are no longer working for you, for whatever reason, then looking at your pain as a doorway may present some new opportunities.

Going through this doorway into an expanded experience of yourself is rarely a quick process. Chronic symptoms take time to establish themselves, and they usually are not going to up and vanish overnight. I am not saying it's impossible for them to vanish overnight. They may. But often it is a process. Sometimes a long process. And it is actually this process that is important. Sometimes it takes a lot of pain to get your attention. The pain may simply be the initiator, the thing that gets you going in a new direction, looking at life in a different way.

Opening that door may mean spending money on health care providers, body workers or counselors. Your insurance policy may not cover these expenses, particularly if you do not choose drugs, surgery or medical doctors. Opening that door may mean slowing down, making space for your feelings and taking the time to ask some pointed questions like, "What is this pain saying to me? Is my body telling me I've gotten off-track? Do I need to make some changes in my life?"

Listening to and learning from your pain may be like opening Pandora's box. It can take you into unknown areas of yourself. It may take time and attention to listen to your pain. There may be feelings locked up in your pain, things which you'd rather not look at. Your pain may ask you to speak up for yourself, change the way you eat, change your line of work, go back to school or leave an unhealthy relationship. It may also awaken your creative energy, your spirituality. It may deepen your relationships, or rekindle your interest in life. It may lead you to a unique lifestyle, happiness, harmony, joy and peace.

Hot or Cold on an Injury?

People frequently ask whether to use hot or cold on an ache, pain or injury. The first thing I ask is "Which feels better?" In traditional Chinese medicine we are always encouraging energy to flow, so we tend to use warmth. Flowing energy is not so different from flowing water. When water gets too cold it freezes. When energy gets too cold it stops flowing and this slows down the healing process. However, if there is inflammation and swelling, cold will help reduce it.

The rule of thumb for an injury is to ice it for the first twenty-four to forty-eight hours. This decreases inflammation and scar-tissue formation. You can put an injured hand or foot into a bowl of ice and water, or you can also use an ice pack wrapped in a cloth, or even put a bag of frozen peas wrapped in a cloth on your injury. If swelling persists, continue icing until the swelling is reduced. Ice the injured area until it feels too cold. Then stop icing it. Do not ice to the point of numbness. Later, you can alternate heat and ice (use an ice pack wrapped in a cloth, then a hot water bottle wrapped in a cloth), to reduce the inflammation and keep your energy circulating. Doing mobilization exercises (moving the joint) under the guidance of a chiropractor, neuromuscular specialist or physical therapist is an important part of healing. With an older injury, use heat to soften the tissue and decrease scar tissue.

Acupuncture can also be used to decrease inflammation and improve circulation. If you are under the care of a chiropractor, doctor, neuromuscular specialist or physical therapist for an injury, follow their recommendations.

Interrupting a Pain Cycle

If you feel pain whenever you do a specific activity, here is a useful technique to interrupt the pain cycle. It involves timing, and you will need an alarm clock or timer.

Before you begin your pain-inducing activity, look at the clock. Then check the time again when you notice the first signs of discomfort, and stop your activity. Perhaps you can work for eight minutes before you feel some pain. Stretch and breathe to release the tension. Remember, from the traditional Chinese perspective, pain is blocked energy. The point here is to stop working *before* you hurt and to unblock your energy with movement and breath.

Now set the timer at seven minutes and go back to work. When the timer goes off, stop working and do whatever feels good to your body. Scrunch up your shoulders and let them drop, breathe deeply, do side stretches, make little circles with your shoulders or massage yourself. Do whatever it takes to release the tension. If you have been given exercises by a physical therapist or neuromuscular specialist, this is a good time to do them. Then reset the timer and go back to work. Gradually you will be able to work for longer and longer increments without experiencing pain.

Joint Pain and Arthritis

Energy seems to easily congest at joints, causing blockage and pain. To alleviate joint pain and facilitate healing, you want to increase the flow of blood and energy through the joint, and increase the flow of lymph away from the joint. It is also important to increase the production of joint lubrication, called synovial fluid, inside the joint to reduce pain. Synovial fluid is increased by appropriate *pain-free* movement. Movement in your pain-free range, no matter how small that movement is, feeds the joint by bringing nutrients into your bones and cartilage. Weight-bearing movement is preferable, but any movement, as long as it is pain-free, is beneficial. Arthritic pain can often simply be a muscle spasm trying to protect an arthritic joint from too much movement. This is why pain-free movement is so important. Also, have your doctor evaluate any joint pain you are experiencing to rule out organic damage or disease.

We all depend on our bodies in our work, whether we are dancers, athletes, or computer programmers. If you suffer from joint pain, it will be valuable for you to work with someone who can teach you how to use your body in a way that minimizes physical stress on that joint. Practitioners to consult include an Alexander teacher, a Feldenkrais® worker, a neuromuscular specialist or a physical therapist.

From the Western perspective, there are two broad categories of arthritis—osteoarthritis and rheumatoid arthritis. Osteoarthritis is a wearing away of cartilage from use, where rheumatoid arthritis is a symptom of a disorder of your immune system. If you suspect you have arthritis, it can be helpful to see your physician for a diagnosis to determine what kind of arthritis you have.

In traditional Chinese medicine there are a variety of reasons why energy becomes blocked at the joints causing arthritic pain. There may be excessive heat, cold, damp, wind, or congested emotions disturbing your energy flow. Traditional treatment varies according to the causes, but in general it focuses on getting the energy moving. As with most joint pain, arthritis responds well to acupuncture. When I treat someone for arthritis, I often send them home with magnets to put on their pain spots when the pain recurs. This makes the treatment last longer.

Generally speaking, when you are lying on the table having an acupuncture treatment, it is a relaxing experience. Most people love it and look forward to it. However, sometimes with arthritis, acupuncture sessions may be uncomfortable. You may experience sensations similar to your arthritis pain while on the table. After the treatment, there is usually a great reduction in your pain level. While uncomfortable treatments happen only occasionally, I do warn people with arthritis of the possibility, so they won't be surprised.

Bursitis is inflammation of the bursa, a fluid-filled sac that provides cushioning between bones and soft tissue. For example, where a tendon crosses over a joint there will be a bursa to keep the tendon from rubbing on the joint. Tendonitis is inflammation of a tendon, the connective tissue that joins muscles to bones. In both cases increasing blood and energy flow through the affected area, and lymph away from it, will accelerate the healing process. Because acupuncture increases circulation so well, it is often an effective treatment for bursitis and tendonitis.

In traditional Chinese medicine, the knees, ankles and heels are governed by the Kidneys. So, when Kidney energy is weak there will be a tendency toward chronic pain, weakness and vulnerability to injury in these areas. Strengthening Kidney energy will support healing in your knees, ankles and heels.

Self-Care Toolbox for Joint Pain and Arthritis

- Acupuncture.
- Consult with an Alexander teacher, a Feldenkrais® worker, a neuromuscular specialist or a physical therapist. Learn to use your body in ways that prevent strain and injury. Often there are specific exercises you can do to strengthen specific muscles surrounding a joint to restore proper joint mechanics. This can allow the joint to heal.
- Magnet therapy.
- Massage.
- Look into dietary modifications for your specific condition. You may want to experiment by avoiding coffee, citrus and dairy products, as well as foods in the nightshade family such as eggplant, peppers and tomatoes, to see if it makes a difference for you.
- Look into nutritional supplements for your specific condition. Glucosamine sulfate, particularly for osteoarthritis, gives some people great relief from joint pain. Glucosamine sulfate is what is in synovial fluid (your joint lubrication), and initial research seems to indicate that cartilage regeneration is possible.

Low Back Pain

It is always important to consult with your chiropractor, doctor, osteopath or physical therapist to evaluate low back pain. Forms of low back pain include: acute pain, chronic pain, spasmodic pain, nagging pain, weakness, numbness, aching, tingling and a radiating sensation through the buttocks, leg and foot. Low back pain may be caused by a variety of problems, such as: organic disease, a disc problem, an accident, an injury such as a sprain or strain, or a pinched nerve as in sciatica. It can develop after surgery, be related to PMS, stress, weak muscles or overstretched ligaments. In traditional Chinese medicine, one is vulnerable to low back pain when Kidney energy is deficient and the muscles of the low back lack adequate energetic support.

Acute low back pain and muscle spasm can be brought on by a small, insignificant movement. You reach for a piece of paper on the floor, and suddenly you are bent over sideways in excruciating pain and can't move. Such problems usually respond well and quickly to a few acupuncture treatments. Very often people report a period of high stress preceding an acute low back episode of this sort. In traditional Chinese medicine we say they have depleted their reserve tank which is located in the lower back region, so the lower back has no energetic support and is vulnerable to spasm and injury. If you find yourself having recurring episodes of acute low back pain and spasm, you might want to notice if your low back is your Achilles' heel that slows you down whenever your stress level gets too high and you are not taking care of yourself. If this sounds familiar, a preventive approach may save you a lot of future pain. When you find your stress level is high, take particularly good care of yourself. Follow the blood sugar regulating diet until the stress passes. Eliminate or minimize your caffeine and sugar intake. Make sure you get enough sleep. Treat yourself to a massage or have an acupuncture tune-up.

Some low back pain is caused by lack of body tone and weak abdominal muscles. In fact your abdominal muscles are not just on the front of your body, but actually go from your front, wrapping around your sides to attach via connective tissue to your back, forming a muscular cylinder. So what may be contributing to your low back pain could be weakness in this cylinder. It connects your pelvis to your upper body, and is responsible for all sorts of movements including standing, sitting, bending, twisting and turning, stretching and reaching. Any weakness in the cylinder will affect these movements, and over the course of a day, when the muscles aren't strong enough, they can become fatigued, ache and go into spasm. If this is true for you, consult with a neuromuscular specialist or physical therapist for help in establishing a regular exercise program, and to learn appropriate exercises to strengthen your abdominal muscles.

Other low back pain is caused by a lack of pelvic stability; the pelvic bones are moving around more than they should because the ligaments that are meant to hold them in place are overstretched.

Symptoms may include chronic low back pain and weakness, and acute pain, numbness and sensation radiating into the buttocks and leg. It feels different for different people. Some examples include feeling like your bones at the back of your pelvis are crashing together in a specific spot that you can point to with one finger, or it may be a diffuse pain, and when you try to move a certain way you get a sensation that your bones are locked together and won't move right at the back of the pelvis at one or both sacroiliac joints. Some people hear a *chunk* sound when they twist or move in certain ways as the bones of the pelvis literally shift. What you want to do is to stabilize the sacroiliac joint. One way you can tell your pelvis is becoming more stable is you will experience less pain and won't hear or feel moving bones in your lower back.

One good indicator of pelvic instability is when your low

THE BONES OF THE PELVIS

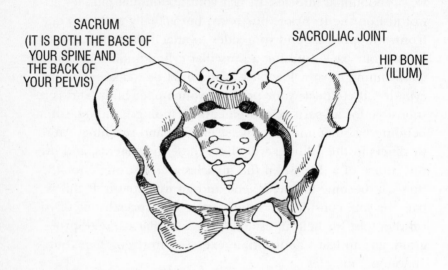

SACRUM
(IT IS BOTH THE BASE OF
YOUR SPINE AND
THE BACK OF
YOUR PELVIS)

SACROILIAC JOINT

HIP BONE
(ILIUM)

back pain is not responding to repeated acupuncture or chiropractic treatments. This may be because your problem is not in your spine and it's not energetic, it is in your sacroiliac joints, so adjusting either your spine or your energy is not going to solve the problem. Massage won't help either. When your ligaments are overstretched, physical stengthening of the muscles in your pelvis is what is needed, for once ligaments are overstretched, they don't become short again. Ligaments don't have contractile fibers the way muscles do. Consult a chiropractor, neuromuscular specialist, physical therapist or osteopath to evaluate the stability of your sacrum. If there is instability, learn exercises for sacral stabilization. Doing your exercises daily is like repairing the foundation of your house. If you experience any increase in your symptoms, contact your neuromuscular specialist or physical therapist for adjustments in your exercises. More pain means you are doing something wrong or they are not the right exercises for you.

Self-Care Toolbox for Low Back Pain

- Have your condition evaluated by your chiropractor, medical doctor, osteopath or physical therapist to rule out organic injury or disease.
- Eat black beans, walnuts and warm foods as recommended in Chapter Seven, Restoring *Qi*, to replenish your Kidney energy.
- Eliminate caffeine and sugar.
- Get enough sleep.
- Reduce stress.
- Increase your awareness of the times when you are vulnerable to a low back spasm, and take care of yourself *before* your back goes out.
- Learn appropriate exercises and stretches for your back and do them daily.
- Bend at your hips, knees and ankles rather than your low back.
- Follow the blood sugar regulating diet. See Chapter Six.
- Acupuncture.
- Chiropractic.
- Neuromuscular training.
- Osteopathy.
- Physical therapy.

Neck Pain

If you stand in front of a full-length mirror, you may notice that your neck is a bit of a bottleneck between your head and the rest of your body. It is easy for unspoken words and unexpressed feelings to get stuck there, blocking energy and causing pain. The first thing you want to do with neck pain is see your doctor for an evaluation to rule out any serious problems. Barring that, you want to unblock the energy that is stuck in your neck, causing you pain.

Sometimes a sudden episode of neck pain occurs when

you are under stress. Someone or something in your life is literally being a pain in the neck. If you are feeling frustrated and angry, and want to blame someone, you may want to review the section in Chapter Ten on using "I" statements. This will remind you to speak from your Heart as opposed to your Liver. Speaking from the Heart takes self-control and awareness. The result is often a cleaner communication with a more satisfying resolution to your conflict. It can also leave you feeling good about yourself, having communicated based on your wants and needs, as opposed to diminishing someone else.

If you have been in a car accident and suffered a whiplash injury it is common to experience spasm, stiffness, pain and limited range of motion in the neck, shoulders and upper back. It is also possible for these problems not to show up immediately after an accident. Later, as the body begins to relax from the trauma, it can start letting go of the muscular armoring. Then the soft tissue damage may become apparent. Acupuncture, chiropractic, neuromuscular training, osteopathy and physical therapy are all effective methods for treating this condition.

Self-Care Toolbox for Neck Pain

- See your chiropractor, doctor, osteopath or physical therapist for an evaluation, diagnosis and treatment.
- Acupuncture.
- If there is a pain-in-the-neck situation in your life, write about it, talk about it, sing it, express it, have a cry. Heighten your awareness of whatever the issue is that is lodged in your neck to dislodge the energy. Verbal expression is especially effective.
- Use the Relaxercise tapes (see Resources at the back of the book) for neck tension.
- Bodywork or massage.
- Use homeopathic arnica—tablets or liquid internally and gel, lotion or oil externally.

Pain Between the Shoulder Blades

It is common to carry tension between the shoulder blades. The upper back can be an emotional area. It is behind the Heart and we tend to armor ourselves here. Expressions such as "being stabbed in the back" or "talking behind her back" reflect this vulnerability.

Ongoing chronic pain, stiffness and tension in the upper back may be indicative of blocked emotional energy. Dealing with the physical pain may go hand in hand with unraveling the emotions beneath it. It is not unusual for people to get angry at their bodies for being in pain, which interferes with their lives. Some people also feel resentment about the time, energy and money they spend dealing with their pain. If you are feeling angry at your body, see if you can recognize that your anger is not helping you feel better, and may even be a part of the problem. Experiment with being kind and gentle with yourself around your feelings, your pain and your resentment. Gentle stretching and yoga can open the front of your body and strengthen your back, which can support an opening of energy in your chest and upper back. Acupuncture can be effective in moving blocked energy and feelings that are lodged between the shoulder blades. Once old feelings are felt and released, there is often a welcomed sense of openness, warmth and aliveness in the chest and upper back.

Self-Care Toolbox for Pain Between Your Shoulder Blades

- Consult your doctor to rule out any serious medical condition.
- Exercise to release tension between the shoulder blades. Stand facing a wall, feet hip-width apart. Bend forward at the hips so your body is at a right angle to the wall. Place the palms of your hands on the wall. Press your feet into the floor and your palms into the wall. Your eyes are

looking at the floor. Push evenly with both hands and breathe into the stretch in your upper back.

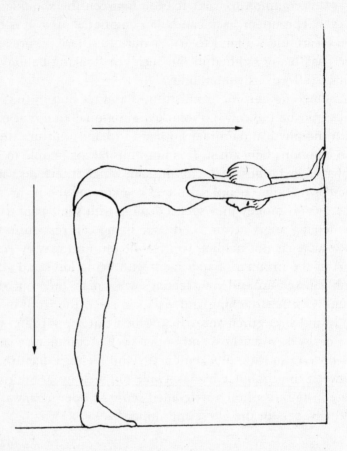

- Massage the points on the center of your palms, known as the *Palace of Weariness.* You may feel an ache up the center of your arm. This is your Pericardium meridian. Close your eyes, breathe into your chest and listen to your Heart.

PALACE OF WEARINESS

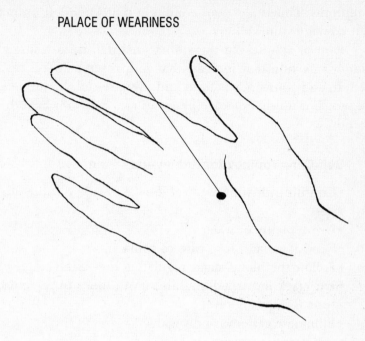

- Acupuncture.
- Breath work such as Holotropic Breath Work, or Rosen work.
- Massage or Traeger work.
- Network chiropractic.
- Physical therapy or neuromuscular training.
- Structural body work such as Heller work or rolfing.

Pain in the Kidney Area

The kidney area is above your waist, in your back, near your lower ribs. Pain in the kidney area can be caused by a bladder infection that is spreading to your kidneys. Other symptoms of a bladder infection may include urgency to urinate, painful urination, blood in your urine and fever. Consult with your medical doctor immediately if you have any of these symptoms. This is a serious condition that when left untreated can damage your kidneys.

Pain or achiness in the kidney area that is not caused by a kidney infection may indicate that your reserve tank is depleted, and your body is tired and overstressed. It can be a red flag to slow down. Self-care practices can help you heal this depletion.

Self-Care Toolbox for Kidney-Area Pain

- Consult with your medical doctor to rule out physical illness.
- Drink plenty of water.
- Slow down and take care of yourself.
- Follow the blood sugar regulating diet. See Chapter Six.
- Eat black beans, walnuts and warm foods to replenish your Kidney energy.
- Eliminate caffeine and sugar.
- Get plenty of sleep.
- Kidney RengenRx, a homeopathic remedy that supports the kidneys energetically.
- Recharge yourself with acupuncture, body work or massage.
- Take a vacation.

Repetitive Motion Syndrome

Repetitive motion syndrome involves pain, numbness and tingling in the forearms, wrists and hands. There is usually tension in the neck, shoulders and upper back as well. This pain frequently develops in response to performing repetitive tasks such as carrying a baby, playing a musical instrument, baking, hairdressing, making jewelry, working at a computer or doing carpentry.

It is important to change your movement cycle, increasing

the variety of your movements, so you are not repeating the problem movement pattern. For example, if you are doing a mailing, don't fold all the letters, then stuff all the envelopes, and then stamp them all. Instead, fold five, stuff five, stamp five. This may seem less efficient, but how efficient is an injury that keeps you out of work for two months? In the long run, it is more efficient to take a bit more time and vary your work pattern.

Emotional stress can be a contributing factor when it manifests as neck, shoulder and upper back tension. Once a repetitive motion injury is resolved, it may recur during periods of stress. Your wrists may become red flags, warning you that it is time to slow down and focus on stress-reduction.

Self-Care Toolbox for Repetitive Motion Syndrome

- Acupuncture. It is extremely effective in treating repetitive motion injuries.
- Learn how to use your body effectively. Consult with an Alexander or Feldenkrais® teacher, a chiropractor, a neuromuscular specialist, an osteopath, or a physical therapist who specializes in repetitive motion injuries.
- You may want to examine if it is *the way* you are doing what you are doing, *or what* you are doing that is the problem.

Shoulder Tension

Shoulder tension can be like an energetic traffic jam in the upper regions of your body. To remedy this you want to redistribute your energy more evenly through your body. This can be accomplished by mentally shifting your thoughts out of your head and into the rest of your body, or by getting up and using your whole body in some form of exercise.

Shoulder tension may also relate to postural or emotional stress. Postural stress may stem from how you use or misuse your body in your work, during long commutes, carrying a baby, talking on the phone with one shoulder up to hold the receiver, sitting at a computer, or holding your head at an angle while you read or write. Many postural stresses are easily remedied by making adjustments in your physical environment such as getting a back-support cushion for your car, a telephone headset, or a back-support chair at your computer. These expenditures can be an excellent investment, as they may prevent more costly physical stress, strain and injury.

Emotional stress may relate to current worries that are generating body tension, or to long-term emotional patterns held unconsciously in your body. This type of stress is not usually resolved as quickly or neatly as postural stress. Which is not to say that postural stress is always so quickly resolved. For posture is so much about habit, and habits are often not easy to change. In fact, habits are often related to our emotional state. In the case of long-term emotional patterns, they have often taken years to develop, and may take years to unravel. Be kind and patient with yourself and these patterns. They have served you well for many years or they wouldn't be there. Thank them for helping you survive physically and emotionally, and let them go with love. As you release old patterns, amidst uncomfortable feelings are often buried essential parts of yourself that you will treasure once you recover them—just as in fairy tales where the dragon guards a cave filled with precious jewels.

Self-Care Toolbox for Shoulder Tension

- Shift out of your head and into your feet. By this I mean take a break and bring your attention into the whole of your body. Stop worrying about whatever thoughts are running through your head and occupying you at that moment. Stand with feet hip-width apart. You may take your shoes off if you like. Relax your shoulders and arms. With the entire sole of each foot on the ground, allow your weight to fall primarily through your heels. Then roll your weight up the outside edges of your feet, across the balls of your feet, down the inside edges and back to your heels. It is as if you were tracing the outline of your foot. You can breathe fully while you do this, first moving in one direction, then reversing to the other. This opens and relaxes the hips, knees and ankles. Soon your whole spine will begin to respond to the movement.

- Shift your energy by shifting your thoughts. Sit in a chair. Close your eyes. Feel your feet on the floor. Notice the difference between your left and right foot. Are your hands resting on your lap or are they on the arms of the chair? Compare the sensations in your left and right arms. Now notice your legs and feet as well. Breathe deeply. Feel your belly puff out when you inhale and pull back toward your spine as you exhale. Notice your thoughts, feelings and sensations. Sense your whole body, and when you are ready, slowly open your eyes and take in your surroundings.
- Exercise.
- Relaxercise. Do the sensory motor learning exercises for shoulder tension.
- Massage the top of each shoulder, between the base of your neck and the tip of your shoulder. Relax, breathe and let your jaw drop as you do this.
- Massage the acupuncture point at the center of each shoulder blade. It is called *Gathering of the Ancestors*. Reach under your arm to massage it on yourself, or ask a friend or body worker to massage it for you. When you find the right spot, it will ache.

GATHERING OF THE ANCESTORS

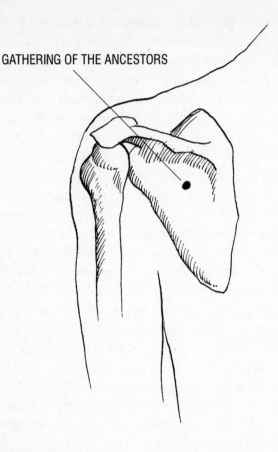

- Buy a telephone headset to free your hands while you talk on the phone.
- When you work at a computer, take regular breaks, get up and move around. Consult an ergonomics specialist to learn proper chair, keyboard and hand positioning to prevent neck and shoulder tension and repetitive motion injuries.
- Acupuncture.
- Chiropractic.
- Physical therapy.
- Consult with postural awareness body workers such as

Alexander teachers, Feldenkrais® teachers, neuromuscular specialists, and rolfers.

Sprains and Strains

Sprains occur when the ligaments around a joint are overstretched, torn or damaged during an injury such as a fall. When an injury affects a muscle or tendon it is called a sprain. When you have a sprain your body will create swelling around it. In this way it makes a cast to stabilize the affected joint. But it also diminishes the flow of blood, lymph and energy through the injury, and this slows down the healing process. Over time most of the swelling will go down on its own, but there will often be some residual blockage which causes weakness and vulnerability. Often after one sprain you will be vulnerable to repeated injuries because the muscles will be weaker from favoring it, and the ligaments have been overstretched, so neither can stabilize the joint as well as before. The muscles will now have to work harder to stabilize the joint, doing the work the ligaments used to do. Strengthening the muscles surrounding an injury is therefore an important part of recovery. It is good preventive care to get treatment to reestablish energy flow through an injured joint.

At the time of an injury, it can be helpful to immediately work on the energy field several inches above the affected area. Of course you will want to ask permission before doing this. If you are injured, you can ask someone to do it for you.

Rub your hands together and run one hand three or four inches above the surface of the skin over the area of the injury, as if you were stroking an invisible energy field. You never touch the body of the injured person or the injury. The more pain the person is in the farther your hand should be from their body. Work from head to toe. This calms and soothes energy that is disturbed by the injury. You will probably feel a static sensation in the hand that is stroking over the area of pain. As you help reorganize the energy, the pain will be reduced and the healing process accelerated.

Self-Care Toolbox for Sprains and Strains

- Elevate the sprain, ice it and rest. You can also wrap an injured joint with an ace bandage to decrease swelling. This not only provides support, but also reminds you to take care of your injury. You will not want to wrap the bandage so tightly that it decreases your circulation. Keep an eye on the color of your toes or fingers. Make sure they remain the same color as the rest of your body. To ice an injury, you can use a bag of frozen peas wrapped in a cloth. Ice it only until it feels too cold. The point of icing is to decrease swelling, not to numb the area so you won't feel it and can keep on using it. If you do over-ice a joint to the point of numbness, wait until normal sensation returns before resuming activity. And don't apply heat to hasten this process, but rather allow room temperature to warm it and bring back normal sensation.
- Rub homeopathic arnica gel, lotion or oil on the sprain.
- Acupuncture. For all kinds of sprains, whether they have happened recently or in years past, leaving residual weakness and vulnerability.
- Chiropractic.
- Energy work.
- Massage.
- Neuromuscular training.
- Osteopathy.
- Physical therapy.

Stiff Neck

Sometimes you wake up and can't turn your neck. People say, "I have a crick in my neck." It is annoying, can cause headaches, and can make the surrounding muscles in your neck, shoulders and upper back go into spasm.

Traditional Chinese medicine says a stiff neck is often caused by wind that enters at the neck, gets stuck and blocks the flow of energy. This can happen when you sit or sleep in a draft, walk outside with your neck exposed on a windy day or sit under an air-conditioning vent. Stiff necks are said to happen more frequently in the spring when there is a lot of wind.

Sometimes a stiff neck is caused by an activity or injury that occurred the day before and only shows up the next morning. Examples of this include impact while playing a sport, talking on the phone with your shoulder up, or reading all day with your head in an awkward position.

Self-Care Toolbox for a Stiff Neck

- Avoid drafts.
- Rub arnica gel, lotion or oil into your neck and shoulders.
- Do the Relaxercise tapes for the neck and shoulders.
- Acupuncture.
- Chiropractic.
- Massage.
- Osteopathy.
- Physical therapy.

Allergies

Allergies can make your life miserable; your eyes itch and swell, your nose runs, you sneeze, can't breathe, can't think. What is going on here?

Your immune system is supposed to recognize and protect you from foreign substances that don't belong in your body and could be harmful to you. If your immune system reacts to harmless substances like dust, mold, pollens, animal dander

and foods as if they were threats to your body, you may experience many uncomfortable allergic symptoms such as: sneezing,
runny or congested nose; itchy, red, puffy, watery eyes; ear congestion; itching in the throat, roof of the mouth and ears;
coughing, wheezing, bronchial congestion and asthma; sluggishness, fatigue and lack of mental clarity; and skin eruptions,
hives and rashes.

In traditional Chinese medicine, allergies have to do with
the Lungs, Large Intestine and Liver. The Lungs include not
only your physical lungs, but also your nose, nasal passages,
skin and protective energy field. The Large Intestine and
Lungs are paired organs in the traditional Chinese system, as
they are intimately connected to each other. For example, the
last point on the large intestine meridian is located on the
outer edge of each nostril and it can be needled during acupuncture to open up a blocked or congested nose. The large
intestine organ is also strongly involved with allergies. A
healthy large intestine supports your immunity. Repeated
courses of antibiotics upset the health of your intestines, and
can contribute to the development of allergies. The Liver is
also intimately connected with allergies. It governs your eyes
which frequently exhibit allergic symptoms, and is responsible
for detoxifying and preparing for elimination of any toxins that
enter your body.

Preventive treatment for allergies involves strengthening
the Lungs and protective energy field, ensuring the health of
your beneficial bacteria colony in the Large Intestine, and supporting the Liver's detoxification pathways both physically and
emotionally.

During allergy season, treat your symptoms with homeopathic remedies. They are remarkably effective in clearing up
symptoms so you can think clearly and function in your life,
without the negative side effects associated with pharmaceutical
allergy medications.

Self-Care Toolbox for Allergies

When your allergy season is approaching:

- Address the imbalances underlying your allergies (usually involving the Lungs, Large Intestine and Liver). It is best to begin this process at least a month before allergy season starts.
- Decongest your liver. See Chapter Nine.
- Take friendly bacteria to restore the bacteria colony in your digestive tract.
- Acupuncture. Schedule a treatment or series of treatments a month or two before your allergy season begins.
- Consult with a naturopath before your allergy season starts for immune strengthening and allergy testing. Great Smokies Diagnostic Laboratory can test for food, spice, inhalant and chemical allergies using a routine blood draw.

When you are experiencing allergies:

- Liver RegenRx. This homeopathic formula is the first thing I recommend to anyone suffering from allergies. It supports liver function and is particularly effective for alleviating eye symptoms.
- Acute Rescue. Bathe your eyes with a few drops mixed with water for especially severe eye symptoms.
- Aller Total, Aller Drain and Airborne. Homeopathic remedies for treatment of multiple allergies to food and pollens.
- Pollinosan. An effective homeopathic remedy that alleviates nasal symptoms associated with allergies. It comes in liquid and tablets. I prefer the tablet form taken under the tongue three times a day. It may take several days to start working, so give it some time before deciding if it works for you. You can take this remedy throughout your allergy season.

- Allergy Relief: Animal Hair/Dander. If you know you will be around animals to which you are allergic, start taking this remedy before you have contact with them, continue taking during contact, and then again after you leave until you are symptom-free.
- Avoid foods and substances that are hard on your liver like alcohol, caffeine, fatty foods and drugs.
- Increase your intake of fresh fruits and vegetables, fresh juices and whole grains.
- Drink plenty of clean water.
- Increase your intake of vitamin C.
- Get plenty of sleep.
- Consult an herbalist for a patent herbal remedy or a custom-made formula to strengthen your immune system and alleviate your symptoms.
- Acupuncture. To strengthen your immune system and alleviate your symptoms.

If you react to molds:

- Minimize your exposure to mold. Don't get under the bathroom sink to clean out the mold. That will stir up mold spores for you to inhale, making your symptoms worse. Instead, ask a family member who is not sensitive to mold to Chlorox the moldy areas of your house, or hire someone to do it. If you have a moldy basement, do not go down there unless you have to, and then wear a face mask. If there is something in your basement that has become moldy and mildewy, do not bring it in your house. If there is something in your house that is moldy or mildewy, get rid of it.

If you are sensitive to household chemicals and perfumes:

- Take an allergic reaction as a clear communication from your body and avoid toxic chemicals whenever possible. Avoid paint, building supplies, and household cleaners.

Use baking soda, vinegar and user-friendly and environmentally-friendly cleaning products.

• If you are sensitive to perfumes, even if you love your perfume, don't wear it. Wash your clothes with lingering scent on them.

Anxiety

Anxiety is a state of uneasiness, agitation and apprehension about future uncertainties. When you are anxious you may anticipate a threatening event or situation, often to a degree that disrupts your normal physical and psychological functioning. There is an overstimulation of your sympathetic nervous system. Symptoms of anxiety include: rapid heart beat, shortness of breath, feelings of panic and panic attacks, inability to sleep, and obsessive thoughts and worries. If you are suffering from prolonged or debilitating anxiety, I suggest consulting with a counselor, psychiatrist or psychologist.

In traditional Chinese medicine, anxiety has to do with deficient Kidney energy and the Heart not being at rest. When the Heart isn't at rest, the Spirit has no home. When Kidney energy is deficient, you are vulnerable to anxiety and fear. In turn, anxiety and fear deplete your Kidney energy. This creates a cycle where fear and anxiety drain the Kidney energy which increases your susceptibility to fear. To ease anxiety, you want to nourish the Heart and Kidneys, and bring them into a state of harmony.

If you are in an ongoing state of anxiety and apprehension, often there is something in your life that is of genuine concern, but you've lost perspective on the subject. Talking about your concerns may defuse the anxiety enough to bring things back into perspective. When your anxieties are running wild and you have no one to talk to, write about them. Get them out on the page so you can see them from a different angle. If it's an ongoing anxiety, write consistently.

Self-Care Toolbox for Anxiety

- Regulate your blood sugar with diet, as low blood sugar can cause feelings of anxiety. See Chapter Six.
- Eliminate stimulants like caffeine and sugar.
- Bring the nervous system back into balance. See Chapter Seven.
- Acupuncture. An excellent way to balance the nervous system.
- Chinese herbs. To nourish the Heart and Kidneys and restore harmony.
- Breathing exercises.
- Yoga.
- Moderate exercise.
- Biofeedback.
- Counseling.
- Meditation.
- Visualization.
- Calms Forte. A homeopathic remedy for relief of occasional nervousness and anxiety.

Asthma

Asthma symptoms involve a constriction of the breathing passages causing shortness of breath, coughing and wheezing. Common triggers for asthma include: cold weather, exercise, exposure to allergens, stress, being premenstrual, catching a cold or flu, or getting a sinus infection. There is an instinctive reaction of fear and panic associated with not being able to get enough air, and anxiety from anticipating not being able to breathe. When treating asthma, it is important to address not only the symptoms of breathing difficulty, but also the fear and anxiety, and any underlying weaknesses that put the body under stress.

If you have asthma, it is important to be under the care of

a medical doctor, and to have your inhalers and medications on hand. It is also reassuring to know that the combination of self-care and acupuncture can be effective in treating asthma. Whether you occasionally use an inhaler, take asthma medication daily, or despite your daily medication are sporadically making trips to the emergency room with uncontrolled asthma attacks, self-care and acupuncture can reduce your reliance on medications and your incidence of asthma attacks.

The foundation of asthma self-care is to reduce susceptibility to allergies, colds and flu by strengthening your overall health and immunity. The less reactive you are, and the fewer colds and flus you get, the fewer asthma attacks you will get, and the less strong medications you will need, particularly prednisone. Prednisone is an essential pharmaceutical support for someone with asthma *and* it is hard on your body. The less you need it, the more you will be funding your strength and resilience. This does not mean you shouldn't take it when you need it. Let me repeat this. *Prednisone is an essential medication for asthma. Take it when you need it.* However, when you take care of yourself and improve your immunity, you will need it less. It will not be an effort not to take it, you simply won't need it as often. Maybe you'll go from needing it eight times a year to twice a year. Then once a year. Then only on rare occasions when you get really sick.

If you are on asthma medication, doing a course of prednisone or using a nebulizer regularly, *do not stop what you are doing.* Complete your course of prednisone as your doctor has prescribed, and continue using your inhalers. Just *add* natural therapies and self-care techniques to your life. Allow your body to become stronger and then see if you require less medication. Allow the high-powered pharmaceutical supports to fall away, gradually and naturally, as your health improves and your need for them diminishes.

Another feature of natural care for asthma is patience. You can expect slow and steady progress with this condition. Think in terms of nine months to a year to reap the benefits of your

self-care and acupuncture work. If you can't afford regular acupuncture, then do self-care on your own. It costs you nothing.
You don't need the acupuncture. It helps. It can speed the
process along. But your actions on a daily basis are most important.

Many people with asthma have a difficult time of year.
Take especially good care of yourself before and during this
time. Once you get through your hard time with little or no
asthma, and without needing prednisone or a trip to the emergency room, you will have leapt a big hurdle, both physically
and emotionally. Your body will not have been subjected to the
usual drain on your reserve tank and so it will be stronger. You
will see that your body can heal and will feel encouraged and
relieved. As the years pass your health will be steadily improving.

If you or a family member have asthma, it is especially important that you avoid putting yourself or that family member
in the position of needlessly being exposed to known allergens,
building supplies, toxic materials and fumes.

Self-Care Toolbox for Asthma

- If you have asthma it is important to be under the care
  of a medical doctor and to have the appropriate inhalers
  and prescription medicines on hand. It is also important
  to go to the emergency room when you are having a severe
  and uncontrolled asthma attack.
- Support your immune system.
- Keep yourself healthy. Prevent colds, flus and sinus infec-
  tions.
- Get plenty of sleep.
- Minimize stress.
- Eat a healthy diet.
- Drink lots of clean water.
- Take vitamin C daily.
- Get regular exercise. Choose an aerobic activity to in-

crease your lung capacity. If cold weather triggers your asthma, join a gym so you can continue exercising indoors during cold weather.

- Find a *Tai Chi* or *Qi Gong* instructor with whom to study.
- Replenish your friendly intestinal bacteria. This will ensure that the first line of defense in your intestines is working for you.
- Avoid anything to which you are allergic, or that is known to aggravate asthma, including: dyes, additives, aspirin and red wine.
- Acupuncture. It is effective in treating asthma. I recommend an extended course of treatment starting out once a week and gradually reducing the frequency of treatment as your need for medications is reduced. Most people find their need for medication, inhalers and emergency room visits reduced significantly when they undertake a course of acupuncture treatment and start practicing self-care.
- See a naturopath for allergy testing. Remove an unnecessary burden from your immune system by temporarily eliminating foods to which you are allergic.
- Massage, shiatsu and various kinds of bodywork can be helpful when you are healing from asthma.
- If emotional stress is a factor, consider doing counseling, biofeedback, or relaxation therapy to address the stress.
- If pollens and dust are causing severe symptoms, consider purchasing an air filter or air conditioner for your house, office or bedroom to give your body a break from these allergens.
- If you are a menstruating woman, take particularly good care of yourself prior to your period, get extra sleep and take extra vitamin C.

When you are under stress and your immune system is vulnerable:

- Get extra sleep.
- Avoid caffeine and sugar.

- Increase your daily dose of Vitamin C.
- Add raw apple cider vinegar, to taste (between ¹⁄₁₆ and ½ of a teaspoonful per glass), to a large glass of water. Drink several glasses like this during the day. This raises your potassium level and oxygenates your blood.
- Keep oscillacoccinium on hand and take at the first sign of a cold or flu. Buy the six-tube pack. Keep some at work, and some at home. If you travel, keep some in your travel kit, purse or briefcase. Remember to take them with you on an airplane, bus or train where you will be exposed to a lot of people breathing the same air in a small space.
- Keep echinacea tincture or tablets in your vitamin cabinet. When you feel a sore throat coming on, immediately start taking echinacea. For echinacea to be effective you must take an adequate dose. Follow the recommendations on your bottle.
- Keep a bottle of zinc tablets in your vitamin cabinet. Suck on them when you feel the beginnings of a sore throat.

Bronchitis

A serious or persistent lung problem should always be evaluated by your doctor, particularly if you have a fever. As the lungs must work against gravity to eliminate congestion, they can be hard to clear. Happily, bronchitis, chronic cough, and weak and aching lungs all respond amazingly well to acupuncture treatment.

If you are suffering from recurring bronchitis ask yourself, "Have I sustained a loss recently? Am I grieving?" I often find that a significant change in immunity follows a major loss. The weight of grief temporarily weakens the Lungs which results in lowered immunity. If you have a recurring lung infection that is not responding to antibiotics, and have suffered a loss, it could be that your immune system is depressed by grief. If so, it may be important to address the grief so your lungs can heal.

Self-Care Toolbox for Bronchitis

- Acupuncture. To support your immune system and clear up the infection. Acupuncture can also help move a persistent grief.
- Rest.
- Take vitamin C.
- Drink plenty of clean water.
- Take echinacea.
- Take grapefruit seed extract tablets, three per day, one with each meal.
- Lung RegenRx. A homeopathic remedy that supports the lungs.
- Metal Element. A homeopathic remedy that not only supports the lungs, but also addresses the emotional states that can accompany lung problems such as loss, grief, melancholy and sadness.
- Grief counseling, when appropriate.

Caffeine Cessation

It is a big transition to shift from running on caffeine and your reserve tank, to using your digestive center. No matter how you approach it, this transition is going to involve work and some short-term discomfort. Everyone is different, however it is reassuring to know that most of the discomfort will pass in three to four days.

You may develop cold symptoms. You probably won't have energy to do much. Inside, your body will be healing. Then you will begin the ongoing process of choosing your digestive center over your reserve tank day by day. You may have periods of feeling exhausted and lousy, as well as periods of feeling pretty good. Give yourself permission to do nothing for as long as you need. The way to change a habit is to live through the times when normally you would rely on it, and instead rely on something else which doesn't damage your health. Each time you do this you are creating new patterns for dealing with stress without injuring yourself. Gradually you get to know and understand your body and its needs.

Before stopping use of caffeine, prepare yourself. Let important people in your life know what you intend to do, and ask for their support. Tell them how they can help. Anticipate stress and have alternative responses. For most people change is a gradual process. It may be three steps forward and one step back. At times you may slip into old habits, especially when you are under stress or during holidays and celebrations. Enjoy these occasional splurges. Instead of judging yourself and feeling guilty, watch how your old habits make you feel. This attitude of the "scientist" does not generate guilt, and it allows you to return more quickly to healthier ways.

Self-Care Toolbox for Caffeine Cessation

- Follow a blood sugar regulating diet. See Chapter Six.
- Find an alternate hot beverage that you like. I recommend Calli tea. It is a green tea, which contains a small amount of caffeine, and Chinese herbs that are good for the liver. Use one tea bag to make at least a quart of tea. Carry it in a thermos and drink it throughout the day.
- Be kind to yourself. You are breaking a habit and the hardest part is at the beginning. Don't give up! Write in a journal, have a massage, write letters, draw pictures, read, watch movies, gaze out the window, call friends. Don't push yourself to be productive. Be gentle and patient with yourself.

Colds and Flus

A cold is one way your body asks you to slow down and rest. If you must push on through a cold, you will be working against the will of your body. If you decide to take an over-the-counter cold remedy to override your body's signals, I recommend you first sit down and have a talk with your body. Tell your body why you are overriding its requests and for how long you must work. Promise yourself some time off to rest. And by all means keep your promise.

It is important not to take your body for granted by treating it like a bottomless reservoir of energy that will always be there for you. In fact, bodies have many needs of their own, quite aside from the agendas in our heads. And because our bodies speak up and rebel, we often resort to a variety of drugs to temporarily silence these unwanted messages.

If you are on your second flu, catch every cold that goes around, have been on any number of antibiotics, are exhausted, or have a persistent cough, you may want to explore natural medicine. Such symptoms often indicate low immunity, weak Lungs, and a deficient protective energy field. There is much you can do with natural medicine to remedy this. Lifestyle, dietary changes and supplementing with vitamins and herbs can turn your health around. And the respiratory system responds enthusiastically to acupuncture.

Self-Care Toolbox for Colds and Flus

- Rest. When you feel a cold or flu coming on, by all means go to bed early and get plenty of sleep. Support your immune system by giving your body the rest it needs.
- Drink plenty of fluids such as water, tea and broth.
- Add raw apple cider vinegar to your water. Drink throughout the day to raise your potassium level and oxygenate your blood.

- Drink gingerroot tea. You can add lemon and/or honey.
- Take vitamin C.
- Take grapefruit seed extract, three tablets per day, one with each meal. It has antibacterial properties.
- Echinacea. It has antiviral properties. Take the full dosage recommended on your bottle throughout your illness. It is best to take it only when you are ill; taken continuously, echinacea loses its effectiveness.
- Garlic. Raw or in capsule or tablet form. If the odor bothers you, there are deodorized garlic supplements available. Garlic has both antibacterial and antiviral properties.
- Gargle with hot salt water for a sore throat.
- Use grapefruit seed extract nasal spray for nasal congestion.
- Acupuncture. To boost your immune system.
- Suck on zinc lozenges for a sore throat to support your immune system.

If you have repeated colds and flus:

- Have weekly acupuncture treatments until you regain your health. When your health is stable, have acupuncture once or twice a month for a while to ensure you are maintaining your health. If your symptoms return, resume weekly treatments.
- See a naturopath for immune system strengthening.
- If you have taken antibiotics, refer to Chapter Eight, the Immune System, and Yeast Overgrowth (candida) in the Self-Care Dictionary.
- Oscillacoccinium. A homeopathic remedy to stimulate your immune system. Can be taken prophylactically in fall and winter to boost your vital force.
- Lung RegenRx. To support the lungs.
- Metal Element. To support the lungs and treat emotional states that are associated with lung-affecting problems such as loss, grief, sadness and melancholy.

- Post Virotox. For exhaustion lingering after a flu.
- Bacteriotox. For lingering bacterial infections.
- When you are well, establish a routine of breathing exercises and aerobic activity to strengthen your lungs and your protective energy field.

If you get a bad flu every year:

- Have acupuncture once a week starting the month *before* your vulnerable time of year to strengthen your immunity. The intention is to break your cycle of respiratory illness, which over the years, especially if it involves taking antibiotics, is progressively weakening your body.
- Take Lung RegenRx starting the month before your vulnerable time of year.
- Take vitamin C daily starting a month before your vulnerable time of year.

Dental Anxiety

For some people, dental work can be stressful. If you are anxious in the dental chair, your anxiety can deplete your adrenal glands and temporarily cause a drop in your immunity. Sometimes chronic conditions flair up following dental work. An example of this is someone with herpes who routinely has an outbreak following dental work. Practicing self-care around dental visits can break this pattern.

Self-Care Toolbox for Dental Anxiety

- Increase your vitamin C intake.
- After your dental visit, recharge your adrenal glands with acupuncture, massage, network chiropractic, or an osteopathic treatment.
- Take Calms Forte before your dental visit. It is a homeopathic remedy for nervousness and anxiety.

- Find a capable *and* kind dentist with an understanding about dental anxiety.
- Let your dentist and dental assistant know how you are feeling. This can decrease anxiety and stress while you are in the dental chair.
- If you have herpes, take nutritional supports like garlic, lauric acid, or HerpEase to boost your immunity before dental visits.

Digestive Disturbances

A healthy diet, good digestion and regular elimination are cornerstones to good health and well-being. Resolving digestive disturbances will not only make you more comfortable, but also remove a major source of stress from your immune system. It is important to have any digestive disturbance evaluated by your medical doctor to rule out physical illness.

The digestive system is highly sensitive to stress and responds well to many forms of natural medicine. Dietary modification, nutritional supplementation and stress reduction can be effective methods of resolving many disturbances of the digestive system. Common problems of the digestive system include: bloating, constipation, diarrhea, flatulence, food allergies, heartburn, hemorrhoids, hiatal hernia, indigestion, irritable bowel syndrome, leaky gut syndrome, peptic and duodenal ulcers (which are of the stomach and small intestine respectively), ulcerative colitis and yeast overgrowth.

The gastrointestinal (GI) tract starts at the mouth and ends at the anus. It is a hollow tube running through your body like the hole in a donut. Things can pass through this tube without ever entering your bloodstream, the rest of your body or activating your immune system. When food is broken down into small enough particles, the nutrients your body needs move through the GI wall and into your bloodstream to be taken to cells throughout your body.

The GI tract is lined with a mucous membrane to protect it from the digestive juices of the stomach and any toxins that might be passing through the digestive system on the way to being eliminated. The integrity of this mucous lining is important for your health. Excess stomach acid, nonbuffered aspirin, and nonsteroidal antiinflammatory drugs like ibuprofin can wear down this mucous membrane, causing irritation and ulceration of the tissue lying beneath. This can increase intestinal permeability, allowing large, partly digested protein particles that should not pass through these walls to do so and get into the bloodstream. This is called "leaky gut syndrome," and it can contribute to the development of food allergies as your immune system reacts to the arrival of "foreign invaders" in your blood.

If you have a flourishing yeast colony in your intestines, the yeast can literally poke holes in your intestinal wall. This also increases intestinal permeability and contributes to leaky gut syndrome. For more information on this, see Yeast Overgrowth (candida) in the Self-Care Dictionary.

Naturopathic training emphasizes optimal digestive function and natural treatment to restore digestive health. If you suffer from digestive disturbance, you may benefit from a Comprehensive Digestive Stool Analysis (CDSA), parasitology screening and permeability profile. Your naturopath will be able to order these tests from such labs as the Great Smokies Diagnostic Laboratory.

Self-Care Toolbox for the Digestive System

- Relax around mealtime.
- Get enough sleep.
- Reduce stress.
- Exercise regularly.
- Deep abdominal breathing.
- Biofeedback.
- Meditation.

- Yoga.
- Activities that shift your nervous system from sympathetic mode to parasympathetic mode will improve your digestive health. See Chapter Seven.
- Take digestive enzymes to facilitate complete digestion. Incomplete digestion can be a contributing factor to the development of food allergies. Do not take if you are suffering from an overly acidic digestive condition such as ulcers.
- Self-check for food allergies. For two weeks follow the blood sugar regulating diet (see Chapter Six) and avoid all wheat, corn, dairy, eggs, nuts, citrus and soy products as well as margarine, shortening, mayonnaise, sugar, white flour and refined and processed food products, salt, alcohol, chocolate and caffeine. Gradually reintroduce each food into your diet and see how you feel. If your symptoms return after eating something then continue to avoid it for a while. Later you can retest it. You may be surprised at how quickly your body-mind communication system becomes reestablished and you are able to know what does and does not work for you. You will also know the consequences of straying from what works best. Sometimes it will be worth it, particularly for special occasions and celebrations.
- Consult a naturopath for allergy testing and treatment. Great Smokies Diagnostic Laboratory can test for food, spice, inhalant and chemical allergies using a routine blood draw.
- Food combining. See Chapter Five.
- Curing Pill. A patent Chinese medicine for upset stomach.
- For constipation, drink more water and increase dietary fiber by eating more whole grains and fresh vegetables. Fiber Formula, TriCleanse and other intestinal bulking products taken with ample water can improve bowel func-

tion. It may take a number of days for your body to adjust to the increase in dietary fiber.
- Acupuncture.
- See a naturopath or nutritionist for dietary recommendations for your condition.

Hair Loss

In traditional Chinese medicine, the Kidneys govern head hair. Loss of head hair indicates that the Kidney energy is weak. In this discussion, I am not talking about hereditary hair loss in men, but rather sudden, unexplained hair loss in women.

Sometimes a woman will suddenly start losing her hair. She may have recently emerged from a major stress or a period of ongoing stress. There may have been a shock, trauma or major loss. Sometimes women start losing their hair after childbirth and breast feeding, when they are depleted from lack of sleep. It also occurs in vegetarians who do not eat enough protein, and women eating poor diets, or following a radical fast or cleanse when their bodies don't have adequate nutrition and strength to sustain a fast or cleanse at that time.

There is often a strong emotional component with hair loss as it is upsetting to lose your hair. This increases stress when what is needed is stress reduction. Treatment involves addressing both the physical and emotional stress. Self-care can channel your anxious energy into constructive activities that replenish Kidney energy and support the growth of your hair.

Self-Care Toolbox for Hair Loss

- Eat a good diet with adequate protein. The blood sugar regulating diet in Chapter Six is a good place to start.
- Get plenty of sleep.
- Reduce stress.

- Eliminate caffeine and sugar from your diet to give your adrenal glands a rest.
- Acupuncture. It calms the nervous system and strengthens Kidney energy.

Headaches

If you suffer from headaches, or suddenly develop headaches, it is important to discuss them with your medical doctor. If you are afraid you have a brain tumor, discuss this fear with your doctor. Silently carrying around such a fear does not contribute to your health.

From a traditional Chinese perspective, there are a number of reasons why people get headaches. For instance, the liver may be taxed by too much caffeine, junk food and alcohol, or by unexpressed emotions, like anger and frustration. Headaches may relate to low blood sugar, poor digestion, constipation, food allergies, or be caused by a sinus infection, a cold or a flu, a hormonal imbalance or lack of sleep. To find out what might be causing your headache, identify where the headache is in your head and look at the circumstances in your life surrounding it.

Self-Care Toolbox for Headaches

Headaches across the forehead often relate to digestive problems. Treatment focuses on improving digestion and elimination.

- Massage Large Intestine 4 and Stomach 36 (see diagram on page 223).
- Acupuncture.
- Eat slowly and chew your food well.
- Try food combining.
- Try digestive enzymes, unless you have an overly acidic stomach condition.

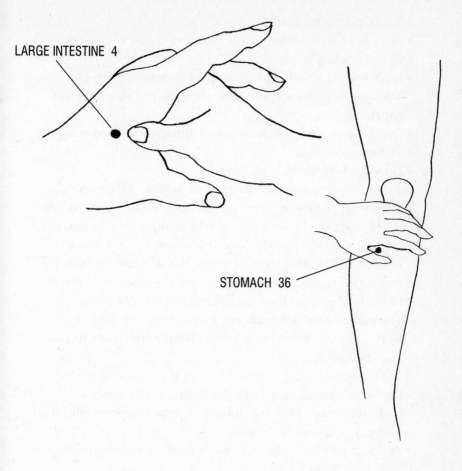

LARGE INTESTINE 4

STOMACH 36

- Eat warm, cooked foods. Avoid raw salads and cold food and drink.
- Consult a naturopath about improving your digestion and elimination.
- Allergy testing. See if you are eating something to which you are allergic.

If you tend to be constipated, encourage daily bowel movements.

- Drink plenty of water.
- Eat whole grains like brown rice and oatmeal. Add bran to your oatmeal.
- Soak several dried organic prunes in water overnight. Squeeze fresh lemon juice on them in the morning and eat them.
- Drink hot water with lemon first thing in the morning.
- Take a daily walk.
- Do yoga with deep breathing.
- Take a fiber supplement either in powder or capsule form with plenty of water. TriCleanse, Fiber Formula and other psyllium husk products add bulk to your stools and act like a scrubbrush in your intestines. Flaxseed swallowed whole with plenty of water has a laxative effect. If you freshly grind flaxseeds and swallow them with plenty of water they also have an antiinflammatory effect on the gut walls. Once flaxseeds are ground they should be stored in the refrigerator in an airtight container to prevent rancidity.
- Take triphala, an Ayurvedic herbal formula that normalizes elimination, enhances digestion and cleanses the large intestine. Take two tablets or one teaspoon with hot water or tea between meals or before bed.
- Support your friendly bacteria colony by supplementing with beneficial bacteria.
- If you experience constipation when you travel, try drinking a cup of Smooth Move tea. Bring these gentle laxative tea bags along when you travel.

Masklike headaches around the eyes often relate to a sinus problem. Treatment involves keeping your sinuses clear and free of infection and treating allergies.

- Acupressure. Sit on a chair with your elbows on a table. Lean your head toward your hands and press your thumbs into the corners of your eyebrows nearest your nose. There is a little notch there, and when you press on it it aches. Relax, breathe deeply, allow your shoulders to drop, and let the weight of your head exert pressure on your thumbs. If you ache along your cheekbones, then press your thumbs along your cheekbones. Find tender spots and lean into them.

- Massage acupressure points located along the top of your head and at the back of your neck at the base of your skull. There are points located outside of the two cords of muscles that run from the back of your head down your neck. They will be sensitive and achy, so work slowly and gently on this area. This works even better if someone else massages it for you. It opens congestion around the eyes, clears vision and helps relieve a sinus headache.
- Acupuncture.
- If you have sinus headaches, check to see if a perfumed or scented body or hair care product is triggering you. Stop using all perfumes and scented products. Notice if it makes a difference in your headaches.
- Sinusitis. A homeopathic product for sinus headaches.
- Read the section on Sinus Infections in the Self-Care Dictionary.

One-sided headaches and headaches at your temples or on the top of your head often relate to the gall bladder and liver. Treatment involves stabilizing blood sugar, regulating hormones, getting enough sleep and calming your emotions. Reduce stress, anger and frustration. Let your energy sink to your feet, and have some quiet time to yourself everyday .

- Regulate your blood sugar with diet. See Chapter Six.
- Massage Gall Bladder 34, Gall Bladder 20, 21 and 41, Triple Burner 5, *Tai Yang*, Liver 3 and Large Intestine 4 (see diagrams on the following pages).

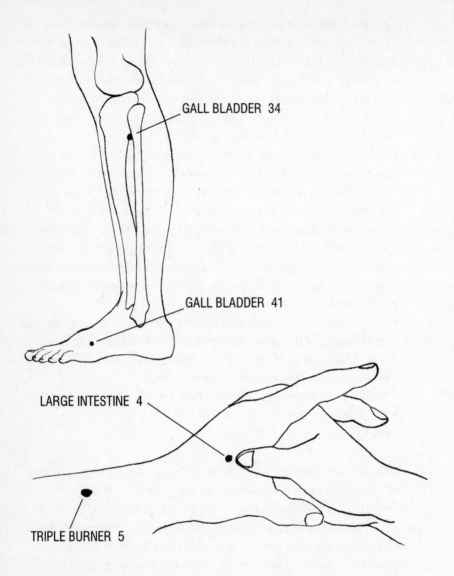

GALL BLADDER 34

GALL BLADDER 41

LARGE INTESTINE 4

TRIPLE BURNER 5

- Acupuncture.
- Consult a Chinese herbalist.
- Go to bed early. Energy runs highest in the gall bladder and liver between 11 P.M. to 3 A.M. When you are asleep at this time you support your gall bladder and liver by allowing them to use that influx of energy for internal healing.

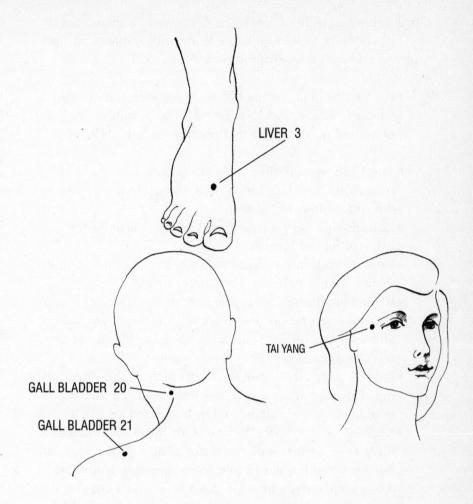

LIVER 3

TAI YANG

GALL BLADDER 20

GALL BLADDER 21

Many people get a second wind during this time and channel that energy into mental activity and "getting things done." I do not recommend this as a regular habit, for just as you have things to do, so does your liver. If you get an energy surge around 11 P.M. and you suffer from headaches, go to bed at 9 P.M. for a few weeks. See if you can be sound asleep by 11 P.M. You don't have to go to bed at 9 P.M. for the rest of your life. Just try it for a week or two and see if it helps your body regain its balance.

Often Liver headaches coincide with a woman's menstrual cycle. Treatment involves regulating hormones, supporting liver function and building strong blood.

- Eat well to build strong blood. Make sure you are eating enough protein and your blood sugar is stable. Try the blood sugar regulating diet recommended in Chapter Six.
- The Chinese herbal remedy, *Dang Kwai Gin*, is a good remedy for building blood. It is a syrup that you take by the spoonful in hot water.
- Consult your acupuncturist or Chinese herbalist for a Chinese herbal formula.
- Do a liver cleanse to improve your liver function and normalize hormone levels. See Chapter Nine.
- If your headache comes premenstrually, try using a natural progesterone product twice daily between ovulation and your period. You can also rub the cream on your neck and temples during a headache.
- Express yourself. Communicate in a clear and direct manner. Do not harbor anger and resentment, and take action when you are depressed or frustrated.
- Establish a calm space in your daily life. Learn meditation. Take a quiet walk daily, not as an aerobic workout, but simply as a quiet respite from your responsibilities. Allow your energy to settle down into your body. Feel your feet on the ground. Relax your shoulders and let your arms swing. Breathe, sigh. Notice your environment. Listen to the birds.

A headache on the top of your head may relate to Liver energy rushing upward because it has lost its roots. Treatment focuses on supporting your roots.

- Drink rice water daily. Simmer a handful of short-grain organic brown rice in a pot of water for an hour or

more. You can add slices of gingerroot for flavor. Drink the broth. Rice water helps nourish your roots much better than plain water.
• Acupuncture.
• Chinese herbs.
• Massage Large Intestine 4 and Liver 3.

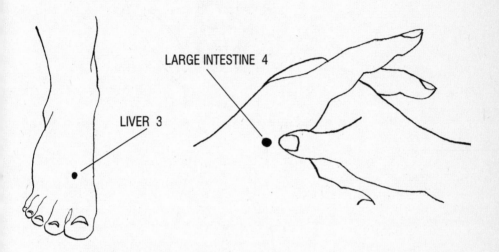

LARGE INTESTINE 4

LIVER 3

Headaches that start at the back of your neck and travel over the top of your head to your eyes are often related to the Bladder meridian. Treatment involves relaxing, releasing upper body tension and shifting your energy into the rest of your body.
• Massage Bladder 2, Gall Bladder 20, 21 and along the outer edges of your feet (see page 231).

THE FOUR GATES (large intestine 4 + liver 3)

HEAVEN

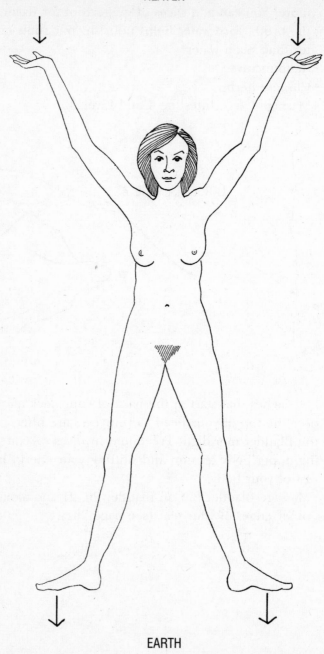

EARTH

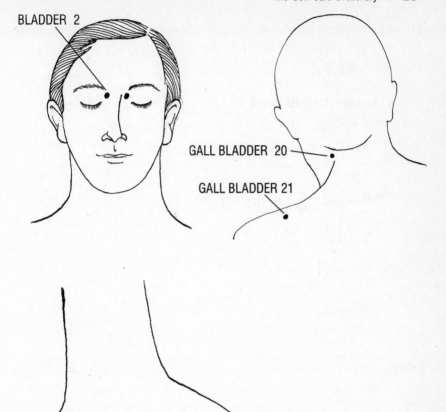

BLADDER 2

GALL BLADDER 20

GALL BLADDER 21

OUTER EDGE OF FOOT

- Acupuncture.
- Sit in a chair with a desk or table in front of you. Rest your elbows on the table and put your thumbs on the inner corners of your eyebrows. Slowly release the weight of your head onto your thumbs and breathe.
- Read the section on neck and shoulder tension in the Self-Care Dictionary and do the exercises recommended there.

Headaches deep inside your head often relate to disturbed Kidney energy. Treatment involves getting adequate rest. Close your eyes. Sleep.

- Massage Gall Bladder 20, *Tai Yang*, Kidney 6, Spleen 6 and Kidney 27.

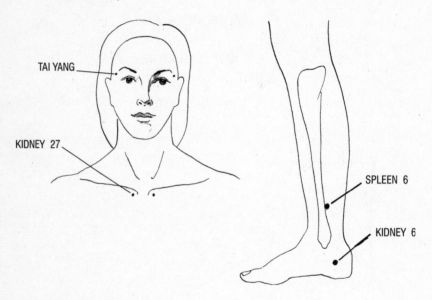

- Acupuncture.
- Stop drinking caffeine.
- Go to bed early. Get enough sleep.
- Read Chapter Seven on Restoring *Qi*.
- Drink rice water.

Insomnia

The Spirit is said to reside in the Heart. If your Heart is disturbed, then your Spirit will have no place to rest, and you will be prone to restlessness, interrupted sleep and insomnia. Some people can't fall asleep. Some people fall asleep and then they wake up and can't go back to sleep. Some people sleep lightly and restlessly and always wake up tired.

A frequent and natural response to occasional insomnia is panic and fear. Panic that it won't end, and fear that you will not be able to function at work or in your life on so little sleep.

It can be helpful to view a short-term insomnia problem as a communication from your body. Sometimes, especially if you normally sleep well, insomnia can be your body's way of saying that it has needs that are not being met during the day. When you can get a minute away from the fear and panic, look at your life and ask yourself what it is in daily life that you want to be doing for which you don't make time. What are you neglecting? There may be a message that wants to come from your inner navigator into your consciousness. Once the message has the opportunity to emerge, and you integrate it into your life, your sleep cycle will often return to normal.

In traditional Chinese medicine it is important to be asleep from 11 P.M. to 3:00 A.M. This is when energy is highest in the Gall Bladder and Liver, and so they have the most energy available to them to do their work.

If you are still up at 11 P.M. when that surge of energy comes through the Gall Bladder and Liver, it will often manifest as overactive mental energy. The Gall Bladder is associated with doubt and indecision, and the Liver with anger, frustration, depression and mental activity. With that sort of energy activated, you may be in for hours of wakefulness. Some people rely on this surge of mental energy to get things done late at night. The problem with this is you are stealing from Peter to feed Paul. The Liver needs that energy to get things done too. Don't waste that internal healing energy on mental activity or worry. To short-circuit this cycle, be asleep before 11 P.M.

Self-Care Toolbox for Occasional Insomnia

- Get up and take some time for yourself. Listen to music. Meditate. Write. Draw. Paint. Daydream. Do what it is you have not made time for in your daily life. See what wants your attention.

- Take Calms Forte, a homeopathic remedy that calms the nervous system.
- Herbal teas or tinctures of passionflower, hops, skullcap and valerian.
- Melatonin.
- Try products such as SleepBlend or MetaRest, or a combination of nutritional, herbal and melatonin sleep aids.
- If noise is disturbing your sleep, or if it is hot out, try sleeping with a small fan on in your bedroom and let the "white noise" lull you to sleep. If it is cold, try using a white-noise machine.

Self-Care Toolbox for Chronic Insomnia

- Eliminate caffeine from your diet. This includes coffee at breakfast, caffeinated sodas and chocolate.
- Start some form of regular exercise; a half-hour walk is fine. Get outside, breathe fresh air and get some sunlight.
- Eat most of your protein in the first half of the day and avoid protein at dinner. This takes a digestive burden off your liver while you are sleeping.
- If noise is disturbing your sleep, try sleeping with a small fan on, a tape of calming sounds, like the ocean, or get a white-noise machine and let soothing sounds lull you to sleep.
- Homeopathic remedies: Calms Forte and Hyland's Homeopathic 23.
- Herbal teas or tinctures of valarian, passionflower, hops and skullcap.
- Melatonin supplements. Some people sleep better when taking melatonin, a hormone that helps regulate cycles of sleepiness and wakefulness. Two melatonin products I

recommend are SleepBlend, a mixture of calcium, magnesium, valerian, passionflower, hops, kava kava, B_6 and half a milligram of melatonin in capsules, and MetaRest, a melatonin product in liquid form with kava kava and B_6. Because you take the liquid in drops, you can fine-tune your dosage to your own needs. Melatonin won't interfere with your dream sleep and you should not be groggy in the morning after taking it. If you are, reduce your dosage.

- If you have been operating with a sleep deficit, it can be helpful to restore your sleep cycle by going to bed at about the same time each night.
- Acupuncture.
- Consult a natural health care provider for help in unraveling your sleep problem.

Self-Care Toolbox for Insomnia from Jet Lag

- Calm's Forte. A homeopathic remedy for insomnia. It will help ease your mind so that you sleep well when you travel. It is fine for children to take it as well.
- Melatonin. Particularly when you have moved through several time zones. Try products like SleepBlend or MetaRest.
- Get several hours of sunlight in the new time zone to help adjust your internal clock.

Jaw Tension

Jaw tension can cause headaches and pain in the face, neck and shoulders, as well as clenching and grinding of your teeth. This can damage your teeth and wear away the protective enamel on the biting surfaces. If you have any of these symptoms it is important to consult your dentist for an evaluation.

Self-Care Toolbox for Jaw Tension

- Consult your dentist for an evaluation.
- Stress-reduction techniques. To release tension that is stored in the jaw.
- Speak up and express yourself. The jaw is where we bite back our words and swallow our feelings.
- Acupuncture. To relax jaw tension.
- Neuromuscular training. For the best results, do your exercises daily.
- Physical therapy. Do your exercises daily.
- Explore emotional issues around self-expression.
- Do sensory motor learning tapes particularly for jaw tension.

Sinus Infections

Your sinuses are located inside your head, next to your nose and above your eyes. When you get an infection in your sinuses your mucus will turn yellow or green. You will probably experience fullness and congestion in your cheeks and around and above your eyes. You may get a masklike headache. If the infection is acute and severe, you may get a fever and experience intense pressure and pain around your eyes, in your cheeks and even in your teeth.

If you suffer from repeated sinus infections and have taken numerous courses of antibiotics and the infections still come back, then natural health care may be a good alternative for you. If you are not in an acute state there are many things you can do to prevent getting to a crisis point. For your natural immunity to be effective, you want ample circulation of blood and lymph through an area of infection. It is like bringing food supplies and new workers into a twenty-four-hour job site. Practice self-care techniques to support your immunity, and keep blood, lymph and energy circulating through your sinuses.

Self-Care Toolbox for Sinus Infections

- Saltwater nasal rinses. The shower is a good place to do this. Make a mixture of salt and warm water and pour it in one nostril and allow it to drain out the other nostril. This clears the sinuses, providing a less welcoming environment for bacteria to grow, and salt kills bacteria.
- Hot showers. Allowing a hot shower to pound down on your congested sinuses can improve circulation and bring temporary relief.
- Hot compresses.
- Recognize your early warning symptoms and take action immediately to nip an infection in the bud.
- Acupuncture. An effective approach for many sinus infections. It stimulates circulation and drainage in blocked and infected sinuses. During and after an acupuncture treatment for a sinus infection you will most likely experience drainage and relief from the congestion and pressure.
- Good diet.
- Plenty of sleep.
- Sinusitis. A homeopathic product for sinus headaches.
- Grapefruit Seed Extract. A natural antibiotic that is helpful for sinus congestion and low-grade infection. Unlike antibiotics, it does not overpower your immune system and leave you out of balance. However, it is neither as strong nor as quick-acting as antibiotics, and you will have to work with it by supporting your immune system. Take in tablet form three times per day, one with each meal. If you are experiencing a strong infection, it may take four or five days for the grapefruit seed extract *and* your immune system to get the infection under control. Your body may need a lot of sleep during this time.
- Grapefruit Seed Extract Nasal Spray. A natural antibiotic nasal spray.
- Acute Rescue Spray. A homeopathic spray that opens,

soothes and heals irritated, inflamed and blocked nasal passages. Take it with you if you have nasal congestion and will be flying. Used before, during and after your flight, it can clear blocked sinuses, making the pressure changes during the flight more comfortable.

- Replenish your friendly bacteria colony following any course of antibiotics.
- Sinuplex. An herbal supplement to keep congested sinuses draining. Take three tablets a day, one with each meal. Very occasionally people have an uncomfortable reaction from taking this tablet. It contains a small amount of Ephedra (*Ma Huang*), a Chinese herb that opens the bronchial tubes and sinuses, is a stimulant and can raise blood pressure. If you have high blood pressure, don't take it. If you feel uncomfortable when you try this product, try something else.
- If you have an acute sinus infection, have a fever or are in pain, see your doctor. If an antibiotic is prescribed, it is important to take the full course as instructed by your doctor.
- If your sinus problems stem from an organic problem such as nasal polyps, you will want to consult a specialist about treatment for them.

Smoking Cessation

Before you quit smoking, start the blood sugar regulating diet recommended in Chapter Six. This will stabilize your energy and moods, and provide you with the inner support you will want to make this change. Also, before you quit smoking it is really important to make a list of alternate behaviors to turn to when you are under stress. When something has pushed you to your edge, it is not a good time to have to come up with alternative coping skills. Help yourself out by planning ahead for stressful situations. Have a list posted prominently so you can turn to it easily. If it says: 1) Go for a walk, 2) Go to the gym, 3) Call Sally, 4) Write in journal, 5) Make a cup of tea, pick one and do it. No thinking needed.

And make a mindmap about the issue of smoking. Mind-mapping is a technique developed by Tony Buzan in the 1970s to develop a more creative and innovative whole-brain approach to thinking. It promotes creativity and can assist you in making new connections in your thinking process. Take a piece of paper and turn it sideways. Write in the middle of the page the word smoking, or cigarettes or quitting, whatever word sums up the situation for you. Then start with that word and write down whatever thoughts occur to you. Keep following the train of your thoughts in words or phrases until you reach an end. Then go back to the word at the center of your page and start another train of thought. A new train of thought can also branch out from any other word on your page. Continue this way until it feels complete. Interesting and helpful information may emerge from this exercise about why you smoke and how you feel about quitting.

Self-Care Toolbox for Smoking Cessation

- Post your alternative behaviors list on your refrigerator. When you want a cigarette, go to that list, pick something and do it. Then, if you still want a cigarette, pick something else from the list and do that.
- Acupuncture. It is especially supportive during the initial withdrawal phase.
- Massage. To nurture yourself and reduce stress.

Vision Problems and Eyestrain

By guest author Jay Kimberley, O.D.

Vision involves a lot more than good eyesight. You can have 20/20 eyesight, which is considered normal, and still have

A MINDMAP FOR SMOKING

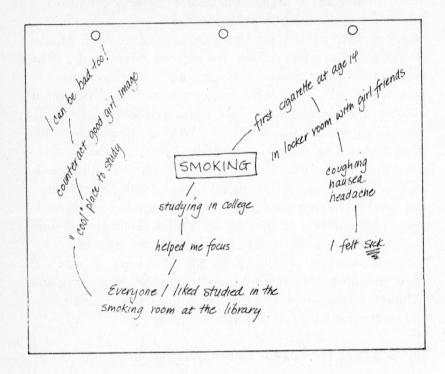

a vision problem. Good vision encompasses, along with 20/20 eyesight, the efficient and comfortable functioning of the eyes' ability to focus, track and converge on what is being looked at, be it a book, computer screen or tennis ball coming at you at 75 mph. Vision also directly influences eye-hand coordination, visual-motor integration, spatial localization and the visual perceptual skills of visual discrimination and visual memory, not to mention concentration and staying visually attended on a task.

If you suspect you are having difficulties in one or more of these areas, I would suggest you have a visual analysis done by a behavioral optometrist. His or her recommendations might include suggestions for better visual hygiene, performance enhancing lenses or vision therapy.

Optometric vision therapy is a program of specific eye exercises designed to remediate and/or enhance specific visual
skills that underlie any visually guided task, be it at work,
school or play.

Resources on vision therapy include:

College of Optometrists in Vision Development
P.O. Box 285
Chula Vista, CA 91912-0285

Optometric Extension Program
2912 South Daimler St.
Santa Ana, CA 92705-5811
(714) 250-8070

*   *   *

When you are reading or sitting at a computer for long
hours, eye motion tends to be limited. This can damage your
vision and be stressful for your body. It is important to allow
your eyes their full range of motion, especially if you stare at a
computer screen all day. A computer can sit there and stare
you down twenty-four hours a day because it is a machine. Neither you nor your eyes are machines. You both need variety
and movement. Even a few minutes of eye exercises can counteract eyestrain, and be relaxing for your entire body.

If you suffer from headaches, eyestrain or double vision,
consult with an eye doctor who does vision therapy. It is possible to improve your vision through working with vision therapy.
Vision therapy can also help children with learning disabilities,
difficulty with concentration and emotional difficulties that are
rooted in visual or perceptual problems and frustrations.

Self-Care Toolbox for Eyestrain

• Let your eyes look out a window and focus on something
  in the distance, then focus on something up close and
  then something in the distance again. Repeat this exercise in shifting focus five or ten times.

- Make circles with your eyes as if you were following the hands of a clock. Rotate your eyes in both directions. Allow your eye muscles to experience their full range of motion.
- Listen to the sensory motor learning tapes for the eyes, and do those exercises.
- There are books on vision therapy with eye exercises to improve vision. Even just a few minutes of eye exercise is very powerful.
- Find a vision therapy course to take.
- If you are having visual or perceptual difficulties, see an eye doctor who offers vision therapy.
- Regular acupuncture can be effective in stabilizing and improving vision.

Weight Gain

Your Body has a natural weight toward which it gravitates. Your natural weight may differ from what you *think* your natural weight should be, and it may vary over the course of your life. What is important is not your size, but rather your actual experience in your body.

There are many factors to considered with weight, and everyone and each situation is different. Lifestyle, habits, emotional state, metabolism, dietary history, what is eaten and when, food allergies and hormonal imbalances may all be involved with weight gain. Some people gain weight because they are overeating, others gain weight while eating very little. First, let's look at weight gain without overeating.

Weight Gain without Overeating

In traditional Chinese medicine we aren't interested in calories or fat. The focus instead is on finding the imbalance in your body and correcting it.

In traditional Chinese medicine everything has a *Yin* and a *Yang* aspect. A harmonious relationship between *Yin* and *Yang* is necessary for balance. The *Yang* aspect has to do with hot, dry energy. The *Yin* aspect has to do with cold, wet energy. In traditional Chinese medicine, a cornerstone to addressing weight gain is balancing the *Yin* and *Yang*, and supporting digestive fire.

Digestive fire fuels digestion, assimilation and the circulation of food and drink. It is associated with *Yang* energy of the Kidneys and Spleen. The Kidney *Yang* is like a pilot light on a stove. Ideally it is always lit and ready to be fired up to support the Spleen *Yang*, which is like the wok on the stove, where digestion and assimilation take place. If the pilot light is burning weakly or not at all, your ability to digest, assimilate and circulate food and fluid will be greatly diminished.

There are two sure ways to weaken digestive fire. One is to weaken the *Yang* aspect of the Kidney energy by expecting too much of your body and not taking care of yourself with ade-

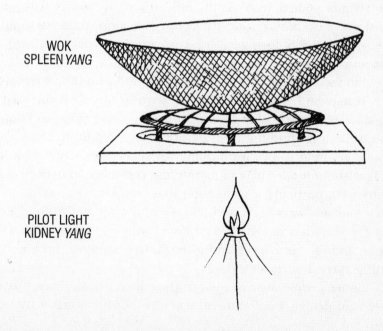

WOK
SPLEEN *YANG*

PILOT LIGHT
KIDNEY *YANG*

quate nourishment, sleep, rest and relaxation. The other is to weaken the *Yang* aspect of the Spleen by eating too much cold, raw food and drink that puts out the digestive fire like a bucket of water on hot coals. Your body's natural temperature is about 98.6 degrees Fahrenheit. When you drink an ice cold diet soda, your Spleen *Yang* has to heat it up to body temperature. This is a waste of digestive fire, particularly if your digestive system is already weak. The remedy for weak digestive fire is not to eat less, or drink more iced tea and diet sodas. Rather it is to eat three meals a day to support your Kidney energy, and to eat and drink only warm food and beverages to support your Spleen energy.

A diet of cold and raw food and drink creates an imbalance between *Yin* and *Yang*. The Spleen becomes damp as a result of too much *Yin*. It loses the ability to circulate body fluids, and they accumulate. In traditional Chinese medicine we call this stagnant *Yin*. The space between your cells becomes filled with stagnant fluid. The more cold, raw food and drink you consume, the weaker your digestive fire becomes and the soggier your Spleen. As the Spleen's ability to circulate fluid decreases, more fluid backs up. The more fluid backs up, the soggier the Spleen gets. It is a vicious cycle. You can eat less and less, but if what you eat is cold and raw, you will continue to feed the imbalance in your body and gain fluid weight.

It may be hard to give yourself permission to eat three hot meals a day. It probably goes against everything that you know about dieting, counting calories and losing weight, not to mention everything you've been doing for years. You may have a lot of fear about food. This can manifest as resistance to trying something new, particularly something that seems so contrary to what you've always been told. However, if what you've been doing for years has not worked or lasted, why not set your resistance aside for one week and give it a try? See how you feel eating three hot meals a day.

Some people are attached to their iced drinks. Even if you love cold drinks, I recommend you give hot beverages a try for a week. Put lemon or lime in hot water to make it more tasty. Drink herbal teas, hot cider or hot milk with almond or vanilla extract for flavor. Find ways to make hot beverages palatable to you.

It takes time to harmonize the *Yin* and *Yang* in your body. Most likely it took years to develop this imbalance, so have patience. Feed yourself three warm meals a day, and focus on how you feel and the quality of your energy. Let yourself relax. Over time, your body shape and size will reflect the inner changes you are making on a daily basis.

Weight Gain with Overeating

Now let's look at weight gain due to overeating. If you are overeating and are overweight or gaining weight, the reason is not a mystery. What is mysterious is why, despite a desire to lose weight, you are compelled to overeat. Often people who overeat have a long history of dieting and deprivation followed by periods of overeating and weight gain. A long history of dieting can turn food and weight into a big problem.

The first thing to do is make some space in your life to take care of yourself. Taking care of yourself means being kind, understanding and compassionate toward yourself. I can't stress how important it is to allow yourself time to relax and nurture yourself. Treat yourself as if you mattered, as if you were very precious. Do not force yourself to do something that you are resistant to doing. Don't force yourself into something before you are ready. When you take care of yourself, in time the natural impulse to make positive changes will just happen. This takes time. It can take years. Be patient. What is of most importance here is that you are learning to take care of yourself.

It is through the days, weeks and years of making space for yourself, treating yourself with kindness, patience and neutrality that allows the small message to emerge. "I want to try something new." It is the space you have created that allows you to hear this message, and the kindness you have learned to generate that will give you the courage to follow it, to try something new. Our minds want to address things head-on, but a more natural way to change a habit is indirectly. You may find yourself backing into it or entering by a side door when you least expect it.

So let's look at some of the imbalances that cause people to overeat. First, take a look at your lifestyle to see if there have been any significant changes recently, such as a change in your metabolism, your stress level or your support system. Have you recently quit smoking? Are you entering menopause? Going through a divorce? Is one of your parents ill? Are you drinking more alcohol? Are you a vegetarian who is eating sugar when your body wants protein?

Then look at the bigger picture. I have noticed a strong connection between overeating, weight gain, depression, lack of exercise and lack of good quality sleep. This combination of factors creates a negative loop that continually feeds upon itself. The best way I know to interrupt this cycle is through regular exercise, improved sleep and keeping blood sugar levels steady.

If you don't get a good night's sleep, you are more likely to overeat because you will be tired and want energy. Caffeine and sugary foods will be tempting, yet both will further deplete your energy, cause erratic blood sugar levels and increase your state of internal imbalance. When you are tired you are less likely to want to exercise. When you don't exercise you are more likely to be depressed. When you are depressed, food is often comforting, and there is a tendency to overeat. Overeating is stressful on your digestive system and this can disturb your sleep. Often when people overeat, they later compensate by skipping meals and not eating for long periods of time. This causes erratic blood sugar levels, and is also hard on your body.

When you feel ready for an experiment, here are two ideas to consider. Choose the one that feels easier to you. Either start a regular exercise routine, or regulate your blood sugar as recommended in Chapter Six. If you feel ready for a big change, try both. Get up, eat a hot breakfast and go for a walk. You may only walk for fifteen minutes. That's fine. Do what you can, what feels good. Keep it enjoyable. Try it for a week and see how you feel.

Exercise will improve your sleep, reduce stress and increase your strength and endurance. It can counter the tendency to overeat, lower your cholesterol and strengthen your bones. Regular exercise is remarkably effective in treating depression, and builds self-esteem and confidence. It improves your metabolism, as the more muscle you have, the more efficient your body is at using the food you eat.

Regulating your blood sugar will stabilize your internal environment, your energy level and mood. It will soothe the panic that accumulates over years of dieting. Over time it will heal your internal depletion and exhaustion.

Notice if you start sleeping better. If your sleep doesn't improve, check out the suggestions under Insomnia in the Self-Care Dictionary. You want to stop accumulating a sleep deficit. The idea is to wake up feeling rested in the morning. Let your body settle into a routine and find comfort and safety there. See how it feels to regularly move your body, and to eat well and enough three times a day.

When you are ready, you may want to look at what and how much you are eating. Let's say you are eating three good meals a day, yet a lot of the food you eat is high in fat. Only when you are ready, try reducing the fat content of each meal. Recognize that one small adjustment creates significant change when practiced over a period of time. Understanding that this may be a long process will help you have patience. As I have said before, this is not about results, this is about taking care of yourself.

Self-Care Toolbox for Dieters

- Eat three meals every day. They don't need to be large meals. Eat at regular intervals, breakfast, lunch and dinner.
- Have hot, cooked foods and hot beverages. Nothing colder than room temperature, including water.
- Cook with *The Ayurvedic Cookbook* by Amadea Morningstar. It is an Indian vegetarian cookbook that uses spices such as ginger, cardamom, coriander, cumin, mustard seed, tumeric, cinnamon, pepper, and garlic to build digestive fire. The food tastes great, is easy to prepare, and the recipes are organized according to the type of energy and organs they heal.
- Acupuncture. To improve digestion, increase circulation of stagnant fluids and restore balance to your body systems.
- Moxibustion (burning Chinese herbs over acupuncture points). To tonify the Spleen and Kidney *Yang* energy. You can receive moxa treatments from your acupuncturist.
- Regular exercise. If you have stagnant fluid, your lymphatic system is probably bogged down with toxic debris. Exercise pumps stagnant fluid out of the lymphatic system and into the bloodstream, so it can be cleared from your body. Take a daily walk to build digestive fire, increase metabolism, improve circulation and stimulate your lymphatic system.
- Bouncing. It is a particularly good form of exercise to circulate stagnant fluid. You can purchase a mini-trampoline bouncer. Bounce every day for half an hour while you listen to music or the news.

Self-Care Toolbox for Overeaters

- Pick a form of exercise you enjoy and do it four or five days a week. Try it for one week. See how you feel. Take a walk, stretch, breathe.
- Experiment with going to bed by 10 P.M. Sleep until you feel rested. If you need naps during the day, take them. There is nothing morally superior about a person who deprives their body of adequate sleep.
- Regulate your blood sugar. See Chapter Six.
- If you have been a long-term vegetarian, your body may need the kind of *Yang* energy that is found only in meat. Try eating some organic chicken soup or organic lamb or beef. If your body responds well to it, include it regularly in your diet. See if your health and energy improve, and if your food cravings change.
- Broil, grill, steam or bake instead of frying and sauteing. Switch to low- or no-fat dairy products. Eat more whole grains and cooked vegetables.

Women's Health

An Introduction

Starting around age thirty-five, progesterone levels start dropping and many women begin to notice changes in their menstrual periods. Periods may become scantier or heavier, come closer together or farther apart. While many of these changes are part of the natural course of a woman's reproductive life, I recommend discussing any changes in your periods with your nurse practitioner or gynecologist at your yearly checkup. If your periods become extreme in any way, it is important to speak with your gynecological health care provider immediately. A simple phone call can ease your mind and provide you with information on how to take care of yourself.

Many women do not get regular gynecological checkups because they have had bad experiences in the past or they are afraid something is wrong and are too scared to face it. If this is your case, I recommend asking the women you know who they see, who they recommend, who is sensitive and skilled. I cannot emphasize enough how important regular checkups are, particularly if you fear something is wrong. Carrying fear around is not constructive for your physical or mental health. Take the time to find a caring and well-trained practitioner. Let them know about your concerns, so they can help you face them. Often things look much worse in the privacy of your mind than they do when brought out into the light of day.

In rural New England where I live, Planned Parenthood of Northern New England provides some of the best women's health care services around. I refer my patients to the women practitioners there, who regularly receive continuing education in women's medicine, and are trained to be sensitive to their patients' emotional as well as physical concerns.

An integral part of a woman's health and well-being is the healthy cycling and balance of the hormones that govern her reproductive life. The four hormones we will discuss here are estrogen, progesterone, follicle stimulating hormone (FSH) and luteinizing hormone (LH).

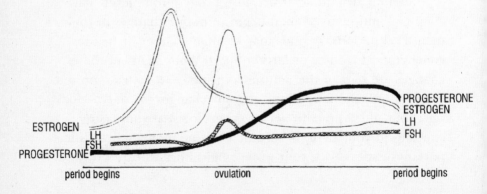

ESTROGEN
LH
FSH
PROGESTERONE

PROGESTERONE
ESTROGEN
LH
FSH

period begins   ovulation   period begins

As you can see in the chart, estrogen levels build up during the first half of your cycle and peak at ovulation. At ovulation a surge of FSH and LH is released from the pituitary gland. Then estrogen levels start declining, and progesterone levels begin to rise. At one point following ovulation, estrogen and progesterone levels are equal. After that estrogen should continue to decrease, and progesterone should continue to rise until a week before your period. Then progesterone levels start dropping off until both hormone levels are low and the uterine lining is shed in a menstrual period.

As a menstruating woman, there are a number of self-care activities that I recommend you incorporate into your lifestyle. They will keep your hormones cycling in a healthy manner, diminish premenstrual discomfort, support healthy breasts and a strong bone structure, and when introduced and integrated into your life during the years when your progesterone levels are gradually dropping, will ensure that you arrive at the door of menopause well prepared physically to go through that next life transition.

Self-Care Toolbox for Menstruating Women

- Get regular weight-bearing exercise.
- Eat a healthy, organic diet.
- Keep your blood sugar well regulated with diet.
- Reduce stress.
- Support liver function.
- Support your adrenal glands.
- Eliminate caffeine, nicotine and other stimulants from your diet.
- Minimize intake of chocolate, sweets and alcohol.
- Many menstruating women who live in cold climates experience better health when eating some organic meat, particularly during colder months.

Bladder Infections

Symptoms of a bladder infection include an urgency to urinate even when there is not much urine there, and burning pain on urination. There is often fatigue associated with a bladder infection as your body fights to control the infection. With an acute bladder infection, your symptoms will be stronger. Urinating will be very painful. You may see blood in your urine, or experience pain in your mid-back. You may run a fever. For an acute bladder infection it is important to see your nurse practitioner or doctor right away. Often you will need to take antibiotics to protect your kidneys, as an acute bladder infection can travel from the bladder up to the kidneys and damage them.

If you are given antibiotics, be sure to take the entire course. That means you take every pill as directed by your doctor, even when you feel better partway through. Some women stop the antibiotic as soon as they feel better. The antibiotic makes them feel lousy and they don't like taking it. This can backfire on you. If you don't take the complete course, some bacteria may live and get stronger, developing a resistance to that antibiotic. Then your infection may recur and you will need a second, stronger antibiotic.

While you are taking antibiotics, watch your sugar intake and follow the blood sugar regulating diet. After you finish the antibiotic, continue watching your blood sugar and take friendly bacteria both orally and vaginally. Many women who take antibiotics for a bladder infection develop a yeast infection afterward. See Yeast Infections in the Self-Care Dictionary for treatment suggestions.

Some women experience chronic bladder symptoms that don't respond to antibiotics. Sometimes this occurs following an acute bladder infection and a course of antibiotics. While an analysis of urine does not show the presence of bacteria, there are still low-grade symptoms of frequent urination and discomfort. In such situations, treatment involves strengthening the immune system and the Kidney energy, working with diet and reducing stress. Herbal remedies and acupuncture can be helpful.

Self-Care Toolbox for Bladder Infections

- If you have blood in your urine, back pain, fever or other acute symptoms, consult your nurse practitioner or doctor immediately.
- Drink cranberry juice. It is preferable to use pure cranberry juice as opposed to the variety that is sweetened. Cranberry makes the walls of the bladder slippery, so the bacteria can't adhere and cause irritation.
- Take cranberry capsules, or combination nutritional products such as CranStat.
- Drink lots of water to flush out the bacteria.
- Drink horsetail tea to clear bacteria out of your kidneys and bladder. Make a big pot of horsetail tea by simmering the herb in water for twenty minutes. Drink half a cup every hour. Do this for a day or two, maximum three days, while drinking lots of water.
- Rest to support your immune system.
- Eliminate sugar, alcohol, caffeine and refined flour products.
- Decrease stress.
- Express your anger. One of my teachers taught that acute bladder infections often follow an episode of unexpressed anger. When I have asked women if they were angry and didn't express it prior to the onset of symptoms, they often have said yes. If you experience repeated acute bladder infections, it may be interesting to look for a connection between the infections, how you were feeling and how you expressed yourself. What makes you angry and how do you communicate it? Do you give yourself permission to be straightforward?
- Some women with chronic bladder infections respond

well to adjusting the pH of their urine. This is discussed in a book called *You Don't Have to Live with Cystitis*, by L. Gillespie.

Breast Care

The incidence of both noncancerous breast lumps and breast cancer is alarming, and many women carry a lot of fear about this. This fear can interfere with doing regular breast exams. However, it is important to get to know how your breasts feel throughout your monthly cycle and if you have lumpy or fibrocystic areas. It is also helpful to learn the difference between soft, movable, tender and cyclically changing fibrocystic lumps, and hard, immobile, more worrisome lumps. It is important to consult with your gynecological health care provider right away if you find a change in one of your breasts.

I recommend doing regular breast massage to get to know your breasts. Wolf Howl Herbal's Breast Balm is great for breast massage. It comes with instructions for six massage strokes that take only a few minutes to do. Doing them in the bath or before you shower is ideal. The balm smells great, and most importantly it switches the focus from "I'm looking for cancer" to "I'm taking care of myself and helping my immune system by increasing the lymphatic circulation in my breasts."

Self-Care Toolbox for Breast Care

- Eat an organic, high fiber diet.
- Increase intake of soy products.
- Increase intake of cruciferous vegetables like broccoli, brussels sprouts, cabbage and onion. This supports the detoxification pathways in your liver.
- Provide nutritional support for your liver.
- Do liver cleansing to improve liver function.
- Maintain a healthy bacteria colony in your intestines.
- Ensure adequate intake of antioxidants like vitamin E and selenium.

- Take nutritional supplements when appropriate, such as FibroBlend and BreastBlend to provide nutritional support for breast tissue.
- Lymphatic drainage massage.
- Self-breast massage.
- Reduce dietary fat, especially animal fat, and dairy products except for yogurt.
- Avoid methylxanthines and caffeine found in coffee, black tea, cola drinks and chocolate.
- Decrease alcohol intake.

Cervical Dysplasia

A diagnosis of cervical dysplasia indicates that there is abnormal cell growth on your cervix. It is generally diagnosed by a PAP smear at your regular gynecological checkup. If your PAP smear results are irregular, ask your health care provider if the irregularity necessitates immediate Western medical treatment, or if the irregularity is mild enough that you can explore alternative approaches to support your immunity and be rechecked in a number of months. Even if you are receiving Western medical treatment, you may want to pursue alternative treatment concurrently to support your immune system.

Factors that can contribute to dysplasia include poor diet, stress and lowered immunity. Therefore, working with dietary improvement, stress reduction, and immune system support can be effective in reversing dysplasia.

Self-Care Toolbox for Cervical Dysplasia

- Regularly see your gynecological health care provider to monitor the health of your cervix.
- Stop smoking cigarettes.
- Eat a fresh, organic, primarily vegetarian diet high in whole grains, vegetables, legumes and fruit.
- Eat only organic dairy and meat products.

- Reduce stress.
- Improve liver function.
- Use introspective techniques such as meditation, visualization, writing, painting or movement to tune in to your reproductive organs. Allow them to guide you in making adjustments to your lifestyle that will raise your immunity and support your sense of well-being.
- Work with the book *Acu-Yoga* by Michael Reed Gach to increase your awareness of and communication with your pelvic area.
- Acupuncture.
- Consult a naturopath.

Endometriosis

Endometriosis is when the tissue that normally lines the uterus grows outside of the uterus. Endometrial tissue can grow in many areas of your body, but most often it is found in the pelvis. This tissue is responsive to hormonal changes. So as your uterine lining grows, swells and bleeds cyclically, so does endometrial tissue in other areas of your body. The swelling can cause pain and the bleeding can cause the buildup of scar tissue.

As endometriosis is responsive to hormonal changes, an imbalance or excess of circulating hormones can exacerbate endometrial symptoms. Dr. John Lee has studied the effects of natural progesterone on endometriosis. He has found that natural progesterone reduces the effects of estrogen, which stimulates the growth of endometrial tissue. Working with natural progesterone, minimizing your exposure to xenoestrogens (foreign chemicals that act like estrogen in your body) and improving your liver's ability to filter old hormones out of your bloodstream can all help reduce endometrial symptoms.

Self-Care Toolbox for Endometriosis

- Eat an organic, high fiber, low fat diet consisting primarily of whole grains, fresh vegetables, legumes, soy products and fresh fruit.
- Eliminate all dairy products.
- Get acupuncture. It increases circulation, improves immunity, reduces stress and supports liver function.
- Improve liver function to improve the hormonal balance in your body.
- Do yoga.
- Work with the book *Acu-Yoga* by Michael Reed Gach to increase your awareness of and communication with your pelvic area.
- Get regular exercise.
- Use natural progesterone cream. Read *What Your Doctor May Not Tell You About Menopause: The Breakthrough Book on Natural Progesterone,* by John Lee, M.D., for more information on this subject.
- Regularly have checkups with your gynecological health care provider.

Fibroids

Uterine fibroids are fibrous nonmalignant growths in the smooth muscle tissue of the uterine wall. They vary in both location and size. Often fibroids cause no symptoms and are diagnosed during a yearly pelvic exam. Your nurse practitioner or gynecologist will feel them when they manually examine your uterus.

Symptoms associated with fibroids depend on their size and where they are located. Fibroids are measured according to how large they make your uterus feel in comparison to a pregnant uterus. For instance, your fibroid may be likened to a twelve-week uterus.

Larger fibroids can cause heavy or irregular bleeding,

cramping, pelvic pain and pressure. This can result in frequent urination, constipation, irritable bowels, and low back pain. In severe cases fibroids can cause hemorrhage. Concern is appropriate if a fibroid is pressing on other organs, causing pain or malfunction, or causing anemia from heavy bleeding.

Generally fibroids are estrogen dependent, and when estrogen levels naturally drop at menopause, fibroids tend to resolve. Knowing this, a woman who doesn't want to lose her uterus may pursue alternative therapies to stabilize her condition until she reaches menopause.

Many fibroids are not problematic and are simply monitored regularly by your health care provider every six to twelve months. If you are experiencing symptoms, you may want to explore natural therapies while continuing to have your medical practitioner monitor you. Acupuncture can be an effective approach for fibroid treatment. If your fibroid is relatively small, acupuncture may be able to shrink it. If the fibroid is large, acupuncture may not be able to shrink it, but can usually resolve uncomfortable symptoms and halt further growth, which may be all that is needed until you reach menopause.

Self-Care Toolbox for Fibroids

- Regularly see your gynecological health care provider for checkups and stay in communication about any major change in your symptoms.
- Eat a warm, primarily vegetarian, organic diet high in whole grains, fresh vegetables, soy products, legumes and fresh fruit.
- Increase dietary fiber.
- Reduce dietary fat and dairy, except for yogurt.
- Eliminate caffeine, chocolate, sugar, white flour products, alcohol and fast foods.
- Support liver function. See Chapter Nine.
- Do yoga.
- Work with the book *Acu-Yoga* by Michael Reed Gach to stimulate circulation in your pelvis.

- Get regular aerobic exercise.
- Use natural progesterone cream or oil. Read *What Your Doctor May Not Tell You About Menopause: The Breakthrough Book on Natural Progesterone*, by John Lee, M.D., for more information on this subject.
- Do castor oil compresses.
- Get acupuncture.
- Consult a naturopath.

Infertility

By guest author Madelyn Jack Goldthwaite, Women's Health Nurse Practitioner

Most people assume that when they decide to have children there won't be any problems in getting pregnant. However, about ten to fifteen percent of couples in the United States who are trying to get pregnant have difficulty conceiving. Many will eventually become pregnant—either on their own or with medical intervention. There have been great advances in fertility evaluations and treatments over the last ten years. But infertility takes a large toll on every aspect of the lives of the people involved. Couples dealing with infertility often describe their lives as roller coasters of hope alternating with disappointment. There is such difficulty in controlling expectations.

Infertility is defined as the inability to conceive after a year of unprotected intercourse. Primary infertility is when a person has never conceived. Secondary infertility is when a person has previously conceived, but has subsequently not been able to become pregnant. In the United States forty percent of fertility problems are male-related, forty percent are female-related and twenty percent are unknown causes or a combination of male and female factors. It is recommended that medical evaluation begin in women under the age of thirty-five if there is no pregnancy after a year without birth control. Fertility declines after the age of thirty-five, so in women over that age, evaluation is recommended when pregnancy does not occur after six months without birth control.

There are many known causes of infertility including con-
genital disorders, hormonal imbalances, environmental factors,
certain medical conditions, infections, medications, sexually
transmitted diseases, and sperm disorders. There are also people that have no known cause for their infertility. Discussion of
the specific causes, evaluation procedures, and treatments of
infertility are beyond the scope of this book. However, there
are some ways to enhance or preserve your fertility and some
known contributing factors to infertility that are helpful to be
aware of.

The timing and frequency of intercourse are basic but key
concepts to getting pregnant. Conception occurs when a
woman ovulates (releases an egg) during her cycle. This occurs
only for a short time, less than twenty-four hours, and about
two weeks before her period. Sperm must be present during
this time for fertilization to take place. Since sperm can only
live about seventy-two hours in the female reproductive tract,
there are only a few days each cycle that are considered a "fertile time." Understanding this and knowing your reproductive
cycle can increase your chances of getting pregnant. There are
resources available that discuss fertility awareness. Your health
care practitioner should also be able to provide you with information on this subject.

Sexually transmitted infections, gonorrhea and chlamydia
in particular, are some of the most preventable causes of infertility. These infections can cause pelvic inflammatory disease in
women which often results in fallopian tube scarring, making
conception difficult. This also increases the risk of tubal pregnancies (pregnancies that implant in the fallopian tubes, causing serious problems if the tube ruptures). Men infected with
gonorrhea or chlamydia are at risk for urethritis and epididy-
mitis—infections that can affect their fertility. It is important, if
you are at risk for sexually transmitted infections, to practice
safe sex and be tested for these infections, even if you do not
have symptoms.

Heavy tobacco, alcohol and recreational drug use may

cause a decrease in the ability to conceive in women and a change in sperm quality in men. If you are trying to conceive, you should limit or abstain from the use of these substances.

Good nutrition is important for fertility. For example, ovulation can be affected if a woman is severely underweight or overweight. Taking folic acid (800 mcg per day) has been found to decrease birth defects. Eating organic foods and minimally processed foods as much as possible decreases your exposure to pesticides and other chemicals which have been implicated in infertility.

There is increasing evidence that exposure to hazardous occupational agents such as lead and toxic chemicals, as well as detrimental environmental agents (contaminated water and air) can affect fertility in men and women. Limiting radiation exposure in the workplace and in medical use is also important.

Certain medications negatively affect fertility. Discuss this possibility with your health care practitioner whenever you are given a medication. Your practitioner may not realize you are trying to conceive.

It is unclear what role stress has on infertility. Dealing with infertility is very stressful on individuals and on couples. It certainly does not help when friends and family give advice such as "take a vacation" or "just relax and you'll get pregnant." Stress affects many aspects of our health, including our immune systems and general sense of well-being. It makes sense that it affects our fertility as well. Looking at your lifestyle and reducing stress whenever possible can help you maintain your balance in an otherwise turbulent time in life.

In addition to stress, the emotional upheaval of infertility can be overwhelming. When seeking medical consultation and treatment, it is important to choose providers who specialize not only in the physical aspects of infertility, but who also address the emotional aspects as well. They should be willing to answer questions, offer information on resources and support, and be honest about what treatments are the most effective and reasonable to pursue. They should also be up-front about when to stop treatments or take a break from interventions. Look for practitioners who use a holistic approach when addressing your needs. Infertility workups and treatments are often expensive and invasive. If you are considering medical evaluation, interview providers to determine who you feel the most comfortable with. In addition, check with your health insurance company about the infertility procedures that may be covered in your plan.

People experiencing infertility often feel very isolated and alone. Support from others dealing with similar issues can be invaluable. Infertility clinics sometimes offer support groups or counseling. RESOLVE is a national infertility organization that provides information about all areas of infertility, including diagnosis, evaluation, treatments, medications, and the need for emotional support. In addition, they have listings of local RESOLVE groups which meet regularly for support and to answer questions.

Finally, complementary therapies such as acupuncture, massage, yoga and naturopathic care may also be helpful in treating infertility and can be used in conjunction with medical interventions to help provide balance.

Resources include:

RESOLVE, Inc.
National Office
310 Broadway
Somerville, MA 02144
(617) 623-0744

References
Hatcher, R.A., Trussel, J., Stewart, F., Stewart, G. K., Kowel, D., Guest, F., Cates, W., Policar, M. S., *Contraceptive Technology: 16th Edition*. (1994) New York: Irvington Publishers, Inc.

* * *

Self-Care Toolbox for Infertility

- Natural progesterone cream. For infertility problems that involve luteal phase defect.
- Decrease stress and make space in your life for a new being. For some people this is all their body needs.
- Eat well.
- Take prenatal vitamins with folic acid.
- Exercise moderately.
- Regulate your blood sugar and take nutritional supplements that support your adrenal glands.
- Cleanse your liver to support balanced hormone levels.
- Consult a naturopath for a nutritional program.
- Acupuncture.
- Chinese herbs.

Mother Roasting

Midwife and acupuncturist Raven Lang writes about a birthing tradition called Mother Roasting which is found in many tribal cultures. While details vary from culture to culture, the intention remains the same. Keep the mother warm and restore her strength and vitality following the birth of a child.

There are three basic components to the tradition of Mother Roasting. The first is rest. The mother rests in bed, caring for her new infant. While she rests, her Kidney energy, which was taxed during the gestation and delivery of her infant, is being restored.

The second component is having health-giving food prepared and served to the mother. Warm foods will rebuild her strength. If she has lost a lot of blood during the birth, her fluid levels can be replenished by warm rice water drinks. These are prepared by slow-cooking a handful of organic brown rice in a big pot of water. Gingerroot may be added for taste.

The third component of Mother Roasting involves keeping the mother warmed by a continuously burning fire. Sometimes it is next to her, sometimes under her bed. Sometimes warm stones are placed in or under the bed. The fire is often tended by the father of the child. He will have gathered and chopped wood throughout the pregnancy, and during the month following the birth he will tend the fire, never letting it burn out. The warmth of the fire rebuilds the mother's warmth.

After a month, when the mother has been properly roasted and her reserve tank has been restored, she will go back to her active role in the family and be able to give of herself without depleting herself.

I often see mothers who are exhausted and depleted. Their reserve tanks were not refilled following pregnancy and birthing. They have been breastfeeding. Maybe they have several children now, and have experienced years of interrupted sleep, nursing and childrearing. When they hear of Mother Roasting they cry, recognizing the depth of their exhaustion. They often feel it is impossible to replenish at this point, that things have gone too far. Yet it is not too late, and better now than never. If you are an unroasted mother, it is time to start roasting yourself. You may not be able to ask your partner to light a fire next to your bed and keep it going for a month while you rest. However, you can ask to have hot dinners cooked for you, or hot tea brought to you in bed.

In *Women Who Run With the Wolves*, Clarissa Pinkola Estes writes about the practice of intentional solitude. "Long ago the word *alone* was treated as two words, *all one.* To be *all one* meant to be wholly one, to be in oneness, either essentially or temporarily. It is the cure for the frazzled state so common to modern women, the one that makes her, as the old saying goes, 'leap onto her horse and ride off in all directions.' Solitude is not an absence of energy or action, as some believe, but is rather a boon of wild provisions transmitted to us from the soul. In ancient times, purposeful solitude was both palliative and preventative. It was used to heal fatigue and to prevent weariness. It was also used as an oracle, as a way of listening to the inner self to solicit advice and guidance otherwise impossible to hear in the din of daily life.''

Self-Care Toolbox for the Unroasted Mother

- Read Chapter Six on blood sugar regulation. Stop running on stimulants like caffeine and sugar. Start feeding your body and allowing your adrenal glands to heal.
- Take hot baths or saunas.
- Go for quiet walks.
- Make time and space for solitude.
- Read by the fire or woodstove.
- Paint.
- Play music.
- Write.
- Nurture yourself.
- Get a massage in a really warm room.
- Have moxibustion at your acupuncturist's.
- Make a bonfire with other mothers and roast yourselves.
- Talk with other tired mothers. Think of ways to roast each other.

Ovarian Cysts

In traditional Chinese terms, cysts are caused by blocked energy causing an accumulation of fluid, fat or whatever is filling the cyst. Ovarian cysts are diagnosed during a manual pelvic exam or with an ultrasound. Symptoms may include changes in the regularity of your periods and pain. Ovarian cysts can come and go quickly, or they may last for several months before resolving. They can recur. Ovarian cysts respond well to acupuncture.

Self-Care Toolbox for Cysts

- Eat a primarily vegetarian diet of fresh, organic, whole, low fat foods.
- Eliminate caffeine, cigarettes, alcohol and sugar.
- Support liver function.
- Improve your bowel movements.
- Get regular exercise.
- Do yoga.
- Work with the book *Acu-Yoga*, by Michael Reed Gach. Do the postures that increase circulation in the pelvis.
- Acupuncture. It increases circulation in the pelvis.
- Consult a naturopath.

Perimenopause

Perimenopause refers to the few years before and after a woman's last menstrual period. The last menstrual period, or menopause, generally occurs between the ages of forty-five and fifty-five.

Menopause is brought on by a variety of hormonal changes in your body. Progesterone levels drop, estrogen levels drop and luteinizing hormone (LH) and follicle stimulating hormone (FSH) levels rise. LH and FSH are produced by your pituitary gland and sent into your bloodstream to tell your ovaries to produce eggs and estrogen. When estrogen is produced it acts as a messenger to the pituitary gland to stop the secretion of LH and FSH. During menopause your FSH levels become high and stay high. This occurs when your ovaries no longer produce estrogen, so there is no messenger telling the pituitary gland to stop producing FSH and LH. This begins a perimenopausal transition that takes place over a number of years.

Some women see their gynecological health care provider for an FSH test. When the result is above a certain point you are technically considered to have entered menopause, whether you are having periods or not.

In Japan, it is reported that women have almost no perimenopausal difficulties *and* a low incidence of breast cancer. When Japanese women come to the United States and eat a traditional American diet, they develop perimenopausal symptoms and breast cancer rates that match those of American women. The traditional Japanese diet, which is particularly high in soy products (a good source of plant estrogens), is thought to be the primary cause for this discrepancy.

There are two varieties of symptoms experienced by many American women during perimenopause. There are the tangible symptoms of which a woman is very much aware. These include: irregular periods, an ongoing feeling of PMS that can last for months, the cessation of periods, disturbed sleep and insomnia, exhaustion, hot flashes and nightsweats, weight gain and not feeling like one's self. Often the emotional symptoms are the most prominent, and they are exacerbated by lack of sleep. These symptoms include: sensitivity, depression, irritability, crying easily and anxiety. Short-term memory loss and poor concentration, as well as changes in vaginal secretions and sex drive can also be associated with menopause.

There are also invisible symptoms of perimenopause, symptoms you may not be aware of, but which nonetheless are of concern. These include osteoporosis and cardiovascular disease.

Osteoporosis

Osteoporosis describes thin, porous bones which are liable to fracture and break. Your bones are continually being torn down, rebuilt and repaired throughout your life. When tearing down happens at a greater rate than rebuilding, then osteoporosis has begun.

Most women over the age of thirty slowly begin to lose bone mass. Women who do not exercise, have a poor diet, smoke cigarettes, and regularly consume caffeine and alcohol often suffer a good deal of bone loss before menopause even begins. The converse is also true; bone mass can be regained by eating a healthy diet, avoiding cigarettes, caffeine and alcohol, and getting regular weight-bearing exercise. So osteoporosis prevention begins during the thirties with regular exercise and a healthy diet.

During perimenopause bone loss accelerates and bones seem to reject calcium. This is a time to be extra attentive to your diet and maintain a steady exercise routine. Several years after the last menstrual period, bone again seems to take in calcium, and you can regain the bone that was lost during perimenopause through appropriate exercise and diet.

Estrogen and progesterone both play a role in the process of maintaining strong bones and so can reduce the incidence of osteoporotic fractures. Estrogen can inhibit the breakdown of bone. Progesterone promotes new bone formation. As progesterone levels naturally begin to drop around age thirty-five, new bone formation also begins to drop. As you approach perimenopause it is common to have periods without ovulating. When you don't ovulate, you don't experience a progesterone surge. Serious bone loss can begin during these years.

Risk factors for osteoporosis include: being small, slender, and of Northern European ancestry; smoking cigarettes (nicotine decreases your estrogen levels and leads to early menopause, bone loss, and increases heart disease); drinking alcohol (it suppresses bone growth); high-stress, a high-protein diet, eating excess sugar, caffeine and salt (all acidify your bloodstream which can cause calcium to be taken from your bones to neutralize the overly acidic blood); drinking colas, carbonated beverages, and eating large amounts of red meat (all are high in phosphorus and contribute toward calcium excretion); not exercising; and having a family history of osteoporosis.

Early signs of osteoporosis noted by Susun Weed in *Menopausal Years* include: persistent backache, severe or sudden periodontal disease, gum infections or loose teeth, sudden insomnia and restlessness, leg and foot cramps at night, and gradual loss of height. She recommends monitoring skeletal loss yearly by measuring the breadth of your arms when stretched out at shoulder height against your height from head to foot.

There is a noninvasive urine analysis test that monitors bone loss and the effectiveness of calcium supplementation available from the Great Smokies Diagnostic Laboratory. Your medical doctor or naturopath can order this test for you. The presence of higher-than-normal amounts of two particular markers indicates a rapid rate of bone loss. A reduction of these markers also indicates a successful treatment program to counteract osteoporosis. Your medical doctor can also monitor your bone density through low-dose X-ray bone density scans.

Cardiovascular Disease

The second invisible symptom that may affect menopausal women is cardiovascular disease. Men traditionally have a significantly higher incidence of cardiovascular problems than women. However, once a woman reaches menopause and her estrogen levels drop, this disparity disappears and women develop heart disease at the same rate as men.

Factors that will support your cardiovascular system include eating a healthy diet, decreasing stress, eliminating caffeine, exercising regularly, and eating soy products regularly. Your doctor can monitor the health of your cardiovascular system with routine blood work to determine your risk factors for heart disease.

About Estrogen

Estrogen stimulates the tissue of the breasts and the uterus. There are three naturally occurring estrogens in your body. E1, estrone, is produced in fat cells from E2. E2, estradiol, is produced in the ovaries. It provides effective relief from hot flashes. E1 and E2 are both strong estrogens and cause cell growth. For this reason, their use is of concern with regard to breast and uterine cancer. E3, estriol, is produced by the ovaries. Its levels are high during pregnancy and it may be protective against breast cancer. E3 is considered a weaker estrogen. It does not cause cell growth as do E1 and E2, and it takes more E3 to control some menopausal symptoms than with E1 or E2. Plant estrogens are also weak estrogens, and seem to block the effects of stronger estrogens in the body.

Natural Hormone Replacement Therapy

There are natural alternatives to artificial hormone replacement therapy. If you choose not to use artificial hormone replacement therapy and you are suffering from perimenopausal symptoms and/or have concern about the invisible symptoms associated with perimenopause, there are natural hormone replacement therapy products available. Natural hormone replacement therapy involves small doses of plant-based estrogens and progesterone. The natural estrogens come from soy products and licorice, the natural progesterone comes from wild yam. They are available in tablets or creams which are generally used daily.

The three estrogens together are called tri-estrogen. There are natural hormone replacement products that include natural tri-estrogen combined with natural progesterone, for women who have no contraindications and have strong perimenopausal symptoms. There is also a product that contains only natural E3 and progesterone. This is the weaker estrogen that is not associated with cancer. I usually recommend this product first for a woman who is having difficulty with menopausal symptoms. These products are low doses of naturally occurring plant-based estrogens and progesterone. They are different from the synthetic, chemically altered hormones that are used in artificial hormone replacement therapy.

You can monitor treatment success of physical and emotional symptoms like hot flashes, insomnia and mood swings through observation. You can monitor your invisible symptoms with the help of your doctor or naturopath as mentioned in the sections on osteoporosis and cardiovascular disease.

Adrenal Glands and Menopause

Your adrenal glands produce hormones, including estrogen and androgens, or male sex hormones, that are related to sex drive. When your ovaries stop producing estrogen, your adrenal glands act as backup and produce some estrogen. This can make your perimenopausal passage easier. If you approach menopause with depleted adrenal glands, you will lack this estrogen buffer. This increases your chances of having a difficult perimenopausal passage. For this reason I recommend that menstruating women maintain and support the healthy functioning of their adrenal glands by practicing self-care activities such as maintaining steady blood sugar, eating well, avoiding stimulants and reducing stress.

Self-Care Toolbox for Perimenopausal Symptoms

- Eat ¾ cup of soy products regularly such as: soy milk, tofu, tempeh or miso.
- In Susun Weed's *Menopausal Years*, she recommends gaining one extra pound a year during perimenopause, up to ten extra pounds. Since fat cells produce estrogen, this additional estrogen can ease your symptoms. She recommends dropping the extra ten pounds after menopause has passed.
- Organic eggs, meat and butter decrease some women's symptoms. Vegetarians suffering from perimenopausal symptoms may want to consider eating some organic eggs, meat and butter.
- Minimize intake of beef and sugar.
- Liver cleansing.
- Use herbal formulas that support liver function and are high in plant estrogens and progesterone, available from herbalists, acupuncturists and naturopaths.
- Support your adrenal glands.
- Use natural progesterone cream to support bone formation.

- Talk with your health care provider about natural hormone replacement products.
- Calms Forte. A homeopathic remedy for insomnia.
- Skullcap, valarian, passionflower and hops in tea, tincture or capsules for insomnia.
- SleepBlend. A combination of melatonin, B_6, magnesium, calcium and herbs for insomnia.
- Meditation.
- Acupuncture.
- Subscribe to *Women's Health Connection* (800-366-6632) for information on women's health care.
- Read Susun Weed's book *Menopausal Years*.
- Contact the Women's International Pharmacy (800-279-5708) for information on natural hormone replacement therapies.
- Avoid carbonated beverages.
- Avoid enriched, refined, canned and processed foods such as: baked goods, boxed breakfast cereals, canned fruit, processed potato products, processed cheese, instant soups and puddings, and luncheon meats.
- Avoid caffeine, alcohol and cigarettes.
- Avoid greens rich in oxalic acid, such as Swiss chard, spinach, beet greens, rhubarb and wood sorrel. (They bind with calcium.)
- Avoid excessive use of fiber pills, bran and nutritional yeast. (They interfere with calcium absorption.)
- Avoid fatty foods.
- Avoid nonorganic meat and dairy products.

Osteoporosis Prevention
- Get some sun daily. You produce vitamin D as the sunlight interacts with the oil on your skin. Vitamin D and calcium work together.
- Moderate weight-bearing exercise, like walking, biking, aerobics or weight-lifting to reduce bone loss. If you love to swim, swim. While it is not weight-bearing exercise, it

does give you the benefits of exercise such as stress reduction and lymphatic circulation, and studies show it
provides some increase in bone mass.

- Yoga. It promotes the absorption of calcium by the bones
  and reduces stress.
- Eat foods high in calcium such as: yogurt, cooked greens,
  broccoli, kale, turnip greens, mustard greens, collards,
  dried figs, raisins, dates, prunes, and corn tortillas which
  are made with lime, a source of calcium.
- Foods high in magnesium such as: leafy greens, legumes,
  buckwheat, tofu, cornmeal and brown rice.
- B vitamins, particularly folic acid and B_6.
- Vitamin C.
- Beta carotene.
- Foods rich in vitamin K such as: green vegetables, pota-
  toes, yogurt, molasses, green tea, kelp, and nettles. Vita-
  min K acts like glue, adhering calcium to your bones.
- Support the friendly bacteria colony in your intestines.
  These beneficial intestinal bacteria produce vitamin K.
- Foods rich in vitamin E, vitamin D, and fish oil such as:
  halibut, sardines, salmon and mackerel.
- Foods rich in boron, such as organic fruits and vegeta-
  bles. They increase your rate of bone formation and support hormone production.
- Manganese, zinc, copper, silicon.
- Drink water with freshly squeezed lemon or raw apple ci-
  der vinegar with or after your meal to facilitate absorption of calcium.
- Whole grains and whole grain products, fresh vegetables,
  legumes, beans and fresh fruit.
- Eat foods such as tahini, tofu, sardines, salmon and yogurt that are high in both calcium and protein.
- Take a comprehensive mineral supplement that is designed for menopausal women.

PMS

Premenstrual syndrome (PMS) occurs one to fourteen days before the onset of your period. Symptoms can range from mild to severe and may manifest both emotionally and physically. Symptoms may increase with age, and become worse with stress, lack of exercise and poor eating habits.

In *Premenstrual Syndrome Self-Help Book,* Dr. Susan Lark addresses the following premenstrual symptoms: anxiety, irritability and mood swings, sugar cravings, bloating, weight gain, breast tenderness, depression, confusion, memory loss, acne, cramps, low back pain, nausea and vomiting. You may experience one or many of these symptoms, and your symptoms may vary at different times in your life.

Often it is the emotional symptoms that most disrupt a woman's life. But before looking at what causes symptoms of PMS and what you can do to address them, let's look at the positive side of the emotional sensitivity associated with PMS.

One wonderful thing about being a menstruating woman is that you get direct feedback from your body every month about what is and isn't working in your life. During the rest of the month you can keep these feelings of dissatisfaction in check. But when PMS arrives and your coping mechanisms go out the window, those things that want your attention can more easily come to the surface. There is a tendency after your period arrives and PMS departs to brush off your emotional outbursts as "just hormones." While hormones can magnify and distort things that are upsetting you, I rarely find the entire situation to be hormonal. Usually the issues about which you are upset premenstrually are unresolved issues that want your attention. These are the bits of gold in the emotional turmoil of PMS.

Clarissa Pinkola Estes writes in *Women Who Run with the Wolves,* ". . . during that time [a woman's menses] a woman lives much closer to self-knowing than usual; the membrane between the unconscious and the conscious minds thins considerably. Feelings, memories, sensations that are normally blocked from consciousness pass over into cognizance without resistance."

While pointing out the value of this premenstrual sensitivity which can give you access to important and perhaps otherwise unavailable information, I am certainly not advocating suffering either emotionally or physically before your period. So let's look at causes and cures of common premenstrual symptoms.

Anxiety, irritability and mood swings are caused by an imbalance in estrogen and progesterone levels. There is too much estrogen circulating in your bloodstream after ovulation. When too much progesterone circulates during this time, there will be a tendency toward depression, confusion and memory loss.

Sugar craving, fatigue and headaches often indicate the need to regulate your blood sugar with diet. Bloating, weight gain and breast tenderness all involve another hormone imbalance causing fluid retention. Acne is due to an increase in male hormones (androgens) during the premenstrual period. Cramps, low back pain, nausea and vomiting relate to an imbalance between Prostaglandin F (which causes the uterus to contract) and Prostaglandin E (which causes the uterus to relax). Many arthritis drugs, like Advil, are prostaglandin inhibitors. They are used successfully to control cramping by inhibiting prostaglandin synthesis. Essential fatty acids like evening primrose oil and borage oil are natural ways to improve a prostaglandin imbalance.

As you can see, many of the problems women encounter during PMS are rooted in an imbalance of hormones. The part of your body most involved in this imbalance is your liver. From the traditional Chinese medical perspective, both physical and emotional toxins can interfere with your liver's ability to function properly. If your liver is congested it will be less able to filter old hormones out of your bloodstream. This buildup of hormones can cause an imbalance. When the liver functions well, you feel even. When your liver is congested you'll feel angry, anxious, jittery, frustrated or depressed.

Cleaning up your diet will support your liver function. It is a strong way to address PMS. If you have been eating erratically or have a nutritionally poor diet, drink coffee, eat doughnuts, candy bars and fast food, you are in for a dietary overhaul. There is much you can learn about what food does for your body, why it is important to feed yourself, and what sort of diet works best for your body. This will take some time. You will be changing your habits, tastes, routines, the way you cook, the foods you buy and perhaps the stores where you shop. Don't expect to do it all and know it all in two weeks. Have patience.

If you already eat a healthy diet, you will want to look at fine-tuning it and perhaps some specific nutritional support for liver detoxification functions.

Self-Care Toolbox for PMS

- Increase your intake of organic whole grains, vegetables, legumes, soy products (tofu, soy milk, tempeh and miso), whole grain pastas, nuts, seeds, and lean meats, chicken and fish.
- Follow the blood sugar regulating diet recommended in Chapter Six. After you have regained your strength and balance, and established communication between your body and your mind, experiment to find a healthy diet that supports you both physically and emotionally.
- Reduce or eliminate: refined sugars, chocolate, alcohol, coffee, tea, soda, aspirin products containing caffeine, fried and fatty foods, dairy, pizza, and foods that are processed and treated with chemicals.
- If you are a vegetarian, and you rely on cheese as your primary source of protein, before eliminating it from your diet, find an alternative protein source that satisfies you.

- Increase magnesium levels. Eat leafy greens, legumes, buckwheat, tofu, cornmeal or brown rice daily.
- Reduce stress.
- Exercise.
- Liver cleansing. See Chapter Nine.
- Pay attention to the issues that arise with PMS. What are the issues in your life that you have been avoiding? What wants your attention?
- Straightforward communication. This keeps your Liver energy flowing smoothly.
- Acupuncture. It decongests the liver so it can filter more effectively both physical and emotional toxins.
- Chinese herbs.
- Consult a naturopath or nutritionist to get a nutritional program, with herbs and nutritional supplements, that is tailored for your body.
- Natural progesterone cream. Used from ovulation until the period arrives, for symptoms relating to an imbalance between your progesterone and estrogen levels. Many women experience a reduction in emotional symptoms as well as physical complaints such as tender breasts, bloating, headaches and cramping when using this cream. Apply to the tender skin of the inner thighs, belly, breasts, neck and inner arms. Your body will absorb it as needed. Because the natural progesterone is absorbed into your fat tissue, you don't want to saturate one area by rubbing it onto the same place everyday. Instead, rotate locations with each application.
- Read Susan Lark's *Premenstrual Syndrome Self-Help Book.*

Post Menopause

Once you are two years beyond your last menstrual period, your bones seem once again to take in calcium. You can rebuild bone mass that you may have lost during perimenopause by working with your diet and continuing to get regular weight-bearing exercise.

Self-Care Toolbox for Post Menopause

- If you gained extra weight during your perimenopausal years, now is the time to slowly take it off.
- If you were eating more eggs, meat and butter to ease your menopausal symptoms, now may be the time to adjust your diet and decrease intake of meat and dairy, except for yogurt.
- Increase the amount of vegetables, legumes, grains and fruit in your diet.
- Eat a mineral-rich diet.
- Read Susun Weed's book *Menopausal Years*.
- Get daily weight-bearing exercise.
- Get some sun daily.

Sexually Transmitted Infections (STI)

By guest author Ellen Starr, Nurse Practitioner specializing in women's health care.

There is a tremendous amount of stigma in our society around sexually transmitted infections. Witness the name change from venereal diseases to sexually transmitted diseases to sexually transmitted infections. These changes have been made over the years in an attempt at clarity. No doubt the changes have also been part of an attempt at softening the visceral reaction we get when we hear "VD." The reality is that these are all infections just like a cold or the chicken pox. It is because they are related to "down there" that we get a wee bit crazy about them. No matter how enlightened we consider ourselves to be, when it comes to our sexuality it is the rare person who handles a diagnosis of genital warts with the same aplomb as a diagnosis of plantar warts. This leaves the medical

provider in a difficult situation. A fine line must be walked between helping someone to keep perspective on their diagnosis
and yet take the idea of protecting themselves from sexually
transmitted infections seriously.

Sexually transmitted infections are a variety of bacterial
and viral infections which happen to be transmitted from one
person to another through sexual contact. While it may only
take one contact, the more sexual contacts a person has, the
greater the risk is of being exposed to such an infection.
Herein lies the negative association. The diagnosis of an STI
implies promiscuity. This is not particularly helpful to the person with an existing STI. It is particularly unhelpful to the person with an STI that they will have for life, such as herpes. On
the other hand, it is important to have a certain amount of respect for these infections, especially those which can kill us,
such that we modify our behavior appropriately to prevent
their transmission to every extent possible.

With the advent of AIDS the push toward condom use in
this country came on strong. It was also assumed early on that
if only we all practiced "safe sex," we would be protected. The
limitations of condom use (slippage, breakage, etc.) quickly led
us to change the concept to "safer sex" and we all began
pushing people to do the best they could do to protect themselves. So what in fact is the best we can do? The best we can
do is to educate ourselves about what infections are out there,
protect ourselves whenever possible, and maintain good health
by supporting our immune systems through healthy lifestyle
choices.

A lot could be written about the numerous infections that
we are faced with. They all have different modes of transmission and different potential for treatment. For example, the
bacterial infections chlamydia and gonorrhea are transmitted
through vaginal, anal and, in the case of gonorrhea, oral intercourse. As a result, condoms offer good protection against
their transmission. Because they are bacterial infections, they
are also easily treated once detected because we have antibiot-

ics which will kill the bacteria. Unfortunately they can be difficult to detect without testing because both men and women can carry either chlamydia or gonorrhea without symptoms.

On the other hand, infections such as herpes (HSV—herpes simplex virus) or genital warts (HPV—human papilloma virus) are viral infections and thereby cannot be killed with antibiotics. While we do have antiviral medications which may affect the course of herpes, it is considered a lifelong infection. Until recently, the virus responsible for genital warts was considered a lifelong infection as well. There is new research, however, which supports the idea that the genital wart virus may actually decrease over time, and may even go away in otherwise healthy people. The tricky thing about these particular infections is that they are transmitted through skin to skin contact and therefore condoms are limited in their ability to afford protection. There are also studies which show that as many as fifty to eighty percent of the general population in this country actually has the genital warts virus and many think that the numbers for herpes are right up there as well. While both of these infections can be very problematic for some people, for others they can be no more than a nuisance. Perhaps most importantly, we don't die from them as we do from AIDS. Our most effective protection against the sexual transmission of HIV (human immunodeficiency virus or the virus which causes AIDS), is still condoms. The threat of HIV still warrants condom use in the case of many if not most sexual contacts.

So where does this leave us? It leaves us needing to keep some perspective on all of these infections. It also leaves us needing to protect ourselves from those infections which really matter and those infections from which we have the power to protect ourselves. The piece that cannot be neglected in all this is the power of maintaining good health.

We are all aware that a strong immune system actually protects us from the assault of various organisms in our environment such as the viruses which cause common colds. A weakened immune system will make us more vulnerable to sexually transmitted infections as well. For example, the transmission of HIV is especially prevalent in needle drug users who share needles, primarily due to direct blood contact. However, it is clear that vulnerability is increased due to having an immune system weakened by chronic drug use.

What is probably less known is the fact that a strong immune system can help minimize the effects of some sexually transmitted infections on our lives. A good strong immune system can help keep outbreaks of infections such as herpes or genital warts at bay. Many are aware of the fact that stress can bring on a cold sore. It is also true that we can rid ourselves of clinically evident genital warts by altering our diet, exercise and sleep patterns, and quitting smoking. The virus may still be present in the body, but a strong immune system can make the actual warts go away and keep them away. Even the most conservative medical providers have acknowledged this connection.

There is powerful evidence that healthy lifestyle choices can impact on every element of our health—including our reproductive health. For example, most people have made the connection in their heads between quitting smoking and decreasing their risk of developing lung cancer. Very few people, on the other hand, are aware that we are beginning to recognize a connection between cigarette smoking and the risk of developing cervical cancer as well. Therefore, it is not exclusively decisions around sexual behavior which will keep our reproductive health in order. Daily decisions about things such as diet and exercise, for example, have a far-reaching effect on our well-being. This includes our risk of contracting sexually transmitted infections as well as our ability to live with them.

All of this adds merit to the concept that respecting and caring for our bodies is the essence of body wellness. We must educate ourselves, make responsible decisions when it comes to our sexual practices, and do our best to stay in good health.

Self-Care Toolbox for Genital Warts
(Adopted from the conservative management protocol of Planned Parenthood of Northern New England)

While following this entire protocol may not be for everyone, following any piece of this protocol can be helpful.

1. Use acid-based soap (e.g., Dove) to wash twice daily from navel to rectum.
2. Wear all cotton underwear, and no underwear at bedtime.
3. Take multivitamins, including 1 mg folic acid daily.
4. Use nonperfumed sanitary pads instead of tampons.
5. Eat a proper diet and develop a rest/exercise routine to manage stress.
6. Do not smoke.
7. Douche with betadine or vinegar solution. Do not douche if you are pregnant or if you have your period. The following are instructions for douching:

   a. Use a gravity-flow (hanging type) douche bag.

   b. Alternate a povidone iodine douche with a white (clear) vinegar douche.

   *Generic povidone iodine costs about ⅓ what the brand-name product (Betadine) costs.

   *If you have any allergic reaction to the povidone iodine (such as itching, burning or discharge), stop medication immediately and call your practitioner.

   *If you are trying to get pregnant, you may choose to avoid douching during your fertile time.

   c. Use 2 tablespoons of solution in 1 pint warm water.

   d. Frequency:

   *2 times per day for 2 weeks

   *1 time per day for 2 weeks

   *1 time every other day until warts are gone

Although this may seem time-consuming, it is something we've found you can do to manage your HPV infection.

* * *

Self-Care Toolbox for Herpes

- Maintain strong immunity. See Chapter Nine.
- Acupuncture. It can reduce uncomfortable symptoms dramatically and support your immune system to eliminate outbreaks.
- Lauric acid. It is a substance naturally found in mother's milk. It interferes with viral replication, thereby reducing the viral load in your body. This reduces the burden on your immune system, and the incidence of outbreaks. I recommend the lauric acid product Monolaurin. You can take one to two capsules per day preventively, increasing your dosage up to six capsules, per day if you start exhibiting symptoms. Capsules are to be taken all at once first thing in the morning with water. Wait one hour before eating.
- Take garlic capsules or tablets at the first sign of symptoms. Continue taking four to eight capsules per day until your symptoms are gone.
- Take HerpBlend. A combination nutritional and herbal formula for herpes.

Yeast Infections (Vaginal)

A vaginal yeast infection indicates an overgrowth of yeast. This often occurs following a course of antibiotics when the healthy bacteria in the vagina are killed. The vaginal yeast population, which is not affected by the antibiotic, then thrives. If you have recurring vaginal yeast infections, you probably have a systemic yeast problem stemming from an overgrowth of yeast in your intestines. When your systemic yeast population is too high it leaves you vulnerable to frequent outbreaks of yeast overgrowth whenever your blood sugar levels get too high as in periods of high stress, and when eating a high sugar diet. Many women with a systemic yeast imbalance experience low-grade vaginal yeast symptoms—such as discharge and itchiness—each month premenstrually.

While prescription and over-the-counter drugs for yeast infections, like Monostat, do kill yeast, they do not reintroduce healthy bacteria. So only half your problem has been addressed. This is one reason why women get recurring yeast infections. They have never regained their healthy vaginal flora. Vaginal suppositories of friendly bacteria are an important part of treatment for a yeast infection to prevent recurrence.

Self-Care Toolbox for Chronic Yeast Infections

- Eat a bowl of yogurt with live bacterial cultures in it daily.
- Follow any course of antibiotics with a course of healthy bacteria both orally and vaginally to prevent yeast overgrowth in the intestines and vagina.
- For recurring yeast infections, see Yeast Overgrowth (Candida) in the Self-Care Dictionary and follow dietary suggestions given there.
- Douche with vinegar to clear out the yeast.
- Douche with a yogurt containing live bacterial cultures to replenish your vaginal bacteria colony.
- Use Fem-Dophilus, a bacterial suppository, or other friendly bacteria capsules to replenish your vaginal bacteria colony.
- If you are prone to yeast infections around your period, just prior to that time, reduce your sugar intake and use Fem-Dophilus to support your bacteria colony.

Yeast Overgrowth (Candida)

Candida Albicans is a yeast that occurs naturally in the digestive tract along with intestinal bacteria. While normal intestinal bacteria contribute to your health and well-being, yeast does not. However, it usually doesn't cause problems unless the healthy balance between the bacteria and the yeast is disturbed, permitting yeast overgrowth.

Symptoms of yeast overgrowth include: allergies; asthma;

acne; fatigue, spaciness and poor memory; food intolerances, cravings for sugar, bread and alcohol, and low blood sugar; headaches; chronic skin rashes, itching and athlete's foot; frequent colds and post-nasal drip; ear pain; gas, bloating, indigestion, constipation or diarrhea; PMS, bladder and yeast infections; sensitivity to environmental pollutants, chemicals, cigarette smoke and perfume; mood swings, depression and anxiety.

The most common cause of yeast overgrowth is an extensive history of antibiotic use. Antibiotics kill bacteria, both the health-giving bacteria and the ones that make you sick. After taking antibiotics, if you immediately replenish your beneficial bacteria colony with a strong bacteria supplement you can prevent many health problems stemming from yeast overgrowth in your future.

However, many people with yeast overgrowth took antibiotics in their teens for acne, oftentimes for several years. They never replaced their bacteria colonies, and now it is years later. The effect of such long-term antibiotic use is often not apparent for many years. When it does become evident, say ten years down the road, yeast overgrowth has become firmly established and the cumulative effect is a moderately to severely handicapped immune system that does not support good health and well-being. At this point, it may often take years to rebuild health and immunity.

Other people develop a milder form of yeast overgrowth over the years from occasional courses of antibiotics, flagyl and steroids like prednisone. Birth control pills, high stress and erratic blood sugar levels will all contribute to an existing yeast overgrowth problem. Diets that are high in sugar, refined carbohydrates, alcohol and junk food, and low in unrefined grains, legumes, and vegetables will also aggravate an existing yeast problem.

Yeast live on sugar from sweets, alcohol, bread, pastries and cookies. When the bloodstream is flooded with sugar, the yeast have their next meal and thrive. As waste products, they excrete alcohol and carbon dioxide gas. Alcohol is toxic to the body, so your liver must detoxify and prepare it for elimination. Carbon dioxide gas causes bloating and flatulence. A strong yeast colony can grow little appendages called mycelia, that can penetrate your intestinal wall. This can lead to "leaky gut syndrome," where your intestinal wall can no longer keep partially digested proteins from leaking into your bloodstream. These proteins, once in your blood, can trigger food allergies as your immune system responds to them as "foreign invaders."

If you suspect you have a leaky gut, there is a test your doctor or naturopath can order evaluating intestinal permeability from the Great Smokies Diagnostic Laboratory, and there are nutritional supplements that you can take to rebuild your intestinal wall and heal leaky gut syndrome.

To reverse this assault on your immune system, you can support your beneficial intestinal bacteria, bifidus and acidophilus. They generate B-vitamins and vitamin K, increase the bulk of your stools so that bowel movements are improved, and inhibit the growth of unhealthy bacteria and yeast in your intestines. They are an important part of your intestinal immune system.

Many people eat yogurt with live acidophilus culture after they have been on antibiotics. This is beneficial—but not enough; to repopulate the bacteria colony of the intestines takes more than this. For bacteria to arrive alive in the intestines, they must pass through an acid stomach and an alkaline small intestine—it's not an easy trip. A strong bacterial supplement taken repeatedly is important to repopulate your intestines with healthy bacteria.

When you start treating yeast overgrowth, you may experience a temporary increase in symptoms. This is called a "die off reaction" and it refers to the increased toxic load that is placed on your body as yeast die and must be eliminated. If you experience increased discomfort when addressing a yeast problem, it may be reassuring and helpful to consult with a health care practitioner who has experience treating yeast over-growth. Although people usually experience improvement within the first month of treatment, the process of rebuilding health takes time. A yeast problem generally develops over many years, and recovery is a gradual process requiring a good deal of patience and work.

Taking birth control pills can exacerbate a yeast over-growth problem as the hormones elevate your blood sugar level which feeds the yeast. If you have yeast-related symptoms such as chronic vaginal yeast infections, and you are on birth control pills, you may want to consider another form of contra-ception. If birth control pills are a form of birth control that works well for you, then you may want to focus on supporting your immune system by regulating your blood sugar with diet to eliminate high blood sugar jags that feed yeast, and supple-menting your diet with yogurt and a strong bacteria supple-ment.

If you have a yeast overgrowth problem and want to get pregnant, it is helpful to address the overgrowth problem *before* getting pregnant. Yeast symptoms often increase during preg-nancy as elevated blood sugar levels throughout the pregnancy feed the yeast.

Self-Care Toolbox for Yeast Overgrowth

- Follow every course of antibiotics with a course of healthy bacteria. Watch your intake of sugar and refined flour products while on antibiotics and in the weeks following antibiotic use.
- Women may want to use vaginal bacteria suppositories to replace the healthy bacteria in their vaginas and prevent yeast infections which commonly follow antibiotic use.
- It is important to note that no matter what sort of anti-yeast supplement or drug you take, it will not replace the friendly bacteria that are essential to healthy intestines and vagina, and a strong immune system. You must also

take a beneficial bacteria supplement and/or supplement with friendly bacteria-containing foods like yogurt with live bacteria culture.

- Be aware that stress raises your blood sugar in the same way that eating sugar does. This feeds yeast.
- Starve the yeast by depriving them of their food source: sugar, alcohol and simple carbohydrates.
- Eliminate foods that are in the yeast, mold and fungus family until the body heals. This includes yeasted breads, mushrooms, moldy cheeses and fermented foods except yogurt.
- Reduce exposure to yeasts, molds and fungi in your environment.
- Take acidophilus and bifidus bacteria supplements with fructooligosaccharides (FOS) to promote the growth of the bifidus bacteria.
- Take natural antiyeast supplements like garlic, caprylic acid, grapefruit seed extract, Pau D'Arco (taheebo tea), omega-3 and 6-EPA fatty acids like flaxseed, evening primrose and borage oils.
- Take a yeast-free multivitamin.
- If you have athlete's foot, wash daily with citricidal skin cleanser.
- Take digestive enzymes to promote digestion and assimilation, unless you have an overly acidic stomach or ulcers.
- Support daily bowel movements with a high fiber diet, psyllium husk powder, plenty of water and exercise.
- Acupuncture. It alleviates the physical stress put on your body during the detoxification process, supports your immune system and speeds recovery.
- Consult your doctor or naturopath for a Comprehensive Digestive and Stool Analysis (CDSA) available through the Great Smokies Diagnostics Laboratory. It tests for intestinal pathogens, including yeast, and includes a sensitivity screening panel for various natural and

pharmaceutical treatments of any pathogens that show up in excess, including yeast.

- Read *The Yeast Connection Handbook*, by William G. Crook, M.D. He has written about yeast overgrowth for years.
- Read *Complete Candida Yeast Guidebook*, by Jeanne Marie Martin. It includes 200 recipes for a candida diet.
- Look in your bookstore for a yeast book that appeals to you.

If you have leaky gut syndrome:

- Avoid nonsteroidal antiinflammatory drugs like ibuprofen;
- Take digestive enzymes, as long as you don't suffer from an overly acidic stomach;
- Take nutrients that support rebuilding the intestinal wall, including: L-Glutamine, NAC, GLA, Gamma oryzanol, vitamin E and Phosphatidyl Choline;
- Take freshly ground flaxseeds with plenty of water.

PART THREE

Stories of
Healing

Asthma

Lori's Story

I've had asthma since the age of eighteen. I am twenty-nine now. Although others in my extended family have had asthma, I never had it as a child. I was diagnosed with asthmatic bronchitis and told that when people get asthma as an adult, they most likely will have it for life. The bronchitis cleared up, but the asthma didn't.

From the age of eighteen to twenty-five my asthma seemed to get progressively worse. I was on so much medication (theodur, brethine, alupent, atrovent and prednisone) that I was spending anywhere from $60 to $100 per month, not including emergency room visits. I was experiencing side effects such as shakiness, nervousness, and mood swings. To top it all off, the medicine was just barely keeping me able to breathe. I was not able to walk down the street, let alone able to walk up one flight of stairs, get on a bicycle, or pick up a tennis racket without getting severely winded and/or experiencing an asthma "attack." Often during the night, my labored breathing or wheezing could be heard in another room. It was frightening for me and anyone who witnessed an attack.

I moved to Vermont in 1989 (age twenty-five) and found that there was some small relief from the asthma during the winter; but it was far from gone. I was still loaded up with drugs.

In April of 1992, I finally decided to give acupuncture a try at the gentle urging of my husband. He tells me that he suggested it to me three or four times before I actually heard him! When I began seeing Deborah DeGraff for acupuncture she spoke with great confidence and sincerity about the positive changes she had seen with other asthma sufferers. I have to say that I was a skeptic about it (having no experience with alternative medical care or choices) but I was so moved by her confidence that I decided to make a commitment to trying acupuncture for at least three months. If at the end of that time I did not see any results, then I would stop the treatment.

From my first visit I realized that I was on to something that could change my life. I was more than a little nervous about the idea of needles being stuck into me, but soon found out that acupuncture is not a painful experience. In fact it is just the opposite. During a treatment I always feel completely relaxed, in a state that I think may be something close to meditation. Afterward I feel energized and rejuvenated.

I noticed real changes in my breathing after several weeks of regular treatment. It took me many months to let go of the fear that I had carried around with me for so long. I had been so afraid of having an attack, that the very act of taking a walk and forgetting to carry an inhaler with me could bring on a severe attack. Letting go of my fear and grasping onto confidence in my body's ability to heal was an important step in my treatment. At the present time I only use inhalers once a week, while at my worst I had needed a replacement every three weeks. I no longer take any of the other medications that I took with regularity. Additionally, I have experienced a great deal of stress reduction and relief from PMS. I truly believe that if I continue treatment, I will not have any asthma symptoms someday very soon. I can't say enough good things about my experience.

[From a letter I received from Lori on February 5, 1994. She had not had an acupuncture treatment for four months.]

"I just wanted to share with you the fact that I haven't used my inhaler in months. How about that?"

When I last talked to Lori on the phone she had had one acupuncture treatment in the past four years. She said, "The asthma has been great. No problems with it." She said she was feeling less fearful and using a preventive inhaler in July, August and September, her difficult months.

Grief

Marilyn's Story
I basically fell apart after my father's death. I became a physical wreck. And I stopped being alive emotionally. I gradually settled into a living-dead kind of existence and accepted it as normal for my age. This lasted for over four years and went from bad to worse, until I met Deb and started getting acupuncture treatments. I didn't realize what bad shape I was in until I started feeling better.

When my father died I was asleep dreaming I was in bed with him in a semi-dark room with an open window. He was talking to someone outside the window that I couldn't see. In another dream, my father and I were taking off in an airplane when we were sucked up into outer space by a hurricane. Once we were in the silence and blackness of space, my father started having radio contact with people he seemed to know out there. . . . Though I was brought up without religion and held no beliefs about consciousness after death, dreams like these actually brought me some solace and relief from the intense pain of grief.

For the first three days after my father died, I felt like a steamroller was crushing my chest every time I woke up and remembered that he was dead. I immediately got sick with a fever and sore throat and started losing weight. I had frequent crying spells, and had a constant cold without congestion that lingered for months. My body was literally weeping.

I became a "night pee-er," waking up several times each night from nightmares in fight-or-flight mode with a tight bladder. I also started having extremely painful periods and other ailments, but cold feet were the thing that bothered me most. At night I would take a hot bath to warm up, go to bed early exhausted and wake up with recurring nightmares.

When I had to be around people, I felt like I had obvious, horrible, bleeding wounds. One particular experience I remember as a surreal nightmare was a surprise birthday party friends had for me about eight months after my father died.

For about two years I had nightmares that my father was dying and I was trying to save him. Finally I had a dream in which my father actually died—he fell into me, dead as a doornail with his eyes open. I woke up so relieved that what I had dreamed was consistent with reality. I felt I had finally moved through the "denial" stage of grief.

Then I started dreaming I was being mugged or attacked. At first the mugger was a one-dimensional villain leaping out of the dark. After at least a year of being terrorized by variations on that theme, I started dreaming about more interesting muggers. They became more complex characters with intelligence and personality. I had my last "mugger" dream when I recognized that the mugger was not only a very attractive and charismatic man but also my father as a handsome young man. I realized that my father's overpowering personality, intellect and personal charisma in a way crushed me as a child. That ended the "mugger" series.

At work I sat in a cubicle next to a man who would always walk a distance around me looking straight ahead in order to get to his desk. He was a very sensitive but straight-as-an-arrow person whose professional image was important to him. When we got to know each other better, he confided in me that he sometimes saw colors around people and that I had a very thick blue-green haze around me that was very disturbing.

By the time I met Deb in a dance class I had moved onto dreams about being on a ship at sea, being tossed around perilously; trying to cross a bridge that was being torn away by raging waters; or being swept into tidal waves and drowning.

I didn't know much about acupuncture but was interested in experiencing it. I told Deb I wanted to wait until I had an injury before trying it. She said I didn't need to have anything wrong with me, I could just have a "tune-up" treatment.

Since then, acupuncture has turned out to be the most powerful intervention on my psyche, not to mention my physical body, that I have ever experienced. Over a period of several months the night-peeing, nightmares and insomnia decreased. The man from work said my aura lost its blue cast and became bright white. My menstrual periods became less painful and my dreams changed.

The first night that I slept all the way through without waking up or getting up to pee, I felt like I had been reborn. I have talked to so many people, especially women over thirty, who get up to go to the bathroom every night and have forgotten what a good night of sleep is.

For me night-peeing and insomnia had become a deeply ingrained and habitual response to stress. At first I had frequent relapses every time I encountered something really upsetting. Then it was as if my body "learned" what to do with stress from the experience of acupuncture, and I learned how to recognize early warning messages from my body.

I started coming back to life, literally noticing how beautiful flowers were as I walked down the street. I changed jobs, moved and took on major new challenges.

I've gained weight, but remain slender (knock on wood). Other ailments and problems I expected would plague me for the rest of my life have disappeared. When new ones appear, or my body doesn't feel right, I go straight for acupuncture to nip it in the bud. I still have setbacks, but my recovery time is faster. I also keep up with regular maintenance treatments.

I still dream a lot (always have), but I don't have recurring nightmares anymore. When I occasionally dream about my father, it is understood he was absent for a period of time due to being dead, but is alive again and living with our family. It's confusing but not at all distressing.

Healing—a Lifelong Process

Susan's Story

If there is one thing I've learned about health and well-being from my years of being a patient of Deb's it is that it is a long-term, lifelong process, not an event isolated in time. Sure there are some things that respond right away to treatment (like the "miracle point" for hemorrhoids), but in my experience, healing takes patience and a certain amount of faith that what I'm doing is right for me and will "work."

I started seeing Deb six years ago. I was in a relationship that was going nowhere and my finances were precarious. While the nonprofit organization I directed and the newsletter I published fed my spirit, they did not keep body and soul together. My financial struggles were especially difficult because I was (still am) a single mother of three boys. But my work fulfilled my purpose and this was extremely important to me, so important that I made what others considered inappropriate choices: I "should" have a "regular" job, with "regular" hours, a steady paycheck, etc. I was also still recovering from a marriage that had at times been emotionally and physically abusive.

What brought me to Deb's office finally, on the advice of a good friend, was I felt like I was separating from my body. I'd be walking down the street and felt myself looking down at my body. I didn't feel in my body. It felt like if I looked in a mirror I'd see a double image of myself. I was not grounded at all and sometimes I'd feel so separate from myself it was hard to breathe. I couldn't hold myself together. It was scary.

Right from the first treatment I felt better. But I knew that healing wouldn't happen overnight because what I had wasn't simple like a cold. It was emotional stuff impacting my physical body and while I knew there were physical things I could do, I also knew that any real change had to come at the emotional and spiritual levels first. Still, I didn't think it would take six years. . . .

As you know from reading this book, Deb's approach is very holistic. On that first visit she found out that I was concerned about my weight (and have been, obsessively, all my life), that I was addicted to a pain reliever due to headaches I'd suffered since my teenaged years (something which I rarely admitted to anyone), had certain emotional attachments around food (I needed comfort foods which happened to be full of fat and/or sugar), and was in a probably unhealthy relationship with a man who was emotionally unavailable to me. I was a mess.

After the first few treatments I felt much better. At least I felt there was only one of me—I wasn't going to fly out of my body anyway. But I resisted making too many dietary changes because of my emotional issues. We worked on my headaches because one of my stated goals was to stop taking medication. I understood, finally, that I was addicted to the drug because of the high caffeine content and that it, in fact, was likely causing the headaches I took it for. This was my pattern: I'd wake up in the morning and take a couple of tablets like some people drink coffee—even if I didn't have a headache, because experience told me I'd have one soon enough. The pills woke me up and gave me energy so I didn't need to eat breakfast. Sometimes I'd take a couple more mid-morning, then more in the afternoon and more at night. I'd take anywhere from six to twelve pain relievers a day and this had been going on for years.

Each time I'd visit Deb she'd ask me, totally non-judgmentally, how I was doing cutting back on the pain relievers. For three years this went on and while I was taking less, I had not quit. Meanwhile, my backaches improved and I began to get a handle on why the relationship I was in was not working, although I still kept hoping it would. I was also doing the same work, loving it, but struggling financially. My relationship with my ex-husband improved as he got the help he needed and some of the stress related to that situation abated.

Finally I decided I was going to do a cleansing diet. This was in March, my birth month, and typically an excellent time for me to start something new. Deb gave me her suggestions and I got the supplies (whole grains, detoxifying teas, fresh veggies, juice, etc.). Then, on the first morning when I reached for the pills I realized that if I was serious about the cleanse I had to stop taking them. So I did.

It sounds simple, but it wasn't. I was in agony. The headache I suffered for about three days was pounding. I tried white willow bark tea but it tasted so vile I couldn't drink it. I rubbed my head with willow bark salve, took an herbal headache preparation, but nothing touched it. For some reason I stuck it out, and after three days the headache was gone. I kept up the cleanse for another three days or so, but I knew the real achievement was stopping the pain relievers. I have not taken one since. What was amazing is that after a short time (a couple of weeks, I think) my energy felt normal and I no longer even thought of pills. I see that those little white pills were a crutch. They gave me something to take, something to assuage the pain I felt, but the pain wasn't really physical, it was emotional. And no pill would help. I was also quite surprised that other people could see the difference in me. They said my face and eyes were clearer and I looked healthier.

It took me so very long to get to this point. For three years it appeared that nothing was happening, then one day I just quit and that was that. Foundation work is what Deb calls it. Regardless, I felt very proud of my accomplishment and this was enormously important to my healing process.

The next couple of years were mostly spent working on emotional issues. But my weight increased and this made me very unhappy. Still, I was unwilling to diet. I had spent most of my life dealing with food issues and weight issues, even going so far as to fast for two weeks and then eat next to nothing for two months after my first son was born. I lost a lot of weight, but then my hair started to fall out! All my life I have been fat, thin, and everything in between and I was sick and tired of it. When dieting I felt deprived, hated myself, felt guilty whenever I ate (no matter what it was); I used laxatives, ate only once a day—my life revolved around food—not eating it and feeling guilty when I did. I knew this was more unhealthy than carrying around extra weight and I made the conscious decision that I would be larger in exchange for a "normal" eating life. Even though this was a conscious choice, I still thought to myself several times a day, "You're so fat, you'll never lose weight." And the underlying emotion was that I was worthless and ugly all due to my size. Intellectually I knew what I was doing, but emotionally I had very little control over it. Eating became almost a rebellious act. I would eat what I wanted, regardless of fat or calories! And I did. And I gained even more weight. What a vicious cycle I was in!

But then this was the next hurdle in my healing—feeling good about my body regardless of its size, knowing that I am a worthwhile person regardless of my size, knowing that I can be healthy and happy regardless of my size.

Then about a year and a half ago a couple of family crises came about that simply changed everything. In January my father broke his hip (he had already suffered a debilitating stroke three years earlier). On the day of his hip surgery I ended the relationship I had been in for six years—the one that was going nowhere. It was sad but exhilarating at the same time. I was so angry—at him and at myself for allowing myself to be in such a negative situation for so long. I felt as if I'd finally come awake.

In April my beloved grandmother died. She was ninety-five and my best friend and mentor. Such a wonderful, wise, loving woman. Suddenly I was the matriarch of the family, a role I did not want and did not feel prepared for. A month later my father had to have his legs amputated due to a complication from diabetes. This also meant that he would have to live in a nursing home, leaving my disabled sister alone in the house in Maine.

Because of all this family stuff I had to put my work on hold. I could not concentrate. Attending meetings, organizing events, etc. were far beyond my ability at that time. I even began questioning the work I was doing. After all, despite numerous campaigns to save forests, stop pollution and all that, the destruction wages on. I felt powerless to stop it and depressed that after all those years of hard work, very little was changed. To make matters worse, the people I had worked with over the years seemed to disappear out of my life when I no longer attended meetings and public events. Sure I'd get invited to the occasional potluck, but no one called to see how I was or to invite me to a family dinner, or over to just talk. I saw with painful clarity that the people I'd thought were my friends were simply colleagues, nothing more. While we all talked a big line about the importance of community and helping one another, it was just that, a big line.

Now maybe this sounds harsh, but it is how I felt. I felt so abandoned and deserted at the time when I needed help. It was my nonactivist friends who came through and this taught me something about real community and how it is created. Real community is built over time on relationships. It isn't created at rallies or meetings or events no matter how exciting or wonderful they feel at the time.

So I decided it was time to make a change. I planned to move to Maine to live with my sister. At first I thought I'd continue my activism in some form there, but after a while it became clear my heart was no longer in it. Just thinking about starting over made me exhausted. What excited me was my relationship with trees and plants, especially herbs, so I decided to open a small herb shop that could educate people about herbs and provide the necessary supplies for people to make their own healing preparations.

Unfortunately I couldn't move right then as my middle son was a senior in high school and I didn't want to move him at that time. So I needed to stick it out in Vermont for another year. At first I called this year my "gray area." Then I decided that I would take advantage of this time to prepare myself emotionally and physically for the change. Thanks to my family I had a little money to tide me over. And I made the choice to spend some of it on myself. In addition to seeing Deb regularly, I started getting a massage every couple of weeks. This was wonderful and helped me feel comfortable about my body—at least comfortable enough to let another woman massage it.

Then one day I was telling Deb about how I noticed that when I sat a certain way at the table I felt bad about myself, but when I sat straight and tall, I felt better. Yet I seemed to naturally fall into the unhealthy posture. At this she recommended I see a friend of hers who is a rolfer. I had been intrigued by rolfing for quite some time but was leery of it because I imagined it was painful. But Deb had never steered me wrong before, so I decided to give it a shot.

To make a long story short, rolfing was so healing for me that I felt like a new person. Now that sounds dramatic and the actual physical changes weren't that dramatic. But how I feel in my body is the important thing. I knew, right after the first couple of sessions, that I had hit upon something that was just right for what I needed at the time.

During this time I made numerous trips to Maine. My home is just over the Maine border from New Hampshire and the White Mountains where I grew up. I noticed on the many trips to Maine that while there I felt better, more energetic, more alive and my body ached much less than when I returned home to Vermont. Why? My own belief is that this place in the Mountains somehow resonates with me, raises my vibrations in a way that says to me "This is home." It is a physical thing I can feel in my body. These mountains know me, they speak to me and comfort me like a mother would. I never felt this way in Vermont and I don't remember feeling this way before I left the White Mountains over twenty years ago either. But I feel it now and it's better than all the bottles of pills I've taken over the years.

It does not seem a coincidence that as I began to feel more at home in my body thanks to acupuncture and the other body work I did, I discovered my true home on Earth and was able to make the decision to move back. Now that I am here, just beginning to do the research to set up my little herb shop (Gaia's Closet), I have few bodyaches. I eat what I would consider "normal." I may have dropped a few pounds, but since I long ago gave up scales, I don't know for sure. But I don't have those negative tapes playing in my head every day (although they do play occasionally) and, in general, I feel wonderful. I am home, both on the Earth and in my body. I have no illusions that I have been "healed." I know that healing is something that happens for as long as we live. But I am excited by the future once again and know that I am up to the challenges—physically and emotionally.

Quitting Smoking

Diane's Story
I was born in New York City in 1947. Both of my parents were smokers. Their brand was Pall Mall. Whenever I saw the advertisement of the neat little bellboy calling out for PPPAAAALLLLLL MAAALLLLL it made me think my folks were really cool. My grandfather smoked Camels. Together, we would play the game, "Where does the camel go when he gets thirsty?" Turning the pack over Grandpa would show me the oasis on the other side. The sheer familiarity of the game as we played it week after week gave me great comfort at age five.

My father had his first heart problem at age forty-two. Thus began my parents' ongoing attempts to give up smoking. This coincided with their request that I promise never to smoke myself. It also coincided with my teenaged years. My family, like so many families of the 1950s, were inexperienced at talking about feelings. Somewhat as a consequence of this problem, I ate my way through the first five years of teenaged life. That is until I discovered cigarettes.

I still remember my first cigarette. I was staring at myself in the mirror at my best friend's house when I took that first drag. It was as if I were inhaling a new self. Puffffff, I was pretty, attractive, smart . . . invincible! I looked up to heaven and said, "Okay, God, this is it. Just let me do this one bad thing and I promise I won't do any of the other bad stuff." Throwing down the borrowed cigarette I went out and bought a pack of my own. And essentially I was not without a cigarette for the next thirty years.

I moved to Vermont as part of the back-to-the-land movement of the late 1960s early 1970s. In terms of health, to say my cigarette smoking was out of character with the rest of my personal vision would be an understatement of gross proportion. There was, however, the element of being a pioneer, a throwback to the French peasant stock from which I'd come. So, I rolled my Top and Buggler tobacco with the best of them; buying Lucky Strikes when I felt flush.

I managed to ignore, deny, etc. and basically kept smoking for many years. I did try to quit when I was pregnant, when my son was four, and when he was thirteen. I usually ended up feeling humiliated after rescuing some teeny, tiny butt from an ashtray, or even worse, from a curb. The emotional pain from these episodes was such that I needed not to voice them, even and especially to myself. But boy would I get angry at you if you tried to intervene. Each time I began smoking again I'd switch brands, though always to the tough guy, nonfiltered brands like my family smoked. I ended my smoking career with Camels.

Quitting smoking was a process for me. Partially, smoking simply stopped working. It stopped keeping the feelings I didn't want to feel at bay. My favorite experience in this process was the day my lungs spoke to me. They said, "Yo, Diane honey, we know you love to smoke. We love you, so we've tried really hard to support you in this thing you love so much. But sweetheart, we just want you to know that although we've done pretty well so far, we're not going to be able to continue without consequences." (Oh no, the dreaded "C" word!) They were so loving, my lungs. None of that harsh, "You better do it or else" stuff. They were so dear, I couldn't resist them.

I used both the patch and a small but motivated group called Smokefree facilitated by a nonsmoking nurse. Amazingly, although it was really hard I didn't miss cigarettes exactly. I longed and longed for something, but somewhere, somehow, I knew it wasn't really a cigarette. I've done a lot more healing work to give voice to the many things I've longed—nay, starved for—when I smoked instead. I haven't smoked in three years. Not smoking is something I'm truly grateful for.

By the way, my grandfather, who was quite a guy, quit smoking at ninety-two! He lived until ninety-four, and died at home with his family around him. May we all be as blessed.

Sleep and Healing from Pneumonia

Susan's Story

Several years ago, I came down with a bad cough. I ignored it for two weeks, figuring it was just that: a bad cough. But then I heard a curious gurgling sound in my chest, almost like polliwogs splashing in a pond, and I realized I was having trouble breathing. When I went to see my doctor, he diagnosed pneumonia. "Don't take this lightly," he said. "You really need rest. Go home and stay in bed for a week."

It was, of course, bad timing. I had three articles due within two weeks. I was feeling like a very busy, very important person. So I made a deal with myself. Since I work at home, I would keep working, but I'd take a nap every afternoon. That way, I figured, I could get my work done and get the rest my doctor prescribed.

For the next week I coughed my way through interviews each morning, took a nap each afternoon, and then wrote into the early evening, when I would collapse on the couch and whine to my husband that I didn't feel well. Then those periods of collapse started coming earlier and earlier. By week's end, I could hardly keep my head up through breakfast. I went to see my doctor and told him I felt worse. "Are you staying in bed?" he asked. I hedged. "If you don't get some rest, I'll stick you in the hospital. Quit working. Lie down. Get some sleep."

In truth, I couldn't do much more than that, so I built myself a blanket-and-pillow fort on the couch. I rented a stack of videos and lined up magazines and books by the bed. But I didn't even have the energy to concentrate on those. Instead, I mostly slept and daydreamed. In fact, I spent whole days contemplating the ceiling, two paintings on the living room walls and my own thoughts.

It was actually very pleasant. As I lay there letting my thoughts drift, I realized I had spent no time in recent years just daydreaming. I was either working, or exercising, or cleaning, or socializing, or planning to socialize, or reading, or watching TV every minute of my waking hours. Sure, my thoughts sometimes drifted as I drove, or bathed, or fell off to sleep, but I was always on my way somewhere else while I did those things, so my thoughts got yanked back to pragmatic things once again. For those five days on the couch, however, I actually got to think about where I was in my life and how I felt about it. My daily project was simply to rest.

I'm not going to say that this experience completely changed my being—I still lead a busy life, still try to do too much, still spend a lot of mental time planning, timing and making lists. But there's a little more space inside now, and I greatly cherish even a few minutes lying back in my garden, or watching the clouds pass my window, or just sitting in the living room sometimes, gazing at nothing much at all. It gives me a little time to think about the big picture—of where I've been, and where I am, and where I'm going. And it gives me a chance to reflect on whether I've been striving too much, leaning in the wrong direction, or forgetting something important—like being rested, feeling at peace or simply enjoying the beauty around me.

Listening to the Pain

Pam's Story

Pain is a powerful entity. It grabs us and says, "Something is wrong, take care of it NOW." We, of course, should be good to these wondrous bodies we are given and take notice when there is discomfort. But for whatever reason, most of us wait until we are barely functioning. When people such as myself relent and go to "the doctor," we are looking for help and relief. We believe they will find what is wrong and facilitate correction.

Seeking answers and relief took me on a long tortuous journey through our medical system. My experience brings to light many aspects of what is wrong with health care now. I have been misdiagnosed, mistreated, not-treated, prescribed medications which never should have entered this body and not received services for fees. This continued for months when it should have been resolved in a few weeks, extremely counterproductive for all parties involved. Perhaps these health care providers were doing the best they could, which is why I am writing to convey these experiences. Not to dwell on the negative, but to share the path that is finally leading back to health.

After all is said and done, we are each responsible for our own health. If a person has a physical problem, as in my case, he or she must make the decision to follow a particular curative program. These decisions are hard ones. Who to go to? Who to trust? How long to wait for results? This can only be answered by asking deeply what is right for you. Do not accept negativity in the form of diagnosis or prognosis. Get other opinions, find another outlook in the form of another doctor or technique. Call health care practitioners and ask what their approach is to a problem such as yours. Ask to meet or talk for five to ten minutes. If they don't have time for that, they won't have time to help you. If you feel good about the contact, after some thought, consider an appointment. Ask questions, read books, know what you are involved with. Seek help with <u>qualified</u> persons from many fields. Sometimes the experienced, caring technicians who do the real work can be very helpful. For example, a physical therapist with a good reputation could be worth seeing early on, instead of waiting to be referred to a "specialist."

My initial "treatment," which consisted of very strong anti-inflammatories, muscle relaxants and a worsening condition, dead-ended in frustration after five months. This led me to complain to my treating physician that <u>my horses</u> would be getting better care

and it would not be bankrupting me. When she asked what care
my horses would be getting, beyond the initial cold packs, anti-
inflammatories and rest (something hard to get for adult humans).
I told her they would get ultrasound, massage, acupuncture, bio-
mechanical evaluation, equipment evaluation and task reevaluation. They would get relief from their pain and inquiry into the
cause. Thankfully, her response was to ask if I would consider
trying something such as acupuncture; and therein started a par-
allel health care journey which was an education in itself.

After speaking briefly to several acupuncturists and assessing
them, one last call came in returning a message I had left. This
acupuncturist was my first choice, although it would be farther to
travel. The phone call impression was that of a caring, personable,
confident professional. It must be hard for practitioners presented
with persons such as I was at that point, overwhelmed with pain,
still practicing denial, depressed by a negative prognosis, angry,
and desperate for relief and answers. For any readers who pursue
acupuncture as a treatment, I hope you have the good fortune to
be treated by someone such as my acupuncturist.

During that first treatment I experienced genuine relief from
the disabling pain in my back. That experience alone gives one
hope. It is not drug induced, but the body's own capacity to come
back to balance. Also, my acupuncturist assured me that I had a
strong underlying vitality, which was important for me to hear.
Due to travel and monetary constraints, we could only do treatments once a week. After a few weeks the fatiguing pain loosened
its grip. I found joy in my life again, and moving and performing
tasks became easier. I was able to go on maintenance treatments,
one every few weeks.

But all was not well. I was still in denial, at an acceptable
plateau, life went on as usual. But the body knows better. And it
said louder, "Listen to me, listen to you." My arms started to
ache. By this time I could see an acupuncturist whose office was
closer to me. But he couldn't stop the progression, only I could. I
had to admit that all this damage was related to my job. My career, my training, my skill, professional development, pride in

helping people with diagnosis everyday, my income . . . how could it be? How could something as seemingly innocuous as microscope and laboratory work be so damaging? I had been in good physical shape so my back took the first hit, unlike others whose arms did.

Then began another round, physical therapy, anti-inflammatories, someone suggested chiropractic, I mentioned ultrasound and someone else massage therapy. At work I was braced and splinted, but real changes weren't made. I wondered why it was illegal to race horses when they are taking anti-inflammatories which mask their pain and lead to breakdowns, but some practitioners are willing to casually prescribe harmful antiinflammatories in similar situations for humans who keep working until they do break down.

Acupuncture and massage made it possible for me to carry on long enough to do serious self-examination and research. I resigned from my job. My reason, besides self-preservation, was that I wouldn't be able to do much good in this world if this process continued. One insightful nurse asked me "Is there anything else you've always wanted to do as a job?" Of course there was; there are so many options and possibilities.

The modalities that helped the most during my injury were the ones that optimized healing. Acupuncture, massage, exercises learned in physical therapy, and ergonomics learned from occupational therapy. Drugs were not necessary. Instead, a good diet and schedule, vitamins, minerals and herbal supplements if used properly help the body optimize its own healing capacity and correct deficiencies, without harmful side effects. For me, this journey was very complex. The one most important thing to relay to anyone facing a health/life crisis is to listen to yourself and your body. You are the only one who can feel and know what is truly going on. I wonder how inhumane treatment can continue in so many sectors of our modern culture. I've seen good and bad practitioners in traditional and alternative medicine, and have been amazed at how the skilled and caring practitioners make such a positive impact.

Look for the good ones in whatever technique is right for

you. Health care is changing and it is an exciting time. In traditional medicine, healing has entered the conversation, and it is more than just wound healing that is being discussed. Doctors are looking at patients holistically, not as isolated symptoms. Integrated, complementary medicine is becoming a reality in many practices. Disease prevention is being recognized as important. We have many choices. Be informed and active in your own care. And remember, be quiet . . . and listen.

Allergies and Cleansing

Tom's Story

At my company I'm unofficially known as the "Food Warden." It seems I have an opinion on what everyone eats, sometimes sneaking up behind someone who is buying candy from the vending machine and whispering, "That's not good for your body!" They're all well aware of my thirty-day cleansing. It's now, after several years, a New Year's event that involves everyone around me. Only from the standpoint that I have a big mouth and so I'm constantly talking about how I am preparing myself for the big day. People around me just have to be prepared to put up with me.

What some may not know is I do this for allergy control, not weight loss. My preparation is fairly simple. Until the big day arrives, I continue to consume all kinds of food and drink. This of course is not my typical diet. The holidays are what put me into a food spin: cookies, cakes, booze and more cookies. I love the holidays, but as they wind down, I look forward to cleansing.

January 2nd is my official start date and by that time I'm ready to begin the cleansing process. The challenge of what I call Food Consumption Control becomes a focused directive for me. Being an ex-cadet, discipline is not a problem. I actually look forward to this commitment. After several years of success, I have fine-tuned it and do not feel hungry. Unfortunately for me, at this point in my life, what I put in my mouth is the only thing I can control.

The true benefit from cleansing is that I can now breathe well, and when I do eat foods that once affected my sinuses, I can honestly say they no longer do. The benefit lasts, and when I begin cleansing the next year, I'm not doing it because I can't breathe. I'm doing it for my entire body and well-being. I might add that the other benefit to the cleansing process is loss of body fat. I'm not looking to lose weight, but loss of body fat is a bonus. The real benefit for me is that the cleansing diet has shaped my everyday diet. I feel healthy! (And nothing feels better!)

Exercise is an almost everyday thing for me and consuming healthy food is part of my life. Sometimes I wonder why I can't just be like the majority of my peer group. They eat everything and anything, rarely exercise and generally just don't care. I guess I just can't settle for being one of those "aging baby boomers"!

ALLERGY CONTROL 30-DAY CLEANSING
as prescribed by Deborah and survived by Tom

Eliminate: Sugar, caffeine, fruit juices, peanuts, shellfish, wheat, beef, pork, liquor, dairy and mushrooms

Consume: Grain, fruit, vegetables, fish, poultry, water

Typical Day:

Breakfast: Oatmeal with bananas, natural applesauce, cinnamon and herb tea

Snack: (10:30 A.M.) Microwave sweet potato, soy butter, pepper and herb tea

Lunch: Salad with greens, carrots, cucumbers, cabbage, red peppers, tomatoes, kidney beans, alfalfa sprouts, turkey, Paul Newman's Vinegar & Oil Salad Dressing and an orange and apple

Snack: (3:30 P.M.) Banana, orange, water

Dinner: Baked fish with soy butter and dill, brown rice, steamed broccoli and carrots, water, orange

Loss and Rebirth

Phillip's Story

In December of 1989, at the age of forty-one and two months after the death of my wife, I found myself confronted with unspeakable pain, unrecognized sorrow and a growing awareness of an abyss that was consuming me and the world around me. Physically this manifested as walking pneumonia, insomnia and deep depression. I was exhausted. I was lost.

Grief was in my chest. The air I breathed, each breath, reminded me of my beloved and caused such pain that I chose, unconsciously, to have more and more shallow breaths. Every cell, every atom in my body felt like it had lost part of its nucleus. Weeping was not enough release from that pain. I took up to 3 mg of Ativan each night in a futile attempt to fight off the insomnia.

With the help of a friend, I began to see an acupuncturist as an alternative to going into the hospital. The acupuncture saved my life. During these sessions my emotions would surface in waves. I embarrassingly joked that anyone listening to the acupuncture sessions might think I was auditioning for "The Exorcist." After the third week, my acupuncturist insisted I see a psychotherapist as a requirement to continue acupuncture. Then and now, I firmly believe there is value in treating people with concurrent acupuncture and psychotherapy.

The acupuncture allowed my body to begin to heal. I would see changes immediately. Such changes included improvement in my eyesight, hearing, smell, breathing, appetite, digestion and the ability to sleep. I had glimpses of a rekindled will to live. It would take me nearly four years to recapture that will fully.

Spiritually for at least two years I was lost. Even after recovering physically, I closely identified with homeless people. I was fascinated by how thin the line was between them (the homeless) and people I knew in everyday life.

I recall an incident, occurring just as I was emerging from a two-year period of celibacy. A wonderfully caring woman in her late thirties sat with me in her car which was parked on a San Mateo street. Now San Mateo at that time had a large number of emotionally disturbed and previously institutionalized people on its streets. So as we discussed my lack of intentions toward forming a committed relationship, it was not surprising that outside, on the sidewalk, a woman who was obviously emotionally troubled, slowly walked by. I had been trying to tell this wonderful lady that I needed more time to deal with my grief.

As I talked, this woman walked slowly by. Her face was so full of pain and fear it was uncomfortable to look at her. As we talked, my lady friend avoided looking at her. I, on the other hand, stared at her. Each step for the woman on the sidewalk was a struggle. She was unaware of us in the car. She looked like she was fighting off fear, as if each step were a conscious choice to move forward. She moved in a strange way, only swinging her arms and legs about six inches in front of her torso, eyes focused on the sidewalk six inches in front of her. She could only occupy that six-inch space as she slowly conquered her fear of the perils facing her.

After watching this struggle I stopped talking. I turned to my friend and asked her what she thought of the woman on the sidewalk. She forced herself to look, shuddered, and said the woman looked deranged. I was silent for a moment, then told my friend that the woman on the sidewalk looked courageous. I told her, "Look, I still have to go where that woman has already been." Her commitment to walking in the face of her fear was a metaphor for what I had to do. I had to face my sorrow.

Sorrow, for me, had two endless vertical walls and no floor. It was an abyss. I could fall and fall and after endless falling I still would not hit a bottom. There was no floor at the bottom. Finally, one day, I decided I needed help. I talked about this to my acupuncturist, who also was a spiritual counselor for me. She listened to what I said about the abyss. I told her of the emptiness, the no-bottom bottom. I was distraught. I told her I felt life had no meaning. She said, This is so. Life only has the meaning we give it.

Sorrow had left a scar. To heal that scar I had to recognize there was nothing I could do to change the things I did or did not do, said or did not say, that may have hurt the one I loved. I could not undo the past. All I could do was accept responsibility for myself and my actions. When I could finally forgive myself, I could live again, breathe again and love again.

Recovering Trust in My Body

Beth's Story

Let's be clear here. I hate needles. Always have. I'm the one the Red Cross volunteer hands the brown paper lunch bag, saying kindly, "You're starting to hyperventilate, hon." Pictures of acupuncture patients with long needles sticking out of their arms, legs or backs have always made me shiver and turn away uneasily. A few years ago, my friend Laurel started acupuncture for her Chronic Fatigue Syndrome, and said it was the only thing that really helped. I listened to her descriptions of treatments and watched her boil dark concoctions of herbs on her kitchen stove, asking questions with the horrified expectancy of a kid who knows the answers will completely gross her out. "I am not doing that. No one is ever going to stick needles in me," I said.

Then I started fainting from hypoglycemia. The second time it happened, I passed out in a crowd of people in the Dupont Circle metro station in D.C., on my way home from a peace march. My friends were alarmed, and I was terrified. I'd known my blood sugar problems were getting worse—no matter how often I ate, I constantly felt a little nauseated, a little light-headed. I was hungry every two or three hours, but eating didn't seem to help for long, and I was always tired. In addition, old back injuries started to give me more and more trouble, and I was immobilized, in severe pain, for days at a stretch. Eventually I was so panicked by my body's accelerating breakdown that even needles seemed manageable in comparison.

I went to my first acupuncture appointment with trepidation. I sat stiffly on an uncomfortable divan in the treatment room while Deb asked me a series of questions. At the first opportunity, "I don't like needles," I said, with a grimace to indicate I was prepared to be brave.

"Oh, I hate getting needles," Deborah said cheerfully. "The other acupuncturists all laugh at me when I see them for treatments, because I'm so squeamish." Her confession shocked me out of my fear for a moment. How could someone who was afraid of needles stick them in other people for a living? I glazed over again as she went on to explain that acupuncture needles were much finer than hypodermic needles. Yeah, yeah, let's just get this over with, I thought.

"Well, we could do a couple of things," Deb said. "I could do a general kind of toning-up treatment for your first session, or we could start by treating your back directly. Which do you think would be best?"

I stared at her, tense and self-conscious. She was the doctor. I didn't know anything about acupuncture! How could I possibly know what would be best? "I . . . I . . . I don't know," I muttered.

"Okay. Hmmmm . . . how about starting with the toning treatment then? I think it'll be a little gentler for you, and you won't have to lie on your stomach on the table, which can be hard for some people. Does that sound all right?"

Minutes later I lay on the table while Deborah gently tapped needles into five points on each side of my body—elbows, wrists (two there), shins, and the top of each foot. It didn't hurt, just as she had said—only a little twinge every now and then. Finally, "Okay, I think that's enough for the first treatment," she said. "Are you comfortable?"

"Yes," I said, and then as she turned to leave the room, "Deborah? Can I see them, the needles?"

"Sure," she said. "Just lift your arms up straight from the shoulders—don't flex your elbows."

Gingerly, I lifted my arms into my field of vision. From each elbow and wrist sprouted long thin silver wires that ended in spiraling spring-like knobs. The silver gleamed against my brown arms, and the fine needles were heavy-headed. They looked so odd and unnatural that I couldn't repress a shudder. Gently I lowered my altered arms back into place along my sides. Deborah left the room, and I dozed uneasily until she came back to take the needles out half an hour later. That night I fell into bed as soon as I got home, and slept deeply for fourteen hours.

Deb suggested that I stop drinking coffee and eating sugar if I wanted to heal my hypoglycemia. I did, and as soon as I got over the withdrawal, I started feeling better. I began going to acupuncture twice a week, and every time, Deb asked me what kind of treatment I wanted. The question stopped throwing me quite so badly, but I still had no answer to it—I just got used to saying, "I don't know," and waiting for her suggestions. Then one day when she asked, I did know. Tentatively, I said, "I think I'd like one of those integrating treatments." When Deb put the needles in that day, I could feel how each point welcomed the needle. Slowly, my knowledge of my body began to awaken, because I was learning how to pay attention.

I started to feel places in my body that were twitchy or restless, where there was an empty not-quite-ache. I began to ask Deb, "Is there a point here?" There always was, and when Deb needled it as part of the treatment, it always made a difference. I located points in my scalp that helped with the headaches I was having. I'd drive along the highway on my daily commute, one hand on the steering wheel and the other buried in my hair, prodding at sore places. I could feel the points that needed needles, little indentations that my fingertips fit into. Sometimes I could feel the meridians connecting them, like a throbbing piece of string under my finger. More and more often I knew what kind of a treatment I needed on any given day, where the energy was blocked and needed to move.

It sounds so mysterious, put that way. It wasn't like a light went on all of a sudden, or angel choirs floated down from the high blue ceiling of the treatment room telling me what I needed to know. It was more like having a hunch, and learning to trust it; noticing the feelings in my body I'd always ignored before and discovering what each one meant. Deborah became a partner in this discovery—when I felt an urge for a needle in a particular spot, she could usually come up with a connection between the work we were doing and that point. She so obviously trusted me, and trusted my body, that I learned to trust myself too.

And then came the moment when I had to trust myself even without Deb's full support. I began to have a persistent feeling of needing a needle in the bottom of my foot, just under the ball. Finally, I asked Deb if there was a point there.

"Ye-es," she replied. "It's a pretty intense one though. I hardly ever needle it. Let me try some other points that work with the same energy."

The other points helped, but the feeling in the sole of my foot didn't go away. I brought it up a couple of other times, and Deb still seemed hesitant. I doubted my own perception. At the same time, I could feel that point in my foot, a kind of restless emptiness wanting to be filled, and the feeling kept getting stronger. I could find the point myself and put pressure on it, and it felt good, but it didn't seem like enough. Finally, one day I said to Deb, "I know you're dubious about this, but unless you think it would be <u>bad</u> for me, I really want you to needle that point, you know, the one in the sole of my foot."

"Kidney One, the Bubbling Spring," she said. "Okay. I <u>hate</u> needling that point. But if you still want it so much, there's got to be a reason. It'll probably hurt, you know." She had me breathe with her and cough, "huh!" as the needle went in. It did hurt, a little—but the relief of feeling the needle in the point and the effect it had throughout my lower body completely outweighed the pain. My legs and torso relaxed. I felt like a conduit for the energy pouring through from my head to my feet and out, as if a plug had been pulled from the end of a pipe, or a river freed from an ice jam. The Bubbling Spring became one of my favorite points, a part of almost every treatment, and it always had the effect of deeply relaxing and grounding me.

In that moment, Deborah and I became true partners in the healing process. Raised in the Western medical tradition, I had been accustomed to deferring to a practitioner's expert knowledge. I had accepted the responsibility of being a wise and careful consumer, but not the deeper one of using my own knowledge of my body to determine the course of treatment, to suggest options outside of those laid before me. I discovered that I was essential to the process, and not as a consumer—not just to choose a doctor well, give her accurate information and follow through on her suggestions—but as a participant, and as a healer. Deborah was trained in Chinese medicine, but I was the only one inside my skin. Our knowledge was complementary—only if we listened to each other and trusted each other could the most powerful healing take place. Deb never stopped wincing when she inserted those Bubbling Spring needles, but her belief in my knowledge of my body never wavered either. Neither of us could heal me alone, but in harmony we could work wonders.

Understanding this connection between my body and my psyche was one of the most profound gifts acupuncture gave me. I found that I couldn't strengthen my back, I couldn't recover from hypoglycemia, without being mindful of my spirit as well. The pain in my back, the disequilibrium in my blood sugar, embodied emotional wounds that I had never been able to heal. They were like chunks of frozen energy, trapped in my body as well as my mind, taking on different forms in each that reflected and magnified the other. Acupuncture dissolved them, and freed the energy to move again. As my back grew stronger and more flexible, I found myself emotionally stronger and less rigid as well. As I worked through the old grief and pain in therapy, my blood sugar stabilized and acupuncture treatments became more effective.

Oh, I don't have hypoglycemia any more, and I can even drink a decaf and eat a cookie now and then. My back is stronger— I've been biking and backpacking again, and as long as I take care with lifting, I can do almost anything without being in pain. I don't wake up in the morning unable to move anymore. But the changes in me are much deeper than those. Acupuncture has released me to move in my life in ways I never could have imagined when I began.

Finding My Path

My Story

My interest in healing began at age twenty when I was fired from my first waitressing job. I had worked one shift and was fired when an employee from the summer before came in and wanted her job back. I was furious. Wanting to do something constructive with all the angry energy running through me, I started running, and felt better. Then I went to the library and emerged with a pile of old herbals and a little book on yoga. Thus began a period of jogging, doing yoga and growing and drying medicinal herbs. Later, after reading Adele Davis, I added nutrition to my list of interests.

After graduating from college I wanted to study with an American Indian medicine man or woman. I had no idea if there still were any, or where to find one or why they would take me on as an apprentice. The idea sank back into my unconscious, and I became involved in powerline activism and the potential hazards of high voltage transmission lines. I moved to Vermont where a huge powerline was planned for construction right down the beautiful Champlain Valley to bring electricity from Hydro Quebec to New York City. At twenty-three I got a job as an Energy Resource Analyst for the State of Vermont.

During that time I had a dream that is still fresh in my mind today. I was trapped in the basement of our house, it was dark, and I was pounding on a trapdoor shouting for help. I woke up standing on my bed, and actually pounding on the ceiling and shouting "Let me out!"

Some part of me was shouting for help and I didn't know

what it was or what it wanted, but I could not ignore it. I knew I was in the wrong job. But what was I supposed to be doing?

I went to the library and took out a book on dream analysis by Freud. It did not help. I had accumulated some vacation time, took three weeks off work and went camping. I played, relaxed, read lots of books, did yoga, and now and again thought about that dream. When I returned to work I picked up the local weekly magazine, and took it back to work to read during lunch. It had an article on holistic health in Central Vermont, with interviews of holistic practitioners. I read an interview with an acupuncturist. A light went on in my head as I read about traditional Chinese medical theory, herbs, nutrition and energy, and how they affect health. I had been interested in health for a number of years, yet Western medicine never made sense to me. This traditional Chinese approach to health made perfect sense. I quit my job and worked with the acupuncturist for four months.

There was a thread running through my experiences and interests, from studying the power grid of New England to studying the power grid of the human body. During this time I made money picking fruit and vegetables on a farm. There was plenty of time in the strawberry fields to think about my future. I wanted a more formal education, but was studying acupuncture right for me? My favorite song at the time was John Lennon's "How Can I Go Forward When I Don't Know Which Way I'm Facing?"

Then one night I had a dream. On waking I could not recall the dream. However I knew I was going to go to San Francisco to study acupuncture. Six weeks later I packed up my car and drove west to California to go to traditional Chinese medical school. And so I became an acupuncturist.

Studying healing, and healing myself became entwined paths. As I studied the traditional Chinese system of health care it opened many doors, yet traditional Chinese medicine did not answer all my questions about health and well-being. I began exploring the riches of the San Francisco Bay Area: body work, therapy, breath work, dance, movement, improvisational theater and voice. For my own sense of well-being, I found I needed to nurture my creative energy and give it voice. Right after graduating from Chinese medical school I took a workshop at the Esalen Institute. My first night there I had a dream:

> I am in a round crater, it is very large, and contains all the strata of vegetative life that one can imagine: conifers, scrubby regions and open space above tree line. I see a fire scar, a burn, it is darker, not living, not growing, there are skeleton charcoal pines standing, and no grass grows. I enter the crater without fear, knowing that although I am alone, there are many others in the crater, and we are all there to explore this crater and perhaps what lies beyond . . .

"The Body Has Its Reasons" was the name of the workshop, and I have found it to be true. The body does have its reasons. I often recall these words when my body is doing something I don't like. If I can muster up the curiosity to wonder why my body is communicating like this, the stalemate is broken. It dispels self-judgment and frustration, and allows my body and my Spirit to communicate with me, teach me, reveal themselves, my Self, to me.

Conclusion

S triking a balance between what our minds want and what our bodies want is important in achieving and maintaining good health. Your wisest guidance comes from inside yourself. Take the time to listen. A conflict between what you think you should do and what your guts tell you is an important red flag. If you override your inner voice you can easily walk into difficulty. Your inner voice is part of your guidance system. Slow down and pay attention to it. Take its opinion into consideration. Listening to your inner guidance requires quiet time, solitude, and awareness. If you are off in your mind thinking about dinner, or what you want to say to someone next week, or going over what happened yesterday, then you won't be able to hear your Lungs say, "This fresh air feels so good. Don't go in just yet, please walk a bit more."

Listening to your body means paying attention, being in the present moment, and being aware of the state of your *Qi*. Your *Qi* is precious. Consider how you use it. Before making a decision, ask your body, "Do I have the energy to do this? Is this a wise way to spend my energy?"

To close, I would like to tell one more story about something that happened to me while I was completing this book. It was a long weekend in the summer, and I had set it aside to write. When I write, I keep myself in balance by planning little outings, walks, hikes or swims with friends. I had just spent an afternoon hiking on some beautiful land a friend of mine was about to buy. Then I got in the car and headed home to write.

I turned on the radio and it was broadcasting a live concert. Hundreds, maybe thousands, of people were celebrating the Fourth of July together at a big outdoor music festival, and here I was going home to write. I started feeling depressed. It was a familiar feeling of disconnection, and I can recall having this feeling as far back as I can remember.

I turned off the radio and put a tape in the tape deck. The speaker on the tape was saying a key to maintaining your power is to accept the situations that life presents to you, and let them transform you. Let them expand you and your thoughts. Just then a new thought popped into my consciousness. The thought was: "No matter what is going on around me, I always have all the loving contact that I need to thrive. Always." It was such a powerful thought I turned off the tape deck to sit with it. My old way of thinking, I realized, assumed that loving contact had to come from outside myself. This wasn't something I consciously remember thinking. It was simply an assumption with which I had been living my life. This bleak feeling was simply asking me to expand my consciousness, to open to what is always there, no matter what!

I understood that taking in this new thought and allowing it to transform me would be a profound shift that could change my experience of life. This new thought filled me with energy. As I let this thought penetrate my consciousness, it felt as if a lightning bolt struck me through the top of my head. This thought was so powerful I felt that if I allowed it to sink down through my body I would be split down the center, like a tree by lightning. This feeling was about reclaiming and owning all of my energy. I joked to a friend on the phone that if she found me with a burn mark down my center, she'd know what to tell everyone at my funeral (a bit melodramatic, I admit). She said, "This thought doesn't sound life-threatening." When I told another friend about it, she really laughed. "You think this thought is going to kill you, Deb, but what I see is that lightning coming in and healing you. You *are* split, and it is going to unite you, make you one, whole, healed." *Arggh* . . . I had to admit, she was right. And as I did, I could feel that lightning bolt eek a bit farther down into my body.

By the time you read this, I expect that that thought will have welded me back together. A whole person, knowing in every cell of my being that I truly have all the loving contact I need to thrive at each and every moment of every day, for always. The power of a thought. I feel blessed by the arrival of this thought. May you also be blessed with thoughts that transform your life and remind you that you are whole.

APPENDIX

Books and Other Resources

Books

Antibiotics
The Antibiotic Paradox: How Miracle Drugs Are Destroying the Miracle, Stuart B. Levy, M.D., Plenum Press, 1992

Diet
Staying Healthy with Nutrition, Elson M. Haas, M.D., Celestial Arts, 1992

Healing with Whole Foods: Oriental Traditions and Modern Nutrition, Paul Pitchford, North Atlantic Books, 1993

The Natural Gourmet: Delicious Recipes for Healthy, Balanced Eating, Annemarie Colbin, Ballantine Books, 1989

Mediterranean Light: Delicious Recipes from the World's Healthiest Cuisine, Martha Rose Shulman, Bantam Books, 1989

The Ayurvedic Cookbook: A Personalized Guide to Good Nutrition and Health, Amadea Morningstar, Lotus Press, 1990

Nourishing Wisdom: A Mind-Body Approach to Nutrition and Well-Being, Marc David, Bell Tower, 1994

Dreams

The Dream Book: Symbols for Self-Understanding, Betty Bethards, Element Books, 1983

Memories, Dreams, Reflections, C. G. Jung, Vintage Books, 1965

Emotional Health

Wishcraft: How to Get What You Really Want, Barbara Sher, Ballantine Books, 1979

Feel the Fear and Do It Anyway, Susan Jeffers, Ph.D., Fawcett Columbine, 1987

Anatomy of an Illness, Norman Cousins, Bantam Books, 1981

The Immune Power Personality: 7 Traits You Can Develop to Stay Healthy, Henry Dreher, Plume, 1996

Focusing, Eugene T. Gendlin, Ph.D., Bantam Books, 1978

How to Get Organized When You Don't Have Time, Stephanie Culp, Writer's Digest Books, 1986

The Dance of Anger, Harriet Goldhor Lerner, Ph.D., Harper & Row Publishers, 1985

Liquid Light of Sex: Understanding Your Key Life Passages, Barbara Hand Clow, Bear & Company, 1991

Care of the Soul: A Guide for Cultivating Depth and Sacredness in Everyday Life, Thomas Moore, HarperCollins Publishers, 1992

Coming Home: The Return to True Self, Martia Nelson, Nataraj Publishing, 1993

The Alchemist: A Fable about Following Your Dream, Paulo Coelho, HarperSanFrancisco, 1993

You Can Heal Your Life, Louise L. Hay, Hay House, 1984

Living with Joy: Keys to Personal Power and Transformation, Sanaya Roman, H. J. Kramer, Inc., 1986

The Artist's Way: A Spiritual Path to Higher Creativity, Julia Cameron, A Jeremy P. Tarcher/Putnam Book, 1992

Love, Medicine and Miracles, Bernie Siegel, M.D., HarperPerennial, 1986

Mindmapping: Your Personal Guide to Exploring Creativity and Problem-Solving, Joyce Wycoff, The Berkley Publishing Group, 1991

The Adventure of Self-Discovery: Dimensions of Consciousness and New Perspectives in Psychotherapy and Inner Exploration, Stanislav Grof, M.D., State University of New York Press, 1988

Exercise

Body, Mind, Sport: The Body-Type Guide to Health, Fitness and Longevity, John Douillard, D.C., Harmony, 1994

Acu-Yoga: Self-Help Techniques to Relieve Tension, Michael Reed Gach, Japan Publications, Inc., 1981

Infertility

The Infertility Book: A Comprehensive Medical and Emotional Guide, Carla Harkness, Celestial Arts, 1995

Overcoming Infertility Naturally: The Relationship Between Nutrition, Emotions and Reproduction, Karen Bradstreet, Woodland Books, 1993

Infertility: The Emotional Journey, Michelle Fryer Hanson, Deaconess Press, 1994

RESOLVE, Inc. National Office, 310 Broadway, Somerville, MA 02144, (617) 623-0744

Naturopathic Medicine

Encyclopedia of Natural Medicine, Michael Murray, N.D. and Joseph Pizzorno, N.D., Prima Publishing, 1991

Sensory Motor Learning Tapes

P.O. Box 5674
Berkeley, CA 94705
(800) 735-7950

Relaxercise A series of six sensory motor learning audiotapes of lessons to counteract postural stress. You do the lessons while sitting in a chair. A soothing voice leads you through small, simple movements that remind your nervous system of a wide variety of movement options. You literally feel chronic tensions melt away. These exercises are *not* to be done while driving a car.

TMJ Health A series of six sensory motor learning audiotapes. A self-help exercise system that offers relief and comfort to those suffering from TMJ problems and symptoms.

Traditional Chinese Medicine

The Web That Has No Weaver: Understanding Chinese Medicine, Ted J. Kaptchuk, O.M.D., Congdon and Weed, 1983

Traditional Acupuncture: The Law of the Five Elements, Dianne Connelly, Center for Traditional Acupuncture, 1992

Vision Therapy

Natural Vision Improvement, Janet Goodrich, Celestial Arts, 1985

College of Optometrists in Vision Development
P.O. Box 285
Chula Vista, CA 91912-0285

Optometric Extension Program
2912 South Daimler St.
Santa Ana, CA 92705-5811
(714) 250-8070

Women's Health

Dr. Susan Lark's Premenstrual Syndrome Self-Help Book, Susan Lark, M.D., Forman Publishing, Inc., 1984

Menopausal Years—The Wise Woman Way: Alternative Approaches for Women 30–90, Susun Weed, Ash Tree, 1992

Preventing and Reversing Osteoporosis: Every Woman's Essential Guide, Alan R. Gaby, M.D., Prima Publishing, 1994

What Your Doctor May Not Tell You about Menopause: The Break-through Book on Natural Progesterone, John R. Lee, M.D.,

Warner Books, 1996

Women's Health Connection: (800) 366-6632—a newsletter about women's health care

Women Who Run with the Wolves, Clarissa Pinkola Estes, Ballantine Books, 1992

You Don't Have to Live with Cystitis, Larrian Gillespie, M.D., Avon, 1996

Yeast Overgrowth

The Complete Candida Yeast Guide Book, Jeanne Marie Martin, Prima Publishing, 1996

The Yeast Connection Handbook, William G. Crook, M.D., Professional Books Future Health, 1996

Diagnostic Tests

General food allergy profile, vegetarian food allergy profile, spice allergy profile and inhalant and chemical allergy profiles. Test for both immediate and delayed allergic reactions through an analysis of your blood.

Comprehensive Digestive Stool Analysis (CDSA), Parasitology Screening and Permeability Profile. Three tests to evaluate different aspects of the health of your digestive tract.

Hormone Profiles. Test reproductive hormone levels, adrenal hormone levels and melatonin levels.

Osteoporosis Risk Evaluation. A urine analysis test to monitor bone loss and effectiveness of mineral supplementation.

Natural Medicine and Body Work Therapies

In general, the best way to find a good health care provider or body worker is through word of mouth. If someone you know and trust has had a positive experience with a practitioner, chances are you will too. However, one word of caution: the bottom line here is to listen to your body. Just because rolfing has been great for your dearest friend does not mean it is appropriate for you. People have different needs at different times. It will not serve you to go with the crowd when your body has other ideas in mind. Trust your instincts in this area. What is your gut telling you?

Here are some questions to ask yourself when choosing from the many varieties of practitioners of natural medicine and body work.

- Am I feeling stuck, exhausted, vulnerable, scared, frustrated, hopeless, curious, ready for change?
- What kind of support do I need now? What would feel supportive to me?
- Do I need comfort and gentleness, or do I want help really digging into a problem area?
- Am I ready for a big change or do I need to integrate the changes that have already happened?
- Do I want a more aggressive approach or a more gentle, noninvasive approach?
- Do I want one session or a series of treatments?
- Do I want just a bit of guidance or do I want a lot of supervision and direction?
- Would I prefer to work with a man or a woman, or doesn't it matter?
- Do I want to be an active participant or a passive recipient?
- Do I want to be educated, taken care of, or both?

Questions you may want to ask your body worker.

- What is your training?

- Is there some sort of accreditation in your field? Have you been accredited?
- Do you have experience working with other people who have had a condition similar to mine?
- Will I be clothed, disrobed, under a sheet or fully exposed during a session?
- How can I expect to feel after a session?
- Do you have any recommendations for me after a session?
- Can we do one session, or do you normally do a series?

Alexander Work

A system of physical re-education and postural awareness based on the work of F. M. Alexander. The focus is on efficient use of the body to achieve relaxed and effortless movement.

The Feldenkrais Method®

The Feldenkrais Method® is a system of neuromuscular re-education based on the research of Moshe Feldenkrais. It focuses on the retraining of the neuromuscular system with small, slow, gentle movements to regain a wide variety of movement options and alleviate pain. For more information about the Feldenkrais Method® you can contact The Feldenkrais Guild® at 524 Ellsworth Street SW, P.O. Box 489, Albany, OR 97321-0143, (800) 775-2118.

Holotropic Breath Work

Based on the work and research of Stanislav Grof, M.D., a more aggressive and cathartic type of breath work that can move you through a lot of emotional material and stuck places quickly.

Lymphatic Drainage Massage

A light, gentle, yet deeply effective massage to move your lymphatic fluid, helping your body to clean house. Excellent when your body is feeling toxic, struggling with an infection or you are doing a cleanse. Be sure to drink lots of water after your massage.

Naturopathy

Naturopathy is a system of medicine using natural therapeutics that recognizes certain principles, most importantly the healing power of nature. It uses natural forms of treatment such as homeopathy, nutrition, herbs, adjustments and acupuncture.

Network Chiropractic

A school of chiropractic care that uses both gentle, nonforce adjustments and more traditional thrust adjustments in a precise sequence to unblock energy. The intention is to gently release tension from the nervous system by clearing blocked emotions and thought patterns with the goal of restoring alignment to the body, mind and soul.

Neuromuscular Specialists

Practitioners who work with injury to the musculoskeletal system and teach exercises specifically chosen to address each individual's problem area.

Rolfing

A deep form of body work that releases holding patterns in the connective tissue. I recommend choosing your rolfer with care, as the nature of the work is to deal in a physical way directly with your body armoring. Your body armoring developed for good reasons, and while it may not be necessary or beneficial for you now, it can still be scary to have it altered. Therefore, feeling comfortable with and trusting your rolfer is important. Initial treatments are done in a series of ten sessions over a period of time so that the connective tissue of the entire body can be released. Often emotional release comes along with this work. It can be helpful to have emotional sup-

port during a series of rolfing sessions. It is great when you are
ready for change in your life.

Rosen Method

A gentle, noninvasive and powerful approach to connecting the body and mind, founded by Marion Rosen. The practitioner is simply present in the moment with gentle touch,
following the natural breath of the client, listening to the client's body, allowing space for the client to listen as well.

Shiatsu and Acupressure

Systems of massage that work with the same energy and
meridians that are used in acupuncture to unblock energy and
restore balance to the body.

Traeger

A gentle, noninvasive form of body work founded by Mil-
ton Traeger, M.D. The body of the client is gently rocked to
release holding and tension patterns. The Traeger practitioner
works in a relaxed, meditative state where she or he is able to
directly impart to the client's nervous system the possibility of
free-flowing movement. This achieves a state of spacious relaxation in the body and mind of the client.

Nutritional Supplements and Homeopathic Remedies

Allergy Research Group—Available from practitioners.

ParaMicrocidin—Natural antibiotic, citrus seed extract capsules. For low-grade, minor or persistent, nonresponsive bacterial and yeast infections, including stomach bugs, upper
respiratory infections and sinus infections.

Apex Energetics—Available from practitioners.

Acute Rescue Spray—A homeopathic nasal spray to unblock congested sinuses and soothe inflamed and irritated nasal membranes.

Aller-Total, AllerDrain, Airborne—Homeopathic remedies for allergy sufferers. For combination food and environmental allergies, and for airborne (pollens, feathers, hair, dust) allergies.

Bacterotox and Post Virotox—Homeopathic remedies to support healing from lingering bacterial or viral illnesses.

Kidney RegenRx—A homeopathic remedy to support the Kidney energy. Especially helpful with chronic low backache or pain or a depleted reserve tank.

Liver RegenRx—A homeopathic remedy to support the liver. Excellent for anyone suffering from allergies, particularly with eye symptoms.

Lung RegenRx—A homeopathic remedy to support the lungs. Particularly useful in chronic lung weakness, or to support recovery during a prolonged respiratory illness.

Metal Element—A homeopathic remedy to support the Lung energy both physically and emotionally.

Water Element—A homeopathic remedy to support the Kidney energy both physically and emotionally.

BioAllers—Available at health food stores and co-ops.

Allergy Relief: Animal Hair/Dander—A homeopathic remedy for allergy symptoms associated with animal hair allergies.

Boiron—Available from practitioners, health food stores and co-ops.

Oscillacoccinium—A homeopathic remedy for colds and flus.

Sinusitis—A homeopathic remedy for sinus congestion and sinus headaches.

Bio/Chem—Available from practitioners, health food stores and co-ops.

Citricidal Nasal Spray—A natural antibiotic nasal spray for those suffering with a sinus infection.

Citricidal Skin Cleanser—A gentle, nondrying grapefruit seed extract gel soap. Good for athlete's foot and other skin rashes.

Citricidal Tablets—Natural antibiotic tablets to treat low-grade, minor or persistent, nonresponsive bacterial infections including stomach bugs, upper respiratory infections and sinus infections.

MetaRest—Melatonin with kava root extract and B$_6$ in capsules or liquid. A natural sleep aid.

Ecological Formulas—Available from practitioners.

Hyland's Homeopathic: Calms Forte—A homeopathic remedy for anxiety, restlessness and insomnia.

Monolaurin—A natural antiviral lauric acid product that is derived from coconut. It reduces viral load by interfering with viral replication. Useful with herpes, chronic fatigue and shingles.

Jarrow Formulas—Available from practitioners.

Antioxidant Optimizer—A vitamin C, antioxidant and herbal formula that seems to be an excellent immune support.

Fem-Dophilus—A vaginal suppository to reintroduce beneficial bacteria to the vagina. For women experiencing yeast infections. This product is to be refrigerated.

Metagenics—Available from practitioners.

Sinuplex—An herbal tablet to support the sinuses, nasal passages and the upper respiratory tract. Contains some *herba ephedra* so not to be taken by those with high blood pressure. If you experience a speedy reaction from taking one then discontinue use.

UltraClear—A powdered beverage mix to be used during cleansing to support the liver detoxification pathways.

UltraClear Sustain—A powdered beverage mix for gastrointestinal support. Supports healing of the intestinal membrane in cases of leaky gut or other gastrointestinal disorders.

Planetary Formulas—Available from practitioners and health food stores.

Hepatopure—A combination herbal formula to stimulate liver cleansing.

TriCleanse—A psyllium-based intestinal bulking agent for intestinal cleansing and toning.

Triphala—A traditional Indian herbal formula to normalize elimination, enhance digestion and cleanse the large intestine.

Tyler—Available from practitioners.

Detoxication Factors—A liver detoxification support formula in capsule form.

Enterogenic Formula—Beneficial bacteria and FOS to support a healthy environment in the intestines. Available in capsules and powder. This product is to be refrigerated.

Fiber Formula—An intestinal bulking agent to improve colon health and regularity of bowel movements.

Oxyperm and Cyto-redoxin—Two antioxidant formulas.

Permeability Factors—A nutritional formula to help reestablish healthy intestinal walls. For people suffering from leaky gut syndrome.

Similase—Plant-based digestive enzymes that work in a broad pH range.

UniKey Health Systems—Available from UniKey and practitioners, (800) 888-4353.

Para-Key and Para-Plus—For treatment of protozoans—little parasites.

Verma-Key and Verma-Plus—For treatment of worms—bigger parasites.

Vitanica—Available from practitioners.

HerpBlend—A nutritional supplement to support an immune system dealing with chronic herpes infections, and for use during an acute outbreak.

OsteoBlend—A supplement designed to maintain bone health.

Women's Symmetry—Women's daily multivitamin and mineral supplement.

Women's Phase I—A combination mineral, vitamin and herbal formula for premenstrual support.

Women's Phase II—An herbal formula for relief of menopausal symptoms.

CranStat Extra—A combination cranberry concentrate and herbal product for urinary tract support.

FibroBlend and BreastBlend—Two products that support healthy breasts.

Sleepblend—A mineral, herbal and melatonin combination sleep support formula.

Vogel—Available at health food stores and co-ops.

Pollinosan—A homeopathic remedy for stuffy, runny, itchy nose associated with allergies.

Wolf Howl Herbals
RR 1 Earthwings Farm
Orange, Vt. 05641
(802) 479-1034

Breast Balm—A good-smelling olive-oil based balm to improve lymphatic circulation in the breasts. For breast massage. It comes with a description of five lymphatic drainage massage strokes to do on yourself. Remember, the lymphatic system resonds to a gentle, light touch.

Recipe for Rice Water
2 Tbs. short grain, organic brown rice
water for boiling
fresh ginger

Put a tablespoon or two of short grain, organic brown rice in a big pot of water. You may add several slices of fresh ginger-root for flavor. Simmer for an hour. Drink the warm broth to nourish Kidney *yin* energy and body fluids. Good for conditions of dryness and depletion.